A Global Green New Deal

Meeting the short-term challenges of reviving the worldwide economy need not mean sacrificing long-term economic and environmental sustainability. A Global Green New Deal (GGND) is an economic policy strategy for ensuring a more economically and environmentally sustainable world economic recovery. Reviving growth and creating jobs should be essential objectives; but policies should also aim to reduce carbon dependency, protect ecosystems and water resources and alleviate poverty. Otherwise, economic recovery today will do little to avoid economic and environmental crises in the future. Part I puts forward the case why a GGND strategy is essential to the sustainability of the global economy. Part II provides an overview of the key national policies, whilst part III focuses on the global actions necessary to allow national policies to work. Part IV summarizes the main recommendations for national and international action, and discusses the wider implications for restructuring the world economy towards "greener" development.

EDWARD B. BARBIER is the John S. Bugas Professor of Economics in the Department of Economics and Finance, University of Wyoming. He has over twenty-five years' experience as an environmental and resource economist, working mainly on the economics of environment and development issues. He is the author of many books on environmental policy, including *Natural Resources and Economic Development* (Cambridge University Press, 2005) and, with David Pearce, *Blueprint for a Sustainable Economy* (2000).

A Global Green
New Deal
Rethinking the Economic Recovery

EDWARD B. BARBIER

United Nations
Environment Programme

CAMBRIDGE
UNIVERSITY PRESS

CAMBRIDGE UNIVERSITY PRESS
Cambridge, New York, Melbourne, Madrid, Cape Town, Singapore,
São Paulo, Delhi, Dubai, Tokyo

Cambridge University Press
The Edinburgh Building, Cambridge CB2 8RU, UK

Published in the United States of America by
Cambridge University Press, New York

www.cambridge.org
Information on this title: www.cambridge.org/9780521132022

First published 2010

Printed in the United Kingdom at the University Press, Cambridge

A catalogue record for this publication is available from the British Library

Library of Congress Cataloguing in Publication data
Barbier, Edward, 1957–
    A global green new deal : rethinking the economic
    recovery / Edward B. Barbier.
        p.   cm.
    Includes bibliographical references and index.
    ISBN 978-0-521-76309-7
    1. Sustainable development–Government policy.   2. Globalization.
    I. Title.
    HC79.E5B358 2010
    338.9′27–dc22   2010008753

ISBN 978-0-521-76309-7 Hardback
ISBN 978-0-521-13202-2 Paperback

No one can possibly have lived through the Great Depression without being scarred by it. No amount of experience since the depression can convince someone who has lived through it that the world is safe economically.

Isaac Asimov

I think if there's a great depression there might be some hope.

Lawrence Ferlinghetti

Contents

Figures

Tables

Boxes

Foreword

A year ago, in October 2008, a beleaguered world that had just been through a spate of shocks and crises – in food, fuel and finance – now found itself in the grip of a global recession the likes of which it had not seen since the 1930s. G20 governments were willing to commit significant fiscal stimulus packages – estimated at more than US$2.5 trillion – towards economic recovery. The question begged to be asked: would the post-recovery economy be sustainable, or would it be prone to the very risks and weaknesses that had led to this latest recession?

To answer this question, and to address the closely related and unsolved challenges of excessive carbon dependency, increasing ecological scarcities and persistent poverty, the United Nations Environment Programme (UNEP) decided to launch, in October 2008, an urgent inquiry into how a "green economy" model could be seeded at this critical time in order to stimulate a sustainable recovery. Named after the original "New Deal" of US president Franklin D. Roosevelt, this inquiry and its recommendations were dubbed a "Global Green New Deal" (or "GGND"), because they were "global" in scope (as befits the challenge of the current recession) and "green" in their principles for a sustainable post-crisis economy. Professor Edward Barbier was nominated to prepare a defining study and recommendation, to be taken to the UNEP General Council in early 2009, to the G8 and G20 meetings soon afterwards and to other fora.

The urgency of this exercise was palpable and essential: every day saw more bad news hit the headlines, and impressive proposed fiscal stimulus packages and wide-ranging reforms were being talked about, but very few were explicitly targeted at a sustainable recovery, as against just a revival of "business-as-usual" GDP growth.

Twenty years ago Ed Barbier co-authored (with David Pearce and Anil Markandya) a path-breaking work on sustainable development called *Blueprint for a Green Economy. Blueprint,* as it is popularly known, challenged traditional notions of the so-called trade-off between environmental stewardship and economic development, and created widespread awareness of what is possible: a "green economy," which thrives through innovation and investment in renewable energy, energy efficiency, materials efficiency and a focus on maintaining natural capital and limiting ecological risks to human progress. Since then Barbier has researched and written extensively on the subject, and so his selection for the challenge of preparing UNEP's "GGND" came as no surprise.

What emerged from this effort was a principled and thorough study on how to address the challenges of this recession with new thinking around the model of a "green economy." Barbier's *Rethinking Economic Recovery: A Global Green New Deal* (*GGND,* for short) was presented at the UNEP Governing Council of Ministers in February 2009, and was widely appreciated. It was further developed by UNEP and many UN sister agencies into a *GGND Policy Brief* for the G20 nations. This helped create a broad understanding and a willingness among nations to explore economic options other than a mechanical return to the "business-as-usual" pattern of unsustainable growth and unsolved global problems.

Ed Barbier's book draws from his work on *GGND,* and presents a logical and structured set of policy analyses and recommendations for both rich and poor nations, addressing the need to reform domestic policies and subsidies, and to improve international policy frameworks in trade, aid and carbon markets. Its suggestion regarding fiscal stimulus packages is to focus around a quarter of these packages (or 1 percent of GDP) on "greening" the economy. In the case of developed economies, this means 1 percent invested in reducing carbon dependency – a key factor for the success of any post-Copenhagen regime. It targets the triple objectives of economic growth and job creation whilst protecting the vulnerable, of reducing climate risks and ecological scarcities (especially freshwater) and of achieving the Millennium Development Goal of poverty reduction.

It asks for nothing less than a shift towards a global economy driven by significant job creation from the growth of resource- and energy-efficient building and construction, the widespread use of modern public transport in mega-cities, the scaling up of solar, wind, wave, thermal and bioenergy in the total energy mix, and sustainable agriculture that reflects the latest thinking in ecosystem management, biodiversity and water conservation. It also addresses the key risks in poor countries, to prevent recession from having its most catastrophic effects on freshwater availability, sanitation, health and the sustainability of primary production.

UNEP's Green Economy Initiative is already taking forward many of the themes and policy solutions described in this book with individual governments around the world, as they seek to reform policies, reinvigorate their economies, re-employ their citizens and address their own challenges of persistent poverty. We are delighted that Ed Barbier's timely book is with us as we do so, providing a rich source of useful reference information and practical advice on a "Global Green New Deal."

Achim Steiner
Executive Director
United Nations Environment Programme

Pavan Sukhdev
Special Adviser and Head – Green Economy Initiative
United Nations Environment Programme
October 2009

Preface

On December 2 and 3, 2008, the United Nations Environment Programme (UNEP) convened a consultative meeting of policy experts in Geneva, under the auspices of its Green Economy Initiative (GEI), to outline possible proposals for a "Global Green New Deal." To participants in that meeting, the need for such a comprehensive global strategy was self-evident: the world was confronted with multiple crises – fuel, food and financial. By December 2008 it was already apparent that the result of these crises would be one of the worst global economic recessions since the Great Depression of the 1930s. The multiple crises threatening the world economy therefore demanded the same kind of initiative that had been shown by the New Deal of US president Franklin D. Roosevelt in the 1930s, but at the global scale and embracing a wider vision. Such a vision would require finding the right mix of policy actions to help stimulate recovery and create jobs while also improving the sustainability of the world economy, enhancing the livelihoods of the world's poor and channeling investments into dynamic economic sectors and at the same time lessening carbon dependency and environmental degradation. The phrase "Global Green New Deal" (GGND) refers to such a timely combination of policies.

The main conclusion of the UNEP meeting in December 2008 was that a report should be commissioned to outline the key elements of a GGND strategy. I was asked to undertake this task by Pavan Sukhdev, the project leader of the GEI, and Hussein Abaza, the chief of UNEP's Division of Technology, Industry and Economics (DTIE), which administers the GEI. The consultancy also received the full endorsement of and support from UNEP's executive director, Achim Steiner.

Given the rapidly unfolding global economic crisis, the timetable set for my task of writing the GGND report was necessarily short. In just over five weeks I produced a draft report, which became the basis for further consultations at UN interagency and expert meetings held at the United Nations in New York from February 2 to 3, 2009. A separate consultation meeting was held at the UN Foundation, Washington, DC, on February 4.

Based on the helpful comments arising from these meetings, as well as numerous comments sent to me by those experts unable to attend, I revised the report in time for its launch on February 16 at UNEP's Twenty-fifth Governing Council/Global Ministerial Environment Forum in Nairobi, Kenya. The report was the key background document for UNEP's *Global Green New Deal: Policy Brief*, which was released in March 2009.[1] That month I was also asked by the UK government to produce a short note based on the GGND report, "The G20 agenda should include implementing a global 'green' new deal," for the macroeconomic policy debate in the run-up to the April 2 London meeting of the twenty largest economies (the G20) in the world.[2]

Since then I have made minor revisions, and in April 2009 I updated the GGND report, which is currently titled *Rethinking the Economic Recovery: A Global Green New Deal* and available through the GEI website.[3] UNEP has also issued a limited print run of the report.

Interest in the report has continued, however, and, thanks to the efforts of UNEP and Cambridge University Press, it should reach a wider audience. With this aim in mind, I have written the

[1] UNEP. 2009. *Global Green New Deal: Policy Brief.* Nairobi, UNEP. Available at www.unep.org/pdf/A_Global_Green_New_Deal_Policy_Brief.pdf.

[2] Barbier, E. B. 2009. "The G20 agenda should include implementing a global 'green' new deal." Debate, "Macroeconomics: A Global Crisis Debate." VoxEU. org, posted March 7, 2009. Available at www.voxeu.org/index.php?q=node/3223.

[3] Barbier, E. B. 2009. *Rethinking the Economic Recovery: A Global Green New Deal.* Report prepared for the Economics and Trade Branch, Division of Technology, Industry and Economics, UNEP, Geneva. Available at www.unep. org/greeneconomy/docs/GGND-Report-April2009.pdf.

following book based on the GGND report. This task involved three principal objectives.

First, transforming a consultancy report into a book has necessarily required changing its structure to make it more readable and accessible. Overall, however, much of the original GGND strategy and discussion of key policies has been retained.

Second, as far as possible, the book has been updated with current information on the state of the global economic crises as well as government plans and policies in response. I have tried my best to do this up until the date of this final typescript (August 2009).

Third, and perhaps most importantly, every effort has been made to improve the "shelf life" of this book. As a result, both the introductory part I and the concluding part IV have been substantially revised to explain why a Global Green New Deal strategy is still relevant for the world economy, even though some analysts believe that the world economy may already be showing signs of recovery.

This latter objective requires further elaboration, as it gets to the heart of the main theme of the book.

In its July 2009 *World Economic Outlook: Update*, the International Monetary Fund (IMF) predicts that any recovery will be weak and uneven, with the global economy expected to contract by 1.4 percent in 2009 and to expand by a modest 2.5 percent in 2010.[4] This suggests that the world economy is likely to be affected by the current economic recession for some years to come.

Faced with the social and economic consequences of a deepening world recession, or at best a weak, unstable and protracted recovery, it may seem a luxury to consider policies that aim to reduce carbon dependency and environmental degradation. Such a conclusion is both false and misleading.

---

[4] IMF. 2009. *World Economic Outlook: Update*. Washington, DC, IMF. Available at www.imf.org/external/pubs/ft/weo/2009/update/02/pdf/0709.pdf.

For one, as the subtitle of this book indicates, at this critical period in world history we still have time to "rethink" our strategy for the economic recovery. This choice boils down to a simple policy question: do we want the recovery simply to revive the existing "brown" world economy on its business-as-usual growth path, or do we want to orient the global recovery towards a "greener" economy that will allow it to avoid future economic and environmental pitfalls?

The key message of this book is that the expanded vision offered by a GGND is critical to the lasting success of a world economic recovery. Reviving growth, ensuring financial stability and creating jobs have to be essential objectives. Unless the new policy initiatives also address other global challenges, however, such as reducing carbon dependency, protecting ecosystems and water resources and alleviating poverty, their impact on averting future crises will be short-lived. Without this expanded vision, simply resuming global economic growth today will do little to address the imminent threats posed by climate change, energy insecurity, growing freshwater scarcity, deteriorating ecosystems and, above all, worsening global poverty. To the contrary, it is necessary to reduce carbon dependency and ecological scarcity not just because of environmental concerns but because this is the correct and only way to revitalize the economy on a genuinely sustainable basis.

In short, as argued in this book, the key elements of any Global Green New Deal should focus on three main objectives:

- reviving the world economy, creating employment opportunities and protecting vulnerable groups;
- reducing carbon dependency, ecosystem degradation and water scarcity; and
- furthering the Millennium Development Goal of ending extreme world poverty by 2025.

Some G20 economies already appear to be working towards some of these objectives, by including "green" investments in their stimulus packages to reduce carbon dependency, enhance economic recovery and create jobs. The full range of GGND objectives cannot be achieved merely through injections of "green" fiscal stimulus investments by a handful of national governments, however. It is unlikely, therefore, that current global green stimulus spending by G20 governments will turn current economic recovery efforts into a global "green recovery." Thus, we return to the fundamental policy question posed by this book: what more must be done to ensure that the world economy is on a recovery path that is more economically and environmentally sustainable?

This is a question that should remain the central concern of global policymakers, not just for the next one or two years of economic recovery but for the next critical decade or so, as we grapple with the ongoing threats posed by climate change, energy insecurity, increasing freshwater scarcity, weakening ecosystems and, most of all, growing global poverty.

Edward B. Barbier
Centennial, Wyoming
August 2009

Acknowledgements

I am grateful to a long list of people who have helped in various ways to make both the original Global Green New Deal report, and then this book, possible.

First and foremost, I am indebted to Pavan Sukhdev, head of the Green Economy Initiative project for the United Nations Environment Programme, for encouraging me in writing the GGND report for UNEP, providing important suggestions and assisting me in revising the UNEP report and promoting its publication as a book. I would also like to thank Hussein Abaza, chief of UNEP's Division of Technology, Industry and Economics, which administers the GEI and is responsible for managing the whole GGND process, including several consultative inter-agency and expert meetings. Finally, I am grateful to Achim Steiner, executive director of UNEP, for his belief in the GGND, his ongoing support of the process, and his tireless efforts to communicate the GGND strategy to policymakers.

I would also like to thank Jay Dowle, communications officer for the UNEP Green Economy Initiative, Fulai Sheng, of the DTIE, and Nick Nuttal, spokesperson, Office of the Executive Director, UNEP.

Thanks also go to Chris Harrison of Cambridge University Press for commissioning this volume and for providing advice on how best to transform the original GGND report into a book.

Many other people also provided invaluable assistance in the preparation of the original UNEP GGND report, which has also influenced this book.

Special thanks go to Joanne Burgess, who read over early drafts of the GGND report in their entirety and provided detailed comments, suggestions and edits. Bill Becker, executive director of the United States' Presidential Climate Action Project, offered important advice and comments. Margie Reis assisted in producing various versions of the UNEP report. Invaluable advice on revising the report for publication as a book has come from Anil Markandya and Michael Toman.

The report also benefited from consultations held at the United Nations, New York, on February 2 and 3, 2009, with experts from, amongst others, the European Environmental Agency (EEA), the International Centre for Trade and Sustainable Development, the International Labour Organization (ILO), the IMF, the Organisation for Economic Co-operation and Development (OECD), various UN agencies (UNCEB, UNCSD, UNCTAD, UNDESA, UNDP, UNECE, UNECLAC, UNEP, UNESCAP, UNFAO, UNFCCC, UNIDO and UNSD), the World Bank and the UN Secretary General's Office. A separate consultation meeting was held at the UN Foundation, Washington, DC, on February 4, 2009, with experts from the Center for American Progress, the Pew Center on Global Climate Change, the Union of Concerned Scientists, the UN Foundation, the World Resources Institute and the Worldwatch Institute. I thank all participants at these meetings for their helpful comments and suggestions, and for sending material for use in subsequent revisions of the original UNEP report on which this book is based.

Specific individuals helped me considerably in drafting the material that appears in the original report and now this book. Heewah Choi, Peter Poschen and Kristof Welslau of the ILO provided the information on the South Korean Green New Deal used in part II. Sanjeev Sanyal provided written input on the general reforms of the financial system, which I have adapted and used in part III. Ben Simmons provided me with the background discussion on enhancing trade incentives, which I have also used in part III. Appendix 1 is based on Trevor Houser, Shashank Mohan and Robert Heilmayr's February 2009 publication *A Green Global*

Recovery? Assessing US Economic Stimulus and the Prospects for International Coordination (Policy Brief no. PB09–3 by the Peterson Institute for International Economics (PIIE) and the World Resources Institute (WRI). My thanks are extended to the authors, Manish Bapna, Ed Tureen, the PIIE and the WRI for allowing the use in this book of the results of this study and copyrighted material. Jacqueline McGlade of the EEA provided me with the information on European environmental taxation used in table 12.1 and Jan Corfee-Morlot of the OECD provided invaluable information on freshwater scarcity and policy that is used throughout the book. Sjak Smulders kindly supplied me with the material for box 11.2, which is summarized from his paper produced at Tilburg University.

Finally, I would like to issue the following disclaimer. Although this book is based on a report that I wrote for the United Nations Environment Programme, the findings, opinions, interpretations and recommendations in this book are entirely mine, and should not be attributed in any manner to the Green Economy Initiative or to UNEP.

Part I   Why a Global Green New Deal?

1 Introduction: opportunity from crisis

2008 will be remembered as the year of multiple global crises. It began with a looming fuel crisis, as well as continued rises in food and commodity prices. Towards the end of the year the world was confronted with a major financial crash, which quickly turned into the worst international economic recession since the Great Depression. By mid-2009 there were signs that the economic recession was easing, but any ensuing recovery has been projected to be long, protracted and vulnerable to further disruption. Global unemployment and poverty are still on the rise, and some economic sectors continue to contract. There is also concern that, as the world economy recovers, it remains vulnerable to the problems posed by other global challenges, such as climate change, energy insecurity, growing freshwater scarcity, deteriorating ecosystems and widespread poverty in developing economies.

These crises have serious implications for human welfare and well-being worldwide, especially in terms of unemployment, poverty and environmental impacts. They may also provide a unique opportunity, however, for governments to come together to promote sustainable economic development at the global level. This book outlines one possible strategy for creating such an "opportunity from crisis."

Faced with the social and economic consequences of a deepening world recession, or – at best – a weak, unstable and protracted recovery, it may seem something of a luxury to consider at this time policies that aim to reduce carbon dependency and environmental degradation. Such a conclusion is both false and misleading, however.

At this crucial juncture in world history there is still time to "rethink" the global economic recovery. This choice boils down to a simple policy question: do we want the recovery simply to revive the existing "brown" world economy on its business-as-usual growth path, or do we want to orient the global recovery towards a "greener" economy that will allow it to avoid future economic and environmental pitfalls?

This book makes the case for the latter approach. The multiple economic and environmental crises threatening the world economy today demand the same kind of initiative that was shown by Roosevelt's New Deal in the 1930s in the United States, but at the global scale and embracing a wider vision. The right mixture of policy actions can stimulate recovery and at the same time improve the sustainability of the world economy. If these actions are adopted, over the next few years they will create millions of jobs, improve the livelihoods of the world's poor and channel investments into dynamic economic sectors. The concept of a "Global Green New Deal" (GGND) refers to such a timely combination of policies.

An expanded vision is critical to the lasting success of a world economic recovery. Reviving growth, ensuring financial stability and creating jobs should be essential objectives; but, unless new policy initiatives also address some of the other global challenges, such as reducing carbon dependency, protecting ecosystems and water resources and alleviating poverty, their ability to avert future crises will be short-lived. Without this expanded vision, simply revitalizing the world economy today will do little to address the imminent threats posed by climate change, energy insecurity, growing freshwater scarcity, deteriorating ecosystems and, above all, worsening global poverty. To the contrary, it is necessary to reduce carbon dependency and ecological threats not just because of environmental concerns but because this is the correct and – indeed – only way to reinvigorate the economy on a more sustained basis.

MULTIPLE GLOBAL CRISES

There is little doubt that we are in the midst of the worst global economic recession since the Great Depression of the 1930s. In 2009, for the first time in decades, the volume of world trade is projected to decline as global per capita income contracts.[1] The number of unemployed globally could rise in 2009 by anything between 29 and 59 million over 2007 levels.[2] Although there are signs that the world economy is stabilizing, the recession is far from over. The International Monetary Fund (IMF) predicts that any recovery is likely to be weak and uneven, with the global economy expected to contract by 1.4 percent in 2009 and to expand by a modest 2.5 percent in 2010.[3]

Although global poverty had been declining before the current economic crisis, projections suggested that by 2015 there would still be nearly 1 billion people living on less than US$1 a day and almost 3 billion living on less than US$2 a day.[4] As the international recession continues to spread and deepen, global poverty trends are expected to worsen. Every fall of one percentage point in growth in developing economies is estimated to consign another 20 million people to poverty.[5]

Alarmed by the state of the world economy, the leaders of the world's twenty biggest rich and emerging economies, which together account for almost 80 percent of the world's population and 90 percent of global gross domestic product (GDP), met in Washington,

---

[1] World Bank. 2009. *Global Economic Prospects 2009: Commodities at the Crossroads.* Washington, DC, World Bank; United Nations [UN]. 2009. *World Economic Situation and Prospects 2009.* New York, UN.

[2] International Labour Organization [ILO]. 2009. *Global Employment Trends: Update, May 2009.* Geneva, ILO.

[3] IMF 2009 (see pref., fn 4).

[4] Based on projections to 2015 of the share of world population living on US$1 a day and US$2 a day in ILO. 2004. *World Employment Report 2004–05.* Geneva, ILO, and 2015 mid-level projections of world population in UN. 2007. *World Population Prospects: The 2006 Revision.* New York, UN, and "World urbanization prospects: the 2005 revision." Online UN database, available at http://esa.un.org/unup. For a comprehensive analysis of global poverty trends from 1981 to 2005, see Chen, Shaohua, and Martin Ravallion. 2008. *The Developing World is Poorer than We Thought, but No Less Successful in the Fight against Poverty.* Policy Research Working Paper no. 4703. Washington, DC, World Bank.

[5] World Bank. 2008. "Global financial crisis and implications for developing countries." Paper prepared for G20 finance ministers' meeting. São Paulo, Brazil, November 8.

DC, on November 15, 2008.[6] Much of the focus of this first ever Group of Twenty (G20) summit was on addressing the immediate financial causes of the current recession, such as enhancing sound regulation and regulatory oversight in the global financial system.[7] In addition, the G20 leaders declared the need to boost economic growth through fiscal stimulus measures, including increases in public spending and investments. Since the Washington summit, many G20 governments have responded by increasing public spending or lowering taxes in order to accelerate economic recovery and create job opportunities (see box 1.1). To date, the total amount of global fiscal stimulus packages is over US$3 trillion, equivalent to nearly 4.6 percent of current world GDP. The largest amounts are being spent by China (US$648 billion, or 9.1 percent of its GDP), Japan (US$485.9 billion, 11.4 percent of GDP) and the United States (US$787 billion, 5.7 percent of GDP).[8]

Box 1.1 Green and total fiscal stimulus of the G20 countries

In their communiqué issued at the April 2, 2009, London summit, the leaders of the G20, the world's twenty largest developed and emerging economies, stressed their commitment to "ensuring a fair and sustainable recovery for all" by stating: "We will make the transition towards clean, innovative, resource efficient, low carbon

---

[6] The members of the G20 include nineteen countries (Argentina, Australia, Brazil, Canada, China, France, Germany, India, Indonesia, Italy, Japan, Mexico, Russia, Saudi Arabia, South Africa, South Korea, Turkey, the United Kingdom and the United States) plus the European Union (EU).

[7] For an overview of the 11 November 2008 G20 summit, see Rao, P. K. 2009. "Moving toward the next G-20 summit." *Global Economy Journal* 9 (1), article 4. Available at www.bepress.com/gej/vol9/iss1/4.

[8] Based on 2007 estimated GDP in terms of purchasing power parity (PPP) from the US Central Intelligence Agency (CIA). "The world factbook." Available at www.cia.gov/library/publications/the-world-factbook/rankorder/2001rank.html. In 2007 world GDP was estimated at $65,610 billion, EU GDP at $14,430 billion, US GDP at $13,780 billion and China's at $7,099 billion. Throughout this book GDP in 2007 is used as the benchmark, since the current global recession is widely regarded as having started in December 2007.

technologies and infrastructure… We will identify and work together on further measures to build sustainable economies."[9]

As the table below indicates, some G20 economies are already including "green" investments in their stimulus packages to reduce carbon dependency, enhance economic recovery and create jobs. Of the nearly US$3 trillion that has been spent worldwide on fiscal stimulus, over US$460 billion has been spent by governments on green investments, mostly by G20 governments.

For example, the US$787 billion American Recovery and Reinvestment Act (ARRA) in the United States includes around US$78.5 billion to retrofit buildings for enhanced energy efficiency, enlarge the mass transit and freight rail network, construct a "smart" electrical grid transmission system and expand renewable energy supply. Additional investments in water infrastructure resulted in a US$94.1 billion green stimulus package. These investments constitute an amount equivalent to 0.7 percent of US GDP over the next two years, and are anticipated to create around 2 million jobs.[10] South Korea has launched a national Green New Deal plan. At a cost of US$36.3 billion from 2009 to 2012, around 3 percent of the country's GDP, the plan invests in low-carbon projects, water management, recycling and ecological protection. The initiative will create 960,000 jobs, with 149,000 new construction jobs in 2009. The low-carbon projects include the development of railroads and mass transit, fuel-efficient vehicles and clean fuels, energy conservation and environmentally friendly buildings. These investments total 1.2 percent of GDP, comprise 95 percent of all South Korea's fiscal stimulus spending and are expected to create at least 334,000 new

---

[9] The full text of the G20 London communiqué is available at www. londonsummit.gov.uk/en.

[10] In addition, the October 2008 Emergency Economic Stabilization Act in the United States also included US$185 billion in tax cuts and credits, including US$18.2 billion for investments in wind and solar power and carbon capture and storage. The 2010/11 federal budget allocates an additional US$9.4 billion to a high-speed rail state grant program and in further clean water investments. For further details, see Robins, Nick, Robert Clover and Charanjit Singh. 2009. *Building a Green Recovery*. New York, HSBC Global Research.

Global stimulus packages and green investments (as of July 1, 2009)

	Total fiscal stimulus (US$ billion)	Green stimulus (US$ billion)			GDP (US$ billion)[b]	GS as % of TS	GS as % of GDP
		Low-carbon[a]	Other	Total			
Argentina	13.2				526.4	0.0	0.0
Australia	43.8	9.3		9.3	773.0	21.2	1.2
Brazil	3.6				1,849.0	0.0	0.0
Canada	31.8	2.5	0.3	2.8	1,271.0	8.3	0.2
China	647.5	175.1	41.3	216.4	7,099.0	33.4	3.0
France	33.7	7.1		7.1	2,075.0	21.2	0.3
Germany	104.8	13.8		13.8	2,807.0	13.2	0.5
India	13.7				2,966.0	0.0	0.0
Indonesia	5.9				843.7	1.7	0.0
Italy	103.5	1.3		1.3	1,800.0	1.3	0.1
Japan	639.9	36.0		36.0	4,272.0	5.6	0.8
Mexico	7.7	0.8		0.8	1,353.0	9.7	0.1
Russia	20.0				2,097.0	0.0	0.0
Saudi Arabia	126.8		9.5	9.5	546.0	7.5	1.7
South Africa	7.5	0.7	0.1	0.8	467.8	10.7	0.2
South Korea	38.1	14.7	21.6	36.3	1,206.0	95.2	3.0
Turkey					853.9		0.0

United Kingdom	34.9	3.7	0.1	3.7	2,130.0	10.6	0.2
United States[c]	787.0	78.5	15.6	94.1	13,780.0	12.0	0.7
European Union[d]	38.8	22.8		22.8	14,430.0	58.7	0.2
Total G20	2,702.2	366.3	88.4	454.7	63,145.8	16.8	0.7
Total other[e]	314.1	7.6	1.0	8.6	6,902.9	2.7	0.1
Global total	3,016.3	373.9	89.4	463.3	70,048.7	15.4	0.7

Notes: [a] Includes support for renewable energy, carbon capture and sequestration, energy efficiency, public transport and rail, and improving electrical grid transmission.

[b] Based on 2007 estimated GDP in PPP terms, from the CIA's "The world factbook."

[c] From the February 2009 American Recovery and Reinvestment Act only. The October 2008 Emergency Economic Stabilization Act also included US$185 billion in tax cuts and credits, including US$18.2 billion for investments in wind, solar and carbon capture and storage.

[d] Only the direct contribution by the European Union is included.

[e] Includes the national stimulus packages of non-G20 EU countries: Austria, Belgium, Greece, Hungary, the Netherlands, Poland, Portugal, Spain and Sweden. The non-EU countries in this group are Chile, Israel, Malaysia, New Zealand, Norway, the Philippines, Switzerland, Thailand and Vietnam.

Sources: Robins, Nick, Robert Clover and James Magness. 2009. *The Green Rebound.* New York, HSBC Global Research; Robins, Nick, Robert Clover and Charanjit Singh. 2009. *A Climate for Recovery.* New York, HSBC Global Research; Robins, Nick, Robert Clover and Charanjit Singh. 2009. *Building a Green Recovery.* New York, HSBC Global Research; and Khatiwada, Sameer. 2009. *Stimulus Packages to Counter Global Economic Crisis: A Review.* Discussion Paper no. 196/2009. Geneva, ILO.

jobs. Over 33 percent of China's US$647.5 billion in total stimulus spending is for energy efficiency and environmental improvements, rail transport and new electricity grid infrastructure. The UK government has devoted around 11 percent of its US$34.9 billion fiscal stimulus to green investments, including announcing in April 2009 its own "green economy" budget, which will feature a range of low-carbon investments aimed at creating 400,000 new jobs over the next eight years.

Although these initiatives are a promising start, they fall short of a major global "green recovery" effort. For example, the large-scale green stimulus programs equivalent to 3 percent of GDP that are planned by South Korea and China are the exception rather than the norm. Of the US$2.7 trillion that G20 economies have already committed to fiscal stimulus since the start of the global recession, about 17 percent has been devoted to low-carbon, energy efficiency or environmental improvement measures – with just a handful of countries involved. In total, green stimulus investments amount to around 0.7 percent of the G20 countries' GDP. Thus, if the G20 is serious about "further measures to build sustainable economies," then it needs to adopt additional initiatives and policies towards this goal, as well as coordinate the timing and implementation of these measures.

2008 was memorable for more than just the global financial upheaval and beginnings of a worldwide economic recession, however; it was also the year of a world fuel and food crisis.

In July 2008 the price of oil peaked at US$145 per barrel. It then fell rapidly as the global recession worsened, reaching a low of US$35 per barrel in January and February 2009. By July 2009 the price of oil had rebounded to approximately $65 per barrel. Other fossil fuel prices have followed similar trends, though natural gas and coal prices have yet to recover as quickly as that of oil. Thus, despite the recession-induced sharp drop in prices, most forecasts predict that the era of "cheap" fossil fuel energy and secure world supplies is over.[11]

Prices of other commodities, especially food and raw materials, have followed fossil fuel trends. Global food prices increased almost 60 percent during the first half of 2008, with basic staples such as grains and oilseeds showing the largest increases. The recent fall in energy and fertilizer prices has reversed this trend somewhat, but food prices in the near term are expected to remain much higher than during the 1990s and more than 60 percent higher than their levels in 2003.

The world economy also faces ongoing global challenges, such as climate change, energy insecurity, growing freshwater scarcity, threats to ecosystems, and widespread poverty in developing economies.

The fourth assessment of the Intergovernmental Panel on Climate Change (IPCC), established in 1988 by the World Meteorological Organization (WMO) and the United Nations Environment Programme (UNEP), confirms that the carbon dependency of the world economy is contributing to global warming.[12] Global greenhouse emissions from human activities have grown since pre-industrial times, rising 70 percent between 1970 and 2004. Higher atmospheric concentrations of greenhouse gases (GHGs) are due primarily to fossil fuel use, with land use change and agriculture providing significant but smaller contributions. The result has been increasing global surface temperatures, sea levels rising at an average rate of 1.8 mm/year since 1961, and disruptions to ecosystems. Greenhouse gas emissions are expected to continue at or above current rates, causing further global warming, sea level rise and ecological damage. Climate change is already linked to an increase in extreme weather events, such as storms, floods and droughts. These events destroy lives, force population migration and contribute to

[11] International Energy Agency [IEA]. 2008. *World Energy Outlook 2008*. Paris, IEA.

[12] IPCC. 2007. *Climate Change 2007: Synthesis Report*. Report of the Intergovernmental Panel on Climate Change [core writing team: R. K. Pachauri and A. Reisinger (eds.)]. Geneva, IPCC.

food shortages. Across all cities worldwide, about 40 million people are exposed to a one-in-100-year extreme coastal flooding event.[13]

The Millennium Ecosystem Assessment (MA) has documented how global economic activity and population growth have affected the world's ecosystems and the various services, or benefits, that they produce.[14] Over the past fifty years ecosystems have been modified more rapidly and extensively than in any comparable period of time in human history, largely to meet growing demands for food, freshwater, timber, fiber and fuel. The result has been a substantial and largely irreversible loss in biological diversity and the benefits provided by ecosystems. The MA found that approximately fifteen out of twenty-four of the major ecosystem services it examined are being degraded or used unsustainably, including freshwater, capture fisheries, air and water purification, and the regulation of regional and local climate, natural hazards and pests.

Poor people in developing countries are particularly vulnerable to the loss of critical ecological services.[15] Nearly 1.3 billion people – over a fifth of the world's population – live in fragile environments found in developing economies (see box 1.2). Almost a half of them (631 million) are composed of the rural poor. They live on lands prone to degradation and water stress, and in upland areas, forest systems and drylands. These marginal environments are areas "where the

[13] Nicholls, R. J., S. Hanson, C. Herweijer, N. Patmore, S. Hallegatte, Jan Corfee-Morlot, Jean Chateua and R. Muir-Wood. 2007. *Ranking of the World's Cities Most Exposed to Coastal Flooding Today and in the Future: Executive Summary*. Paris, Organisation for Economic Co-operation and Development [OECD] (extract from Environment Working Paper no. 1). The top ten cities in terms of exposed population are Mumbai, Guangzhou, Shanghai, Miami, Ho Chi Minh City, Kolkata, Greater New York, Osaka-Kobe, Alexandria and New Orleans.

[14] MA. 2005. *Ecosystems and Human Well-being: Current State and Trends.* Washington, DC, Island Press.

[15] OECD. 2008. *Costs of Inaction on Key Environmental Challenges.* Paris, OECD; United Nations Development Programme (UNDP). 2008. *Human Development Report 2007/2008: Fighting Climate Change: Human Solidarity in a Divided World.* New York, UNDP; Sukhdev, Pavan. 2008. *The Economics of Ecosystems and Biodiversity: An Interim Report.* Brussels, European Communities.

people's links to the land are critical for the sustainability of communities, pastures, forests, and other natural resources" (see box 1.2).[16] In developing regions, those countries with a larger fraction of their population living on fragile lands also tend to have a higher incidence of rural poverty (see figure 1.1).

Box 1.2 The global poor and fragile environments

The table below indicates that over one-quarter of the people in developing countries – almost 1.3 billion – survive on "fragile lands," which are defined by the World Bank as "areas that present significant constraints for intensive agriculture and where the people's links to the land are critical for the sustainability of communities, pastures, forests, and other natural resources."[17] These populations living on fragile land in developing countries account for many of the people in extreme poverty, living on less than US$2 per day, and include 518 million living in arid regions with no access to irrigation systems, 430 million on soils unsuitable for agriculture, 216 million on land with steep slopes and more than 130 million in fragile forest systems. In other words, the economic livelihoods of the people living on fragile lands are directly and indirectly affected by the services provided by surrounding ecosystems.

Figure 1.1 further illustrates that rural poverty is correlated with the fraction of the population in developing countries found on fragile lands. As the figure indicates, the sample of sixty countries that have substantial numbers of people living in fragile environments – ranging from 20 to 30 percent of the population to over 70 percent – also have a high percentage of the rural population living in extreme poverty (45.3 percent on average). What is more, the incidence of

---

[16] World Bank. 2002. *World Development Report 2003: Sustainable Development in a Dynamic World: Transforming Institutions, Growth and Quality of Life*. Washington, DC, World Bank: 59. See also Comprehensive Assessment of Water Management in Agriculture. 2007. *Water for Food, Water for Life: A Comprehensive Assessment of Water Management in Agriculture*. London, Earthscan, and Colombo, Sri Lanka, International Water Management Institute.

[17] World Bank 2002: 59 (see fn 16).

Distribution of world's population and rural poor on fragile land

(a) Distribution of world's population[a]

Region	Population in 2000 (millions)	Population in fragile lands	
		Number (millions)	Share of total (%)
Latin America and the Caribbean	515.3	68	13.1
Middle East and north Africa	293.0	110	37.6
Sub-Saharan Africa	658.4	258	39.3
South Asia	1,354.5	330	24.4
East Asia and Pacific	1,856.5	469	25.3
Eastern Europe and central Asia	474.7	58	12.1
OECD group[b]	850.4	94	11.1
Other	27.3	2	6.9
Total	6,030.1	1,389	23.0
Total developing economies[c]	5,179.7	1,295	25.0
Total Latin American, African and Asian developing economies[d]	4,677.7	1,235	26.4

(b) Distribution of rural poor in developing regions[e]

Region	Rural poor on favored lands (millions)	Rural poor on fragile lands	
		Number (millions)	Share of total (%)
Central and South America	24	47	66
West Asia and north Africa	11	35	76

Table (*cont.*)

Sub-Saharan Africa	65	175	73
Asia	219	374	63
Total	319	631	66

Notes: [a] From Barbier, Edward B. 2005. *Natural Resources and Economic Development*. Cambridge, Cambridge University Press: tab. 1.7, and adapted from World Bank. 2002. *World Development Report 2003: Sustainable Development in a Dynamic World. Transforming Institutions, Growth and Quality of Life*. Washington, DC, World Bank: tab. 4.2, which defines fragile lands as areas that present significant constraints for intensive agriculture and where the people's links to the land are critical for the sustainability of communities, pastures, forests and other natural resources; they include arid regions with no access to irrigation, areas with soils unsuitable for agriculture, land with steep slopes and fragile forest systems.

[b] The OECD group of countries includes Australia, Austria, Belgium, Canada, Denmark, Finland, France, Germany, Greece, Iceland, Ireland, Italy, Japan, Luxembourg, the Netherlands, New Zealand, Norway, Portugal, Spain, Sweden, Switzerland, the United Kingdom and the United States.

[c] World total less OECD group.

[d] World total less OECD group, eastern Europe and central Asia, and other.

[e] Adapted from Comprehensive Assessment of Water Management in Agriculture. 2007. *Water for Food, Water for Life: A Comprehensive Assessment of Water Management in Agriculture*. London, Earthscan, and Colombo, International Water Management Institute: tab. 15.1, which equates fragile lands with marginal lands, or areas with the greatest potential for land and water degradation – i.e. land with highly weathered soils, steep slopes, inadequate or excess rainfall, and high temperatures.

rural poverty rises when developing countries have more of their populations concentrated on fragile lands.

The tendency for the rural poor to be clustered in the most marginal environments is also supported by studies at the regional and country level, although there can be important differences within and between countries. For example, researchers from the World Bank have examined the "poverty–environment nexus" in three of the poorest countries in southeast Asia – Cambodia, Laos and Vietnam.[18] In Cambodia, the core poor in rural areas appear to be located in areas that are already heavily deforested; on the other hand, poor populations tend to be more concentrated in the lowlands rather than steeply sloped lands. In Laos, the poorest provinces in the north and northeast also have the highest incidence of poor rural populations, who appear to be concentrated in forested areas and the highlands. In Vietnam, large poor populations confined to steep slopes exist in the provinces comprising the northern and central highlands, but extensive rural poverty is also found along the north central coast and the Red River delta.

The rapid growth of rural populations in the developing world is being outpaced by the even faster growth of urban populations. In 2007 2.38 billion people, approximately 44 percent of the population of developing countries, lived in urban areas.[19] By 2019 half the developing world will live in cities, and by 2050 5.33 billion people, or 67 percent of the population in developing countries, will inhabit urban areas. This brisk pace of urbanization means that the growing populations in the cities will be confronted with increased congestion and pollution and rising energy, water and raw material demands.

---

[18] Dasgupta, Susmita, Uwe Deichmann, Craig Meisner and David Wheeler. 2005. "Where is the poverty–environment nexus? Evidence from Cambodia, Lao PDR, and Vietnam." *World Development* 33 (4): 617–38; Minot, Nicholas, and Bob Baulch. 2002. *The Spatial Distribution of Poverty in Vietnam and the Potential for Targeting*. Policy Research Working Paper no. 2829. Washington DC, World Bank.

[19] UN. "World urbanization prospects: the 2007 revision, executive summary." Available at http://esa.un.org/unup.

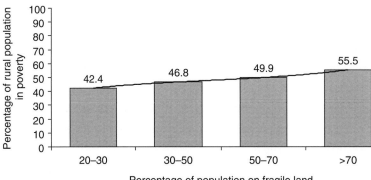

FIGURE 1.1 The location of the rural poor in developing regions
Notes: Developing regions are defined as low- and middle-income countries in Africa, Latin America, Asia and Oceania, based on World Bank
definitions (countries with 2003 gross national income [GNI] per capita
of $9,385 or less), from World Bank. 2006. *World Development Indicators
2006.* Washington, DC, World Bank. Percentage of rural population in
poverty is also from World Bank. 2006. *World Development Indicators
2006.* Washington, DC, World Bank. Percentage of population on fragile land is from World Bank. 2002. *World Development Report 2003.*
Washington, DC, World Bank: tab. 4.3. Number of observations is sixty
countries, of which twenty-four have 20 to 30 percent of population on
fragile land, twenty-nine have 30 to 50 percent, five have 50 to 70 percent
and two have more than 70 percent. The mean average rural poverty rate
across all countries is 45.3 percent, and the median is 43.1 percent.

Although such environmental problems are similar to those faced
by industrialized countries, the pace and scale of urban population
growth in developing countries are likely to lead to more severe and
acute health and welfare impacts.

The rural and urban poor face severe water problems in particular. One in five people in the developing world lacks access to
sufficient clean water, and about half the developing world's population, 2.6 billion people, do not have access to basic sanitation. More
than 660 million of the people without sanitation live on less than
US$2 a day, and more than 385 million on less than US$1 a day.[20]

[20] UNDP. 2006. *Human Development Report 2006: Beyond Scarcity: Power,
Poverty and the Global Water Crisis.* New York, UNDP.

The scarcity of freshwater supplies relative to increasing demand, and the lack of clean water and sanitation available for millions of the poor in developing regions, point to another looming global problem: an emerging water crisis.

Collectively, these global economic and environmental challenges are severely constraining the ability to sustain prosperity in developed economies and to achieve the Millennium Development Goals (MDGs) in the developing world.

In sum, the world economic recession of 2008/9 is embedded in a series of overlapping global crises. On the one hand, there is the current contraction in the world economy, trade and employment, which is the most pronounced downturn since the Great Depression of the 1930s. The severity of the current recession should not distract us, however, from the other global economic and environment problems that preceded it – and which will return if we fail to address them urgently. To some extent, the recession may have given us temporary respite from some of these problems, such as energy insecurity and increasing greenhouse gas emissions. The recession is worsening global poverty, however, which is likely to increase the numbers of the world's poor as well as increase their vulnerability to climate change, ecological degradation and food and fuel crises.

GREEN FISCAL STIMULUS AND THE G20

There are encouraging signs that some major economies have taken seriously the threat posed by these multiple global crises.

As we have seen, at the April 2, 2009, London summit, the leaders of the G20 stressed their commitment to "ensuring a fair and sustainable recovery for all" by making "the transition towards clean, innovative, resource efficient, low carbon technologies and infrastructure."

As box 1.1 indicates, some G20 economies appear to have acted on this objective, by including "green" investments in their stimulus packages to reduce carbon dependency, enhance economic recovery and create jobs. The recovery program in the United States includes investments amounting to 0.7 percent of US GDP over the next two years and is anticipated to create around 2 million jobs. South Korea's Green New Deal plan is equivalent to around 3 percent of GDP and is expected to create 960,000 new jobs by 2012. Over a third of China's stimulus spending is for energy efficiency and environmental improvements, rail transport and new electricity grid infrastructure, while the UK government has devoted around 11 percent of its fiscal stimulus to green investments and aims to create 400,000 new jobs over the next eight years.

As box 1.1 makes clear, though, these initiatives may be a promising start, but they fall short of a major global "green recovery" effort. Of the nearly US$3 trillion that has been spent worldwide on fiscal stimulus in response to the recession, over $460 billion has been spent by governments on green investments. The vast majority of the green stimulus spending has been by the G20. As of July 1, 2009, however, of the $2.7 trillion in total fiscal spending by the G20 economies, only about 17 percent has been devoted to low-carbon, energy efficiency or environmental improvement measures. In total, green stimulus investments amount to around 0.7 percent of the aggregate G20 GDP.

Not all G20 economies have responded to the recession with low-carbon and environmental investments. As figure 1.2 indicates, just two countries, the United States and China, account for over two-thirds of the global expenditure on green fiscal stimulus. The world's largest economy, the European Union, has contributed substantially less to green recovery efforts. The governments of key European economies, such as France, Germany, Sweden and the United Kingdom, are spending much less on low-carbon and environmental investments than the major Asia-Pacific economies, Australia, Japan and South Korea. Several G20 governments have not committed any funds to green stimulus, including the large emerging market economies of Brazil, India and Russia (see box 1.1).

As shown in figure 1.3, green stimulus measures and investments amount globally to around 15 percent of all fiscal stimulus spending during the current recession. Only a handful of economies have devoted a substantial amount of their total fiscal spending to

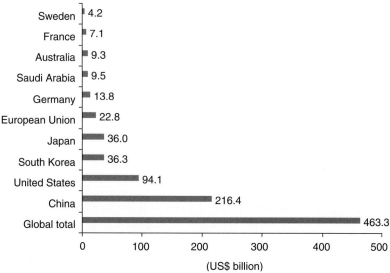

FIGURE I.2 Total green stimulus spending by country
Notes: Based on box I.I. The figure displays the top ten economies by total amount of green stimulus spending.

green investments, however. The most notable is South Korea, whose Green New Deal plan accounts for nearly all of its fiscal response to the recession. China currently apportions around a third of its total fiscal spending to green measures. Over one-half of the direct contribution of the European Union to spending under the European Recovery Plan is for low-carbon investments, but, as indicated in figure 1.3, the overall size of this investment is relatively small. In comparison, the United States has made a sizable commitment to green stimulus measures in the American Recovery and Reinvestment Act, though they still comprise only 12 percent of the act's budget. Overall, most G20 governments have been conservative in allocating substantial amounts of their stimulus spending to low-carbon and other environmental investments.

As a result, as figure 1.3 indicates, low-carbon and environmental investments by most G20 governments account for 0.7 percent or less of GDP during the current recession. Large-scale green

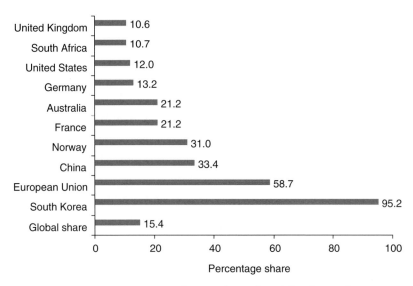

FIGURE 1.3 Green stimulus as a share of total fiscal stimulus
Notes: Based on box 1.1. The figure displays the top ten economies by green stimulus spending as a percentage of total fiscal expenditure.

stimulus programs such as the 3 percent of GDP planned by South Korea and China are the exception rather than the norm.

Current global green stimulus spending by G20 governments is therefore unlikely to initiate the global "green" recovery promised in the April 2009 G20 communiqué. It is also questionable whether low-carbon and other environmental investments on their own can have much impact on economies in which fossil fuel subsidies and other market distortions, as well as the lack of effective environmental pricing policies and regulations, diminish the incentives for stimulating both public and private investment in green sectors. In addition, the green stimulus spending of G20 governments is directed primarily to their own economies. Less effort has been devoted to assisting developing economies, which are expected to face worsening poverty and environmental problems as a result of the global recession. Green fiscal spending by individual governments will also have little impact on the global problems of ecological degradation, climate change and energy insecurity, especially if such spending is not coordinated across major economies, is supported by only a handful of G20 governments, and remains small relative to the size of most economies.

Thus, if the G20 is serious about its stated aim to "further measures to build sustainable economies," then it needs to adopt additional initiatives and policies towards this goal, as well as coordinating the timing and implementation of these measures. To understand why a more comprehensive and coordinated effort is required by the G20, the rest of this introduction outlines briefly the danger posed by business-as-usual growth and why a Global Green New Deal is an important alternative for "rethinking" the economic recovery. ⸻

BUSINESS-AS-USUAL GROWTH

The indications are that, if the world economy fails to shift from a business-as-usual-growth path once it has recovered, avoiding future global environmental and economic crises may be difficult.

Given the current fossil fuel dependency of the world economy, once growth resumes the oil price could rise significantly. For example, the IEA suggests that global energy demand will rise by 45 percent by 2030, leading to a significant increase in real fossil fuel prices. The IEA trend projection expects the oil price to rise to US$180 per barrel once growth resumes.[21]

The impact of higher fossil fuel prices will be felt throughout the global economy, but especially by the poor. In 2008 rising fuel prices cost consumers in developing economies US$400 billion in higher energy expenditures and US$240 billion in dearer food. The accompanying rise in food prices led to an increase in the number of people worldwide affected by poverty of between 130 million and 155 million.[22] Such increases in energy prices will worsen the problem of global energy poverty. Billions of people in

[21] IEA 2008 (see fn 11).
[22] World Bank 2009 (see fn 1).

developing countries have no access to modern energy services, and those consumers who do have access often pay high prices for services that are erratic and unreliable. Among the energy poor are 2.4 billion people who rely on traditional biomass fuels for cooking and heating, including 89 percent of the population of sub-Saharan Africa, and another 1.6 billion people who do not have access to electricity.[23]

Even if demand for energy remains flat until 2030, just to off-set the effect of oilfield decline the global economy will still need 45 million barrels per day of additional gross production capacity – an amount approximately equal to four times the current capacity of Saudi Arabia.[24] With the resumption of world economic growth on a business-as-usual path, though, fossil fuel demand is unlikely to stay constant, despite the rise in energy prices. As we have seen, the IEA expects a 45 percent increase in global energy demand by 2030.[25] Rising consumption of fossil fuels will worsen energy security concerns for carbon-dependent economies, in terms of an increased concentration of the remaining oil reserves in a smaller number of countries, the risk of oil supply disruptions, rising energy use in the transport sector and insufficient additions of oil supply capacity to keep pace with demand growth.[26]

A world economic recovery that revives fossil fuel consumption will accelerate global climate change. Based on current trends, greenhouse gas emissions will also increase by 45 percent in 2030, to 41 gigatonnes (Gt), with three-quarters of the rise generated by China, India and the Middle East.[27] Without a change in the carbon dependency of the global economy, the IEA warns that the

[23] Modi, Vijay, Susan McDade, Dominique Lallement and Jamal Saghir. 2005. *Energy Services for the Millennium Development Goals*. Washington, DC, World Bank, and New York, UNDP.

[24] IEA 2008 (see fn 11).

[25] IEA 2008 (see fn 11).

[26] IEA. 2007. *Oil Supply Security 2007: Emergency Response of IEA Countries*. Paris, IEA.

[27] IEA 2008 (see fn 11).

atmospheric concentration of GHGs could double by the end of this century, and lead to an eventual global average temperature increase of up to 6°C.[28] Such a scenario is likely to cause a sea level rise of between 0.26 and 0.59 meters, and severely disrupt freshwater availability, ecosystems, food production, coastal populations and human health.[29] According to the Stern Review, with 5 to 6°C warming, the world economy could sustain losses equivalent to 5 to 10 percent of global GDP, with poor countries suffering costs in excess of 10 percent of GDP.[30]

The world's poor are especially vulnerable to the climate-driven risks posed by a rising sea level, coastal erosion and more frequent storms. Around 14 percent of the population, and 21 percent of urban dwellers in developing countries, live in low-elevation coastal zones that are exposed to these risks.[31] By the 2070s it is thought that 150 million urban dwellers will live in areas prone to extreme coastal flooding events.[32] The livelihoods of billions – from poor farmers to urban slum dwellers – are threatened by a wide range of climate-induced risks affecting food security, water availability, natural disasters, ecosystem stability and human health.[33] For example, as shown in box 1.1 and figure 1.1, the rural poor in developing regions

---

[28] IEA 2008 (see fn 11).

[29] IPCC 2007 (see fn 12).

[30] Stern, Nicholas. 2007. *The Economics of Climate Change: The Stern Review.* Cambridge, Cambridge University Press. Although the estimates in the Stern Review of the economic damages of climate change are widely cited, as Richard Tol has shown, any such estimates are affected by the choice of discount rate and equity weights, and are subject to large uncertainties. See Tol, Richard S .J. 2008. "The social costs of carbon: trends, outliers and catastrophes." *Economics: The Open-access, Open-assessment E-journal* 2 (2008–25). Available at www.economics-ejournal.org/economics/journalarticles/2008–25. For example, Tol finds that the estimates in the Stern Review are highly pessimistic, even compared to other studies that employ low discount rates on future damages.

[31] McGranahan, G., D. Balk, D. Anderson and B. Anderson. 2007. "The rising tide: assessing the risks of climate change and human settlements in low elevation coastal zones." *Environment and Urbanization* 19 (1): 17–37.

[32] Nicholls *et al.* 2007 (see fn 13).

[33] OECD 2008 (see fn 15); UNDP 2008 (see fn 15); Sukhdev 2008 (see fn 15).

tend to be clustered in areas of ecologically fragile land, which are already prone to degradation, water stress and poor soils.

Global ecosystems and freshwater sources are also endangered by an economic recovery that ignores environmental degradation. As discussed above, one of the more alarming findings of the Millennium Ecosystem Assessment has been the extent to which the past half-century of global economic activity and population growth have led to the despoliation or unsustainable use of major ecosystem services worldwide, including freshwater, capture fisheries, air and water purification, and the regulation of regional and local climate, natural hazards and pests.[34] A return to business-as-usual growth in the world economy would probably continue these worsening ecological trends.

Once again, it is likely to be the poor in developing regions who are disproportionately affected. For example, global water scarcity manifests itself as a water poverty problem for the world's poor. One of the biggest health and economic problems facing the poorest households in developing countries is the lack of access to sufficient clean water and basic sanitation.[35] If a worldwide economic recovery fails to tackle the emerging problem of global water scarcity, or if it makes the problem worse, then more and more of the world's poor will be unable to afford improved access to clean water and sanitation.

As a result, even the claim that business-as-usual growth will reduce global poverty significantly is questionable. Although the current economic recession is likely to consign more people to extreme poverty, a return to business-as-usual growth may not necessarily reduce world poverty significantly. It is true that, from 1981 to 2005, the number of extreme poor fell globally by slightly over 500 million, from 1.9 billion to 1.4 billion.[36] Resuming business-as-usual growth is unlikely to reduce poverty rapidly over the coming

[34] MA 2005 (see fn 14).
[35] UNDP 2006 (see fn 20).
[36] Chen and Ravallion 2008 (see fn 4).

decades, however. As noted previously, even before the current global economic recession it was estimated that, by 2015, there would still be nearly 1 billion people living on less than US$1 a day and almost 3 billion living on less than US$2 a day.[37] Improving the livelihoods of the remaining poor may be an intractable problem under a business-as-usual growth scenario. One reason, as we have seen, is to do with the areas where many of the poor are located and how they survive. In general, about twice as many poor people live in rural as in urban areas in the developing world.[38] Moreover, as indicated in box 1.2, well over 600 million of the rural poor currently live on lands prone to degradation and water stress, and in upland areas, forest systems and drylands that are vulnerable to climatic and ecological disruptions. A world economic recovery that does not also address directly the problems of energy and water poverty, climate change and ecological risks will have little impact on improving the livelihoods of many of the world's poor.

A GLOBAL GREEN NEW DEAL

Meeting the short-run challenges of reviving the worldwide economy and creating jobs must not mean sacrificing long-run economic and environmental sustainability. Carefully designed economic policies, investments and incentives aimed at immediate global economic recovery and employment creation should be made compatible with reducing the carbon dependency of the world economy, protecting vulnerable ecosystems and alleviating poverty. Ignoring the latter objectives would instead provide just a "temporary fix" to

---

[37] Based on projections to 2015 of the share of world population living on US$1 a day and US$2 a day in ILO 2004 (see fn 4) and 2015 mid-level projections of world population from UNDP 2006 (see fn 20).

[38] Chen, Shaohua, and Martin Ravallion. 2007. "Absolute poverty measures for the developing world, 1981–2004." *Proceedings of the National Academy of Sciences* 104 (43): 16757–62. Chen and Ravallion note that the US$1-a-day rural poverty rate of 30 percent in 2002 is more than double the urban rate, and that, although 70 percent of the rural population lives on less than US$2 a day, the proportion in urban areas is less than half that figure.

the world economy, perpetuating long-run economic instability and continuing environmental deterioration.

The premise of this book is that the current economic crisis has brought governments together to instigate a worldwide recovery. International cooperation over financial and economic policy in response to the current global recession is perhaps the most important achievement of the Washington and London G20 summits in 2008/9. This progress on international policy coordination by the major world economies should also be used to address other important global economic, social and environmental challenges.

Addressing both short-run economic recovery and other global challenges will require bold measures by world leaders. Seventy-five years ago, during the depths of the Great Depression, President Franklin D. Roosevelt of the United States launched a series of wide-ranging programs to provide employment and social security, reform tax policies and business practices, and stimulate the economy. The programs instigated under Roosevelt's New Deal were implemented over a short period, and the scale of the investments and expenditures was sufficiently large – equivalent to approximately 3 to 4 percent of US GDP during this period – to affect the structure not just of the US economy but even of the world economy.

The multiple crises facing the world today demand the same kind of government leadership as shown by Roosevelt's New Deal in the 1930s, but at the global scale and embracing a wider vision.

Efforts to revive the world economy should not stop at simply recreating the same pattern of global economic development of the past. Instead, serious consideration must be given to new and bold measures that not only stimulate economic growth and employment opportunities but also move the world economy further along the path of more environmentally sustainable development. There is a need to "green" the world economy as we revive it, not rebuild the old "brown" one. For developed countries, the objective should be to revive economic prosperity while demonstrating that restructuring the economy with a view to reducing carbon dependency and environmental impacts is feasible. For developing countries, the objective should be to ensure that moving to a more sustainable economy will at the same time help achieve the Millennium Development Goals. As the economist Jeffrey Sachs has argued, we must not lose sight of the global objective of ending extreme poverty by 2025.[39]

In sum, what the world needs urgently today is not just increased public spending to quicken economic recovery and create employment opportunities. Such an injection of spending, even if it is the US$3 trillion of fiscal stimulus that has been spent so far during the current recession, is necessary but not sufficient. Instead, what is called for is a new "Global Green New Deal" to meet the multiple global challenges.

The package of policy, investment and incentive measures comprising a GGND must therefore have three principal objectives.

- Revive the world economy, create employment opportunities and protect vulnerable groups.
- Reduce carbon dependency, ecosystem degradation and water scarcity.
- Further the Millennium Development Goal of ending extreme world poverty by 2025.[40]

Achieving these objectives will require national actions by governments as well as global coordination of these efforts and additional international actions. Such a worldwide policy initiative is imperative. As noted above, the green stimulus initiatives of some G20 economies are a promising start, but they do not on their own comprise a GGND. A concerted and coordinated global effort could, however, achieve such a GGND over the next couple of years.

The aim of a GGND strategy should be to revive the international economy and to forge a new global economic development model based on reducing environmental harm and scarcities, training workers for

---

[39] Sachs, Jeffrey D. 2005. *The End of Poverty: Economic Possibilities for Our Time.* New York, Penguin Books.

[40] The original goal set by the UN was 2015, but, given the current global recession and its impacts on world poverty outlined above, a more realistic deadline now is 2025.

twenty-first-century skills, creating new employment opportunities and reducing the carbon dependency of all economies. The scale of investments and spending required will be large and the timeframe for implementing such measures is short. Nonetheless, the opportune moment for instigating the Global Green New Deal is now.

At no other time in recent world history has it been possible to achieve a worldwide consensus over a package of policies that can converge on attaining all three fundamental objectives. The purpose of this book is to provide a framework, or "blueprint," for policy discussion on what a GGND might look like.

This book should therefore be seen as the first step in the process of developing a GGND. The focus is mainly on framing the broad dimensions of this strategy, adding important examples and explanations wherever possible, but it is necessarily limited in the details, development and discussion of specific policy recommendations.

The organization of the remainder of the book is as follows.

Part I has made the case as to why a GGND strategy is essential to the economic and environmental sustainability of the global economy.

Part II provides an overview of the key components of the GGND that are the basis of national actions by individual governments. The broad strategies for national action are outlined, and specific measures for each strategy are assessed for their impact on a sustained and "greener" economic recovery. The different national-level actions and the challenges faced by governments in high-income (mainly OECD) economies, large emerging market economies (e.g. transition and middle-income economies, including Brazil, China, India and Russia) and low-income economies are all identified and discussed.[41]

---

[41] According to World Bank. 2008. *World Development Indicators 2008.* Washington, DC, World Bank, high-income economies are those in which 2006 GNI per capita was $11,116 or more. In contrast, low- and middle-income economies are those in which 2006 GNI per capita was $11,115 or less. Most high-income economies consist of those countries that comprise

Part III focuses on the actions necessary at the global level to facilitate national governments' efforts to overcome the challenges they face in implementing the GGND strategy and to enhance the sustained economic benefits gained from such policies. Of particular concern are the constraints faced by the emerging market and low-income economies as they strive to accelerate economic development, expand trade opportunities and alleviate widespread poverty.

Part IV concludes the book by summarizing the main findings and the recommendations for national and international action under the proposed GGND and discussing the wider implications of the proposed policies for creating employment opportunities, inducing technological innovation, overcoming fiscal deficits and restructuring the world economy. The final chapter looks to the future, at the challenges and opportunities for creating a truly "greener" world economy.

the Organisation for Economic Co-operation and Development. The countries currently in the OECD are, from Europe, Austria, Belgium, the Czech Republic, Denmark, Finland, France, Germany, Greece, Hungary, Iceland, Ireland, Italy, Luxembourg, the Netherlands, Norway, Poland, Portugal, Slovakia, Spain, Sweden, Switzerland, Turkey and the United Kingdom and, from other regions, Australia, Canada, Japan, Mexico, New Zealand, South Korea and the United States. A few of these OECD countries do not meet the World Bank's definition of "high-income" economies, however, such as Hungary, Mexico, Poland, Slovakia and Turkey.

Part II The Key Components of a Global Green New Deal

The policy debate over developing a "blueprint" for greening modern economies has been with us for some time.[1] The multiple global crises of the past couple of years have brought renewed attention on the possible convergence between green economy initiatives and short-term solutions to resolving these crises.

The food crisis of the past several years spurred the United Nations in 2008 to assemble a High-Level Task Force (HLTF) to recommend international policies to ameliorate the crisis. The HLTF formulated a comprehensive plan of coordinated actions at the national and global levels, with short-, medium- and long-term objectives to boost agricultural production, trade and sustainability. The HLTF plan also called on donor countries to double financing for food assistance, other types of nutritional support and safety net programs, and for an increase in the percentage of aid to be invested in food and agricultural development from the current 3 percent of overseas development assistance to 10 percent within five years.[2]

In response to the growing concerns over climate change and fossil fuel dependency, policy think tanks in the United States have been urging the new US administration of President Barack Obama to consider specific measures to ensure the development of a "low-carbon" economy.[3] In its 2008 yearbook, the United Nations

---

[1] An early and influential contribution to this debate was Pearce, David W., Anil Markandya and Edward B. Barbier. 1989. *Blueprint for a Green Economy*. London, Earthscan. A ten-year retrospective and update appeared as Pearce, David W., and Edward B. Barbier. 2000. *Blueprint for a Sustainable Economy*. London, Earthscan.

[2] High-Level Task Force on the Global Food Crisis. 2008. *Comprehensive Framework for Action*. New York, UN.

[3] See, for example, Podesta, John, Todd Stern, and Kit Batten. 2007. *Capturing the Energy Opportunity: Creating a Low-carbon Economy*. Washington, DC, Center for American Progress [CAP]; Becker, William S. 2008. *The 100 Day Action Plan*

Environment Programme documented the growing numbers of companies worldwide instigating environmental policies and investors pumping billions of dollars into cleaner and renewable energies.[4] A "Green New Deal" was proposed for the United Kingdom as early as July 2008.[5] A similar focus on building a "green recovery" in the United States was launched soon afterwards, and it became the policy "White Paper" that inspired the green stimulus investments proposed by the Obama administration and passed by Congress as the American Reinvestment and Recovery Act in February 2009.[6] Finally, as noted in chapter 1, South Korea's economic recovery package, entitled a "Green New Deal," prioritizes many low-carbon spending initiatives, and China has also devoted an amount equivalent to almost 3 percent of its GDP to a low-carbon stimulus (see box 1.1). Other G20 governments have also included spending on reducing carbon dependency as part of their economic recovery efforts.

These initiatives are an encouraging sign of increasing receptiveness by the international community for a Global Green New Deal. As emphasized in chapter 1, to be truly global such a strategy must encompass the widespread adoption by national governments of fiscal measures and other policies in the short term that will expedite economic recovery and create jobs while being consistent with the medium-term objectives of reducing carbon dependency, environmental deterioration and extreme world poverty. To achieve these

to Save the Planet: A Climate Crisis Solution for the 44th President. New York, St Martin's Press; and McKibbin, Warwick, and Peter Wilcoxen. 2007. "Energy and environmental security." In Brookings Institution. Top 10 Global Economic Challenges: An Assessment of Global Risks and Priorities. Washington, DC, Brookings Institution: 2–4.

[4] UNEP. 2008. UNEP Year Book 2008: An Overview of Our Changing Environment. Geneva, UNEP.

[5] Green New Deal Group. 2008. A Green New Deal: Joined-up Policies to Solve the Triple Crunch of the Credit Crisis, Climate Change and High Oil Prices. London, New Economics Foundation.

[6] Pollin, Robert, Heidi Garrett-Peltier, James Heintz and Helen Scharber. 2008. Green Recovery: A Program to Create Good Jobs and Start Building a Low-carbon Economy. Washington, DC, CAP.

aims, such a package of initiatives must be adopted quickly, in the next year or two. To be effective, the scale of additional investments and programs must be large, much more than the "green measures" in current proposals by G20 governments for additional spending over the next one to two years to revive the world economy (see box 1.1).

Part II elaborates on the key components that could comprise a timely and effective GGND. These components are based on a strategy aimed at two broad objectives:

- reducing carbon dependency; and
- reducing ecological scarcity.

Chapters 2 and 3 highlight how national actions to achieve each of these goals can also achieve the more immediate aims of stimulating economic growth, creating jobs and reducing the vulnerability of the poor. Although the specific priorities, policies, investments and incentive mechanisms adopted by each national government will differ with the economic, environmental and social conditions of the individual economy, examples are provided of the type of successful initiatives that have been adopted or could be implemented. As far as possible, each measure discussed is assessed for its impact not just in terms of environmental objectives but also in terms of the economic goals of instigating a speedy economic recovery, creating jobs, sustaining growth and reducing the incidence of poverty.

Because the economic, environmental and social conditions vary considerably from economy to economy, governments will face markedly different challenges in implementing national-level actions to achieve these goals. The various challenges faced by governments and the actions required to tackle them are likely, in particular, to differ for three distinct groups of economies: the high-income economies that comprise the OECD; large emerging market economies, such as transition and middle-income economies, including Brazil, China, India and Russia; and low-income economies, which face the most severe constraints in implementing any global GND strategy.

Chapter 4 outlines the challenges that confront developing economies in particular. Chapter 5 concludes part II by summarizing the main national actions that are essential for the success of the proposed GGND and outlining the US$36 billion Green New Deal of South Korea, which contains many of the national actions advocated in this book.

2   Reducing carbon dependency

A critical component of the Global Green New Deal is the necessity of reducing the carbon dependency of the world economy.

As indicated in box 2.1, although the greenhouse gas intensity of the world economy may have declined from 1990 to 2005, overall global emissions have risen. They are projected to rise even further over the next twenty-five years, with fossil fuel energy use continuing as global populations increase, the world economy grows and poorer economies develop. Thus, reviving economic growth in today's carbon-dependent world economy will simply contribute to both the rising demand for and combustion of fossil fuels and increased GHG emissions.

In 2005 the top ten emitters of GHGs were either rich economies (e.g. the United States, the European Union, Japan and Canada) or large emerging market economies (e.g. China, Russia, India, Brazil, Mexico and Indonesia). Together, the top emitters accounted for over 70 percent of the world's total GHGs (see box 2.1). By 2030, however, this situation is likely to have changed. Emissions from energy sources alone will more than double for the developing world, increase by nearly 30 percent in transition economies and rise by 17 percent in the OECD. By 2030 developing economies will account for more than a half of the world's GHG emissions from energy use, and China's share could be close to a third. Other large emerging market economies, such as India and Russia, will also continue to contribute significantly to global emissions.

Box 2.1 Greenhouse gas emissions, carbon dependency and the world economy

In 2005 the top ten emitters of greenhouse gases were either rich economies (e.g. the United States, the European Union, Japan and Canada) or large emerging market economies (e.g. China, Russia, India, Brazil, Mexico and Indonesia). Together, the top emitters accounted for over 70 percent of the world's total GHGs. During the last period of sustained growth in the world economy, from 1990 to 2005, GHG emissions worldwide rose by over a quarter, though it is worth noting that the rate of increase was faster still in countries other than the top ten emitters.

Because carbon dioxide alone accounts for nearly three-quarters of the world's greenhouse gas emissions, and, with other carbon-based gases, contributes over 90 percent of total emissions, the CO_2 equivalent measure of GHG emissions is a good approximation of the overall carbon dependency of the world's economy. This dependency is therefore reflected in the greenhouse gas intensity of economies, the tonnes of CO_2 equivalent GHG emissions per million international dollars of gross national product. With the exception of Brazil, from 1990 to 2005 all the top ten emitters reduced the GHG intensity of their economies, with the largest reductions occurring in China, the European Union and India. The rest of the world reduced the GHG intensity of their economies no more than modestly, however, by around 13 percent. Overall, there was about a one-fifth decline in the GHG intensity of the world economy.

Although the declining GHG intensity of the world economy is encouraging, the trend does not suggest that the overall carbon dependency of economies and regions is being reduced significantly. Projections suggest that the growth in GHG emissions for most economies and regions will continue until 2030. The energy sector currently accounts for over three-quarters of the world's GHG emissions, and almost all is from the combustion of fossil fuels. As global populations increase, the world economy grows and poorer countries develop, the increased use of fossil fuel energy will cause

Global greenhouse gas emissions (million tonnes of carbon dioxide equivalent), 1990–2005[a]

	1990	2005	Change	Average annual growth (%)	Total growth (%)	Share of world total 2005 (%)
China	3,593.5	7,219.2	3,625.6	4.8	100.9	18.6
United States	5,975.4	6,963.8	988.5	1.0	16.5	18.0
European Union[b]	5,394.8	5,047.7	−347.1	−0.4	−6.4	13.0
Russia	2,940.7	1,960.0	−980.7	−2.7	−33.3	5.1
India	1,103.7	1,852.9	749.2	3.5	67.9	4.8
Japan	1,180.0	1,342.7	162.6	0.9	13.8	3.5
Brazil	689.9	1,014.1	324.2	2.6	47.0	2.6
Canada	578.6	731.6	153.0	1.6	26.4	1.9
Mexico	459.5	629.9	170.4	2.1	37.1	1.6
Indonesia	332.6	594.4	261.8	3.9	78.7	1.5
Top ten emitters	22,248.7	27,356.3	5,107.6	1.4	23.0	70.6
Rest of world	8,456.2	11,369.6	2,913.4	2.0	34.5	29.4
World	30,704.9	38,725.9	8,021.0	1.6	26.1	

Notes: [a] Excludes land use change as a source of GHG emissions. In 2005 world GHG emissions consisted of carbon dioxide (CO_2, 73.6 percent of total), methane (CH_4, 16.5 percent), nitrous oxide (N_2O, 8.5 percent), hydrofluorocarbons (HFCs, 1.0 percent), perfluorocarbons (PFCs, 0.3 percent) and sulfur hexafluoride (SF_6, 0.2 percent). A tonne is a metric ton.
[b] Includes all twenty-seven economies comprising the European Union. In 2005 the top three EU emitters were Germany (977.4 million tonnes of CO_2 equivalent), the United Kingdom (639.8 million tonnes) and Italy (565.7 million tonnes).
Source: Climate Analysis Indicators Tool (CAIT), version 6.0, 2008, produced by the World Resources Institute (WRI), based in Washington, DC.

Global greenhouse gas intensity of economies (tonnes of CO_2 equivalent per million 2000 international US\$), 1990–2005[a]

	1990	2005	Change	Average annual growth (%)	Total growth (%)
China	2,869.4	1,353.6	−1,515.8	−4.9	−52.8
United States	751.2	561.7	−189.5	−1.9	−25.2
European Union[b]	561.5	387.4	−174.2	−2.4	−31.0
Russia	1,570.2	1,154.4	−415.8	−2.0	−26.5
India	1,076.6	759.1	−317.5	−2.3	−29.5
Japan	368.2	346.9	−21.3	−0.4	−5.8
Brazil	637.7	640.6	2.8	0.0	0.4
Canada	774.6	647.4	−127.1	−1.2	−16.4
Mexico	601.7	536.6	−65.1	−0.8	−10.8
Indonesia	894.9	839.7	−55.2	−0.4	−6.2
Top ten emitters	1,010.6	722.7	−287.9	−2.2	−28.5
Rest of world	753.6	656.1	−97.5	−0.9	−12.9
World	882.1	689.4	−192.7	−1.6	−21.8

Notes: [a] Excludes land use change as a source of GHG emissions. In 2005 75.2 percent of world GHG emissions were from energy, 16.7 percent from agriculture, 4.9 percent from industrial processes and 3.8 percent from waste. In the energy sector, 32.6 percent of world emissions came from electricity and heat generation, 14.2 percent from transportation, 13.7 percent from manufacturing and construction, 10.0 percent from other fuel combustion and 4.6 percent from fugitive emissions.

[b] Includes all twenty-seven economies comprising the European Union.

Source: CAIT, version 6.0, 2008.

Global greenhouse gas emissions (million tonnes of CO_2 equivalent), 2005–30[a]

	2005	2030	Change	Average annual growth (%)	Total growth (%)	Share of world total 2030 (%)
World	26,620	41,905	15,285	1.80	57.40	
OECD	12,838	15,067	2,229	0.60	17.40	36.0
European Union	3,944	4,176	232	0.20	5.90	10.0
Japan	1,210	1,182	-28	-0.10	-2.30	2.8
United States	5,789	6,891	1,102	0.70	19.00	16.4
Transition economies[b]	2,538	3,230	692	1.00	27.30	7.7
Russia	1,528	1,973	445	1.00	29.10	4.7
Developing economies[c]	10,700	22,919	12,219	3.10	114.20	54.7
China	5,101	11,448	6,347	3.30	124.40	27.3
India	1,147	3,314	2,167	4.30	188.90	7.9

Notes: [a] IEA projections from energy sources of GHG emissions only.

[b] Economies of the former Soviet Union and Eastern Europe.

[c] Low- and middle-income economies from Africa, Asia, Latin America and the Middle East.

Source: CAIT, version 6.0, 2008.

GHG emissions to rise. Thus, reviving economic growth in today's carbon-dependent world economy will simply contribute to both the rising demand for and combustion of fossil fuels and increased GHG emissions.

In 2030 a carbon-dependent world economy is projected to produce close to 60 percent more GHG emissions from energy combustion than it does today. Growth in emissions will occur in the high-income OECD economies, but to a level just 17.4 percent higher than today. Japan's emissions might fall, and the European Union's emissions may increase by less than 6 percent. Much of the growth in OECD emissions is likely to come from the United States, which may show a 19 percent increase. The large increase in global GHG emissions is likely to come from transition and developing economies, however. Emissions by 2030 will more than double for developing economies, led by large increases in India and China. Emissions from transition economies will rise by nearly 30 percent, led by Russia. By 2030 China's share of GHG emissions could be close to one-third of the world total, and all developing economies together could account for the majority of emissions.

As noted in chapter 1, the implications for global climate change are worrisome. Without a change in the carbon dependency of the global economy, the International Energy Agency warns that the atmospheric concentration of GHGs could double by the end of this century, with an eventual global average temperature increase of up to 6°C.[1] Such a scenario is likely to cause a global sea level rise of between 0.26 and 0.59 meters, and severe disruption to freshwater availability, ecosystems, food production, coastal populations and human health around the world.[2] According to the Stern Review, with 5 to 6°C warming, existing estimates of the overall costs suggest an average 5 to 10 percent diminution in

[1] IEA 2008 (see ch. 1, fn 11).
[2] IPCC 2007 (see ch. 1, fn 12).

global GDP, with poor countries suffering costs in excess of 10 percent of GDP.[3]

Reducing carbon dependency in the world economy is not just about averting global warming, however. An increasing number of studies have emphasized the importance of reducing fossil fuel use in order to enhance national and global energy security. The vulnerability of today's economies to oil shocks is now well established.[4] The IEA predicts that the risk of oil supply disruptions has grown in recent years and will continue to grow in the near future, given the continued demand growth for fossil fuels by carbon-dependent economies, the increased concentration of the remaining oil reserves in a smaller number of countries, the concentration of oil use in the transport sector and insufficient additions to oil supply capacity to keep pace with demand growth.[5] The problem is exacerbated by the decline in production from major oilfields. As discussed in chapter 1, although the world's oil reserves are sufficiently large to meet future demand for oil, even if this demand were to remain flat until 2030, 45 million barrels per day of additional gross production capacity – approximately four times the current capacity of Saudi Arabia – needs to be found worldwide just to offset the effect of oilfield decline.[6]

Increasingly, reducing the carbon dependency of the world economy is seen as a means of addressing at one and the same time the twin global objectives of achieving energy security and climate change mitigation.[7]

---

[3] Stern 2007 (see ch. 1, fn 30). See also Tol 2008 (ch.1, fn 30), however, who finds that these estimates in the Stern Review are highly pessimistic, even compared to other studies that employ low discount rates on future damages.

[4] Hamilton, James D. 2008. "Oil and the macroeconomy." In Steven N. Durlauf and Lawrence E. Blume (eds.). *The New Palgrave Dictionary of Economics*, 2nd edn., vol. VI. London, Palgrave Macmillan: 172–5. Available online at www.dictionaryofeconomics.com/dictionary; Jiménez-Rodríguez, Rebeca, and Marcelo Sánchez. 2005. "Oil price shocks and real GDP growth: empirical evidence for some OECD countries." *Applied Economics* 37 (2): 201–28; World Bank 2009 (see ch. 1, fn 1).

[5] IEA 2007 (see ch. 1, fn 26).

[6] IEA 2008 (see ch. 1, fn 11).

[7] Becker 2008 (see pt II introd., fn 3); McKibbin and Wilcoxen 2007 (see pt II introd., fn 3); Pascual, Carlos, and Jonathon Elkind (eds.). *Energy*

Results from country case studies of the Czech Republic, France, Italy, the Netherlands and the United Kingdom reflect a generally worsening trend to 2030 in terms of CO_2 emissions and energy security, if these economies do not reduce significantly their carbon dependency.[8] Import dependency on fossil fuels is reaching 100 percent for the small island developing economies in the Asia-Pacific region, and fossil fuels (in China, India, Indonesia, the Philippines, Thailand and Vietnam) provide more than three-quarters of final energy consumption.[9] It is the increasing carbon dependency of these Asian and other developing economies that not only places them at great risk from future disruptions to global fossil fuel supply but also ensures that they will become the main source of global greenhouse gas emissions by 2030 (see box 2.1).

Energy security and vulnerability to climate change take on a completely different dimension for the world's extreme poor. A large fraction of the population in developing countries has no access to modern energy services, and those consumers who do have access often pay high prices for services that are erratic and unreliable. Approximately 2.4 billion people in developing countries, including 89 percent of the population of sub-Saharan Africa, rely on traditional biomass fuels for cooking and heating, and another 1.6 billion people do not have access to electricity.[10] The combination of extreme poverty and low human development limits the capacity of the global poor to manage and adapt to rising energy costs and increasing climate risks.

The World Bank has found that the sharp rise in oil prices over the past five years has had a direct impact on global food prices,

Security: Economics, Politics, Strategies, and Implications. Washington, DC, Brookings Institution Press; IEA. 2007. *Energy Security and Climate Policy: Assessing Interactions.* Paris, IEA; United Nations Economic and Social Commission for Asia and the Pacific [ESCAP]. 2008. *Energy Security and Sustainable Development in Asia and the Pacific.* Bangkok, ESCAP.

[8] IEA 2007 (see fn 7).
[9] UN ESCAP 2008 (see fn 7).
[10] Modi *et al.* 2005 (see ch. 1, fn 23).

with a disproportionate impact on the world's poor. For example, the resulting higher food prices from 2005 to 2007 increased the poverty headcount among urban populations in developing countries by 2.9 percent and among rural populations by 2.1 percent.[11] As discussed in chapter 1, the urban poor in developing countries are particularly at risk from the climate-driven impacts of rising sea level, coastal erosion and more frequent storms. Around 14 percent of all developing country populations, and 21 percent of their urban dwellers, live in low-elevation coastal zones that are particularly vulnerable to these risks.[12] Box 2.2 summarizes the vulnerability of billions of poor people in developing regions to a wide range of similar climate-induced risks.

Moving to a low-carbon world economy is not just a necessary action in order to address mounting concerns over global energy security and climate change; it is also imperative for improving the human development prospects of the world's poor.

A GGND implemented over the next couple of years can put the world economy on a development path to achieve these objectives, and at the same time boost short-run economic recovery and create millions of jobs worldwide. Achieving these multiple goals will, in turn, require progress simultaneously in five main areas:

- improving energy efficiency and conservation;
- expanding "clean energy" supply options;
- improving the sustainability of transport;

Box 2.2 Vulnerability of the world's poor to climate-induced impacts

The United Nations Development Programme has identified five key transmission channels through which climate-induced impacts severely affect the livelihoods of the poor.

---

[11] World Bank 2009 (see ch. 1, fn 1).

[12] McGranahan *et al.* 2007 (see ch. 1, fn 31). The authors estimate that, in comparison, 10 percent of the global population lives in the high-risk low-elevation coastal zones.

Transmission channel	Physical impacts of climate change	Effects on vulnerable populations
Agricultural production and food security	Affects rainfall, temperature and water availability for agriculture in vulnerable areas.	Drought-affected areas in sub-Saharan Africa could expand by 60 to 90 million hectares (ha) by 2060. All developing countries could experience losses in agricultural production by 2080. The number of malnourished globally could rise to 600 million by 2080.
Water stress and water insecurity	Changed run-off patterns and glacial melt will affect water availability for irrigation and human settlements.	An additional 1.8 billion people could be living in a water-scarce environment by 2080.
Rising sea levels and exposure to climate disasters	Sea levels could rise rapidly with accelerated ice sheet disintegration, and warming seas could fuel more intense tropical storms.	330 million people could be displaced through flooding, including 70 million people in Bangladesh, 22 million in Vietnam, 6 million in Egypt and the populations of small island states in the Caribbean and Pacific. 344 million people could experience more devastating tropical cyclones.

		The 1 billion people currently living in urban slums on fragile hillsides or flood-prone river banks face acute vulnerabilities.
Ecosystems and biodiversity	Around one-half of coral reef systems have suffered bleaching from global warming, and increasing ocean acidity is a long-term threat to marine ecosystems. With 3°C of warming, 20 to 30 percent of terrestrial species could face extinction.	The 1 billion people currently living in urban slums on fragile hillsides or flood-prone river banks face acute vulnerabilities. The economic livelihoods of the 1.3 billion rural poor living in fragile environments of developing regions (see box 1.2) will be severely impacted.
Human health	Major diseases could spread.	An additional 220 to 400 million people could be exposed to malaria; dengue fever is also expected to spread.

Source: UNDP. 2008. *Human Development Report 2007/2008: Fighting Climate Change: Human Solidarity in a Divided World.* New York, UNDP.

- adopting economy-wide policy measures to discourage carbon use (such as cap-and-trade, carbon taxes, etc.); and
- at the same time, increasing the availability of affordable and sustainable energy services (e.g. lighting, heating for cooking, etc.) for the world's poor.

The remainder of this chapter provides examples of the type of national actions that can be adopted by various national governments in these areas. The next section reviews comprehensive proposals that would alter drastically the carbon dependency of three major world economies, China, the European Union and the United States. The evidence from these three economies, which together account for more than a half of world GDP, suggests that implementing these plans would also stimulate new economic sectors, increase the demand for skilled work and create jobs, thereby boosting overall economic recovery and sustaining growth. The potential for implementing similar proposals in other countries is also discussed. A separate section looks at policies and actions for improving the sustainability of transport, which is an essential component of any low-carbon national strategy.

CREATING LOW-CARBON ECONOMIES

Together, China, the United States and the European Union account for half the world's emissions of greenhouse gases, and, under existing policies, these three economies will still be the largest source of these emissions in 2030 (see box 2.1). Although any Global Green New Deal should not rest solely on reducing carbon dependency in these three economies alone, achieving this aim for China, the European Union and the United States would clearly have a major impact on moving the global economy to a lower-carbon development path. Moreover, a number of proposals and studies have shown that it is possible to reduce fossil fuel energy use and greenhouse gas emissions in the three economies significantly while at the same time encouraging new economic sectors and employment opportunities. Other OECD and large market economies, especially the major contributors to global GHG emissions, might find it useful to adopt strategies similar to these proposals for China, the European Union and the United States. Governments in low-income economies might also consider adopting some elements of the various strategies for creating low-carbon economies whilst promoting a "green" economic recovery.

As indicated in box 2.3, China is already committed to policies that will introduce more energy saving and green energy supply options, in order to achieve the twin objectives of improved energy security and reduced carbon intensity of economic production. As discussed in chapter 1, over a third of China's $648 billion stimulus package is allocated to energy efficiency and environmental improvements, rail transport and new electricity grid infrastructure. Thus, of all the G20 members, China has one of the largest green stimulus packages, allocating 3 percent of its GDP for such investments, with the total spending on low-carbon initiatives alone amounting to 2.5 percent of its GDP (see box 1.1). In addition, China is the world's largest recipient of carbon emission reduction credits under the Kyoto Protocol's Clean Development Mechanism (CDM), collecting at present around US$2 billion in tax revenues from these CDM credits.

Box 2.3 describes a number of studies showing that China could accelerate its transition to a low-carbon economy by adopting innovative economic policies and instruments, including carbon taxes, other emission taxes and the careful targeting of subsidies. The costs of such policies are often more than offset by ancillary benefits, such as improved air quality, increased agricultural productivity, the development of new economic sectors and technologies, improved employment and reduced poverty. The Chinese economy would also gain from an increase in employment and sectoral growth opportunities. Currently, China's renewable energy sector is an important source of exports, has a value of nearly US$17 billion and employs close to a million workers. The expansion of this sector as part of a low-carbon strategy would provide a needed boost to employment and growth prospects in the country.

Box 2.3 Reconciling carbon dependency and economic development in China

The adoption of measures to reduce fossil fuel energy use in China, and thus its greenhouse gas emissions, is driven in large part by energy security concerns, especially the country's overreliance on coal. From 2000 to 2005 China's energy consumption rose by 60 percent, accounting for almost half the growth in world energy consumption, and between 1990 and 2005 its GHG emissions rose by 80 percent. Coal accounts for nearly 70 percent of China's energy consumption, mostly for electricity generation. At present China imports almost a half of the oil it consumes, and it is likely to be importing 60 to 80 percent of its oil by 2020.

China's current energy security initiatives with potential climate mitigation impacts include a number of measures to improve energy efficiency and conservation as well as to expand its energy supply options. China's 11th five-year plan has the overall goal of reducing energy consumption per unit GDP by 20 percent below 2005 levels by 2010. Meeting this target is projected to reduce China's GHG emissions by over 1.5 billion tonnes of CO_2 equivalent, or 10 percent below current emission trends. The overall national target is allocated among all provinces and industrial sectors, including the most energy-intensive, and incentives are included to encourage enterprises to meet targets. In addition, China is embarking on policies to retire inefficient coal-fired power plants and industrial factories. There are also a range of policies to increase energy efficiency in buildings, industry and consumer goods. Moreover, China has set a target of producing 16 percent of its primary energy from renewable sources, including hydropower, by 2020, which is more than double its current capacity. Finally, over one-third of China's $648 billion stimulus package is allocated to energy efficiency and environmental improvements, rail transport and new electricity grid infrastructure. Thus, of all the G20 members, China has one of the largest green stimulus packages, allocating an amount equivalent to 3 percent of its GDP for such investments (see box 1.1).

China is also the largest source of Clean Development Mechanism carbon emission reduction credits, accounting to date for over one-quarter of registered projects and over one-half of average annual reductions in emissions from the CDM. Most of China's CDM credits arise from reductions of hydrofluorocarbons and the capture of landfill methane and nitrous oxide. A significant portion of the US$2 billion in tax revenues collected by these CDM credits in China is being used to finance investments in further CDM projects, in renewable energy supply and in R&D in climate change mitigation and adaptation technology.

Although adopting improved energy saving and alternative energy supply options are important components in any climate mitigation strategy for China, recent proposals have suggested that China could achieve more ambitious reductions in its carbon dependency by adopting a carbon tax policy along with complementary economic instruments and subsidies. A study by Kristin Aunan and colleagues shows that carbon taxation could be used to reduce overall GHG emissions by 17.5 percent while still producing net economic gains for the economy. The costs of the policy would be more than offset by the ancillary health benefits from improved air quality in urban areas and the gains in agricultural productivity and higher rural incomes. Carbon tax revenues could be used to fund research in energy efficiency, renewable energy, carbon sequestration and low-energy urban development. Mark Brenner and colleagues have suggested that carbon charges could be implemented through a Chinese "sky trust," whereby revenues are recycled to the public on an equal per capita basis to reduce income inequality and poverty. The authors find that around 70 percent of the population would emerge with more net income from the sky trust, and poverty across China would be reduced by 20 percent. Scenarios developed by Hao Wang and Toshihiko Nakata show that a carbon tax combined with a sulfur dioxide (SO_2) emissions charge could generate revenues sufficient to develop clean coal technology for electricity generation. Up to 25 percent of SO_2 emissions and 29 percent of CO_2 emissions could be eliminated, and clean coal technology would provide around a third of all future electricity generation, with an overall net gain for the Chinese economy in terms of electricity prices.

Increased investments in China's burgeoning renewable energy sector and other "clean technologies" could have a major impact on developing new economic growth and export sectors. China has set ambitious targets for biomass generation from sugar cane (20 gigawatts [GW] by 2020), and it is already the world's third largest ethanol producer. China has now surpassed the United States to become the world's third largest producer of solar panels, which are currently mostly for export, and is the largest global producer of solar water heaters. China already produces 80 percent of the world's energy-saving lights and is planning to become a major wind turbine manufacturer. Investments in clean technologies in China increased from US$170 million in 2005 to US$420 million in 2007.

Employment in China's renewable energy sector, 2007

	Wind power	Solar PV	Solar thermal	Biomass	Total
Generation	6,000	2,000		1,000	9,000
Manufacturing	15,000	38,000	400,000	15,000	468,000
Service	1,200	15,000	200,000	250,000	466,200
Total	22,200	55,000	600,000	266,000	943,200
Output value (US$ million)	3,375	6,750	5,400	1,350	16,875

Source: Renner, Michael, Sean Sweeney and Jill Kubit. 2008. *Green Jobs: Towards Decent Work in a Sustainable, Low-carbon World.* Geneva, UNEP.

The development of these new industries could impact significantly on employment in China. As the table above shows, the renewable energy sector of China has a value of nearly US$17 billion and already employs close to a million workers, including 600,000 in solar thermal, 266,000 in biomass generation, 55,000 in solar photovoltaics (PV) and 22,200 in wind power.

Sources: Aunan, Kristin, Terje Berntsen, David O'Connor, Therese Hindman Persson, Haakon Vennemo and Fan Zhai. 2007. "Benefits and cost to China of a climate policy." *Environment and Development Economics* 12 (3): 471–97; Brenner, Mark, Matthew Riddle and James K. Boyce. 2007. "A Chinese sky trust? Distributional impacts of carbon charges and revenue recycling in China." *Energy Policy* 35 (3): 1771–84; Downs, Erica. 2006. *China.* Brookings Foreign Policy Studies, Energy Security Series. Washington, DC, Brookings Institution; Heggelund, Gørild. 2007. "China's climate change policy: domestic and international developments." *Asian Perspective* 31 (2): 155–91 (available at http://cdm.unfccc.int/Statistics/index.html); Kim, Margaret J., and Robert E. Jones. 2008. "China: climate change superpower and the clean technology revolution." *Natural Resources and Environment* 22 (3): 9–13; McKibbin, Warwick J., Peter J. Wilcoxen and Wing Thye Woo. *Preventing the Tragedy of the CO_2 Commons: Exploring China's Growth and the International Climate Framework.* Global Working Paper no. 22. Washington, DC, Brookings Institution; Pew Center. 2007. *Climate Change Mitigation Measures in the People's Republic of China.* International Brief no. 1. Arlington, VA, Pew Center on Global Climate Change; Renner, Michael, Sean Sweeney and Jill Kubit. 2008. *Green Jobs: Towards Decent Work in a Sustainable, Low-carbon World.* Geneva, UNEP; UN ESCAP. 2008. *Energy Security and Sustainable Development in Asia and the Pacific.* Bangkok, ESCAP; Wang, Hao, and Toshihiko Nakata. 2009. "Analysis of the market penetration of clean coal technologies and its impact in China's electricity sector." *Economic Policy* 37 (1): 338–51; Zeng, Ning, Yihui Ding, Jiahua Pan, Hijun Wang and Jay Gregg. 2008. "Climate change: the Chinese challenge." *Science* 319: 730–1; and Zhang, ZhongXiang. 2008. "Asian energy and environmental policy: promoting growth while preserving the environment." *Energy Policy* 36 (10): 3905–24.

The example of China from box 2.3 illustrates how the effective implementation of policies for energy efficiency and conservation, increasing clean energy supply options and carbon pricing policies and other economic instruments can be used in a large emerging market economy to foster a transition to a low-carbon economy. Several studies have shown that a similar set of policies can induce such a transition across all Asian economies, including low-income nations.[13] For example, by 2006 India had already accumulated US$2.6 billion in investments in sustainable energy supply, second only to China (US$4.0 billion) among developing economies. If India invested substantially in end-use energy-efficient management, it would reduce energy consumption by about 45 percent by 2030. Similar savings could be achieved by the entire Asia-Pacific region (including Russia).[14]

The adoption of a low-carbon development strategy by China and the rest of Asia could therefore provide important global leadership to other large market, transition and developing economies in terms of the potential of a new development model while stimulating a much-needed short-term economic boost and boosting job opportunities. As discussed in chapter 1, three other major Asia-Pacific economies, Australia, Japan and South Korea, have also signaled a commitment to promoting low-carbon investments as part of their strategy for economic recovery. Overall, the Asia-Pacific region accounts for 63 percent of all global green stimulus spending during the current recession, with most of the investments targeted to reducing carbon dependency. China accounts for two-thirds of the region's government spending on low-carbon investments, Japan around 12 percent, South Korea 10 percent and Australia 3 percent.[15] Chapter 5 discusses in more detail the low-carbon national actions of these major Asia-Pacific nations, especially the Green New Deal launched by South Korea.

---

[13] See, for example, Carmody, Josh, and Duncan Ritchie. 2007. *Investing in Clean Energy and Low Carbon Alternatives in Asia.* Manila, Asian Development Bank [ADB]; Renner, Michael, Sean Sweeney and Jill Kubit. 2008. *Green Jobs: Towards Decent Work in a Sustainable, Low-carbon World.* Geneva, UNEP; UN ESCAP 2008 (see fn 7); and Zhang, ZhongXiang. 2008. "Asian energy and environmental policy: promoting growth while preserving the environment." *Energy Policy* 36 (10): 3905–24.

[14] UN ESCAP 2008 (see fn 7). See also Shukla, P. R. 2006. "India's GHG emission scenarios: aligning development and stabilization paths." *Current Science* 90 (3): 384–95.

[15] Robins, Clover and Singh 2009 (see ch. 1, fn 10).

As illustrated in box 2.4, an ideal opportunity exists in the United States to merge short-term interests in creating job opportunities and stimulating economic recovery while transitioning in the medium term to a lower-carbon economy. Such a policy would involve two major components: an immediate "green" fiscal stimulus and the introduction of a carbon pricing policy. Elements of the first component are already in place, at least partially. The US$787 billion American Recovery and Reinvestment Act of February 2009 includes around US$78.5 billion to retrofit buildings with energy-efficient equipment, expand mass transit and freight rail, construct a "smart" electrical grid transmission system and expand renewable energy supply. These investments have the potential to create 1.5 million new jobs through investments in energy efficiency and clean energy strategies. Such an investment program needs to be accompanied by the development of a comprehensive cap-and-trade system for greenhouse gas emissions, however, which could eventually pay for low-carbon investment programs by generating US$75 billion a year in revenues from permit sales. An additional element of the carbon pricing policy would be the immediate elimination of all federal tax breaks and subsidies for the US oil and gas industry, which currently amount to at least US$6 billion annually. In essence, this two-part strategy would represent an important component of a national Green New Deal for the United States.

Box 2.4 Reconciling economic recovery and carbon dependency in the United States

As indicated in box 1.1, the US$787 billion American Recovery and Reinvestment Act of February 2009 includes around US$78.5 billion to retrofit buildings for energy efficiency, expand mass transit and freight rail, construct a "smart" electrical grid transmission system and augment renewable energy supply. Additional investments in water infrastructure resulted in a US$94.1 billion green stimulus package. In addition, there is cautious optimism about the introduction of a comprehensive cap-and-trade system to limit CO_2 emissions. Consequently, an ideal opportunity exists in the United States to merge the short-term aim of stimulating economic recovery and employment opportunities with the creation of a lower-carbon economy in the near future. Various studies have shown that such objectives are complementary.

For example, the Union of Concerned Scientists, backed by leading scientists and economists, has called for an 80 percent reduction in US greenhouse gas emissions below 2000 levels by 2050. A 2007 report by the Center for American Progress outlines a ten-year strategy, including increased energy efficiency, investments in clean energy and a carbon pricing policy, that would realign the US economy along such a low-carbon development path. The carbon pricing policy has two key components: an economy-wide cap-and-trade system to reduce greenhouse gas emissions by 50 to 80 percent in relation to 2000 levels by 2050 and the elimination of the US$6 billion per year federal tax breaks and subsidies for the US oil and gas industry. The proposed cap-and-trade system would auction all the permits across all businesses in the economy, but companies unable to meet their emission quotas would have to purchase permits from the federal government or from other companies. An initial 10 percent of the projected US$75 billion a year in revenues generated could be allocated to businesses operating in energy-intensive sectors to compensate their shareholders, employees and local communities. Half the remaining revenues could be distributed to low- and moderate-income households to help offset any energy price increases that may occur during the transition to less carbon-intensive energy use. Any other cap-and-trade revenues would be put into R&D and investments for raising the energy efficiency of the economy and the development of clean energy technologies.[16]

---

[16] As an alternative to such an economy-wide cap-and-trade system for the United States, Rob Stavins of Harvard and Bob Repetto for the Presidential Climate Action Project advocate the implementation of an "upstream"

The policies envisioned in the 2007 CAP report aim to develop a ten-year strategy for transforming the United States into a low-carbon economy. A second CAP report in 2008 demonstrates that a "green economic recovery" program enacted over the next two years could start the transition to the low-carbon economy, revitalize US economic growth and create millions of high-skilled jobs. The report proposes a US$100 billion initiative over the next two years, which could be paid for with proceeds from auctions under a greenhouse gas cap-and-trade program implemented over the same period. This fiscal stimulus would create 2 million jobs by investing in four energy efficiency and renewable energy strategies:

- retrofitting buildings to improve energy efficiency;
- expanding mass transit and freight rail;
- constructing a "smart" electrical grid transmission system; and
- developing renewable energy – namely wind power, solar power and next-generation biofuels (i.e. cellulosic rather than corn-based fuels, such as agricultural plant waste or dedicated crops such as grasses and algae) and other bio-based energy.

As the table below indicates, the additional 2 million jobs created by the green recovery program would include over 935,000 new jobs across a range of highly specialized as well as general industries. In addition, another 586,000 jobs would be created indirectly in manufacturing and service sectors associated with the main energy

cap-and-trade system that limits sales of fossil fuels in the US economy. Under such a system, permits would be calibrated to the carbon content of each fuel type and would be required of the first sellers of such fuels, to be enforced at petroleum refineries, natural gas distribution points, coal mine shipping centers and ports for imported fuels. First sellers could trade their permits, and overall greenhouse gas emission targets would be imposed to limit the total permits issued. See Repetto, Robert. 2007. *National Climate Policy: Choosing the Right Architecture*. Report prepared for the Presidential Climate Action Project. New Haven, CT: Yale School of Forestry and Environmental Studies, Yale University; and Stavins, Robert N. 2008. "Addressing climate change with a comprehensive US cap-and-trade system." *Oxford Review of Economic Policy* 24 (2): 298–321. For an assessment of different cap-and-trade policy options and their distributional implications for the United States, see Burtraw, Dallas, Richard Sweeney and Margaret Walls. 2008. "Crafting a fair and equitable climate policy: a closer look at the options." *Resources* 170: 20–3.

Job creation by a US green recovery program

Direct employment activity	Type of job created (total jobs: 935,200)
Building retrofitting	Electricians, heating/air-conditioning installers, carpenters, construction, roofers, insulation workers, truck drivers, building inspectors.
Mass transit/freight rail	Civil engineers, rail track layers, electricians, welders, metal fabricators, engine assemblers, bus drivers, dispatchers, locomotive engineers, railroad conductors.
Smart grid	Computer software engineers, electrical engineers, operating engineers, electrical equipment assemblers and technicians, machinists, team assemblers, construction, electrical power line installers and repairers.
Wind power	Environmental engineers, industrial production workers, managers and supervisors, iron and steel workers, millwrights, sheet metal workers, machinists, electrical equipment assemblers, construction, equipment operators, truck drivers.
Solar power	Electrical engineers, electricians, industrial machinery mechanics, welders, metal fabricators, electrical equipment assemblers and installers, construction equipment operators, construction workers.
Advanced biofuels	Chemical engineers, chemists, chemical equipment operators and technicians, machine operators, farmers, agricultural workers and supervisors, truck drivers, agricultural inspectors.

Table (*cont.*)

Direct employment activity	Type of job created (total jobs: 935,200)
Indirect employment effects	**Type of job created (total jobs: 586,000)**
Associated manufacturing and service job creation	Forest products, hardware, iron and steel, transportation.
Induced employment effects	**Type of job created (total jobs: 496,000)**
Additional job creation through increased income expenditures	Retail and wholesale.

Source: Pollin, Robert, Heidi Garrett-Peltier, James Heintz and Helen Scharber. 2008. *Green Recovery: A Program to Create Good Jobs and Start Building a Low-carbon Economy.* Washington, DC, CAP.

efficiency and renewable energy sectors. Finally, nearly half a million new retail and wholesale jobs would be created across the United States through the induced effects of additional spending of income by the directly and indirectly employed workers. Although the US$78.5 billion in low-carbon stimulus investments included in the ARRA is modeled on the CAP green recovery program, the final amount allocated is much less than US$100 billion. Nevertheless, the low-carbon strategy in the ARRA should still have a considerable job impact, perhaps creating around 1.5 million new jobs in the economic sectors outlined below.

Other studies and proposals, such as those by the Presidential Climate Action Project, suggest that a US$500 billion investment over ten years would create 5 million new jobs across the United States. Additional income and employment opportunities could occur if substantial induced technological changes arise in the US economy through complementary policies that promote "climate-friendly technological change," along the lines suggested above. A report by Larry Goulder for the Pew Center on Global Climate Change points out that combining "direct emission policies," such as a cap-and-trade system, with R&D subsidies for encouraging private sector investment in increased energy efficiency and clean energy technologies may have a powerful induced technological innovation effect (see also box 2.6). Similarly, another Pew study by Dale Jorgenson and colleagues demonstrates that the right combination of carbon pricing policies, complementary fiscal policies and a redistribution of revenues substantially reduces the costs of any climate mitigation policy for the US economy.

Sources: Becker, William S. 2008. *The 100 Day Action Plan to Save the Planet: A Climate Crisis Solution for the 44th President.* New York, St Martin's Press; Goulder, Lawrence. 2004. *Induced Technological Change and Climate Policy.* Arlington, VA, Pew Center on Global Climate Change; Jorgenson, Dale W., Richard J. Goettle, Peter J. Wilcoxen, Mun Sing Ho, Hui Jin and Patrick A. Schoennagel. 2008. *The Economic Costs of a Market-based Climate Policy.* White Paper. Arlington, VA, Pew Center on Global Climate Change; McKibbin, Warwick, and Peter Wilcoxen. 2007. "Energy and environmental security." In Brookings Institution. *Top 10 Global Economic Challenges: An Assessment of Global Risks and Priorities.* Washington, DC, Brookings Institution: 2–4; Podesta, John, Todd Stern and Kit Batten. 2007. *Capturing the Energy Opportunity: Creating a Low-carbon Economy.* Washington, DC, CAP; Pollin, Robert, Heidi Garrett-Peltier, James Heintz and Helen Scharber. 2008. *Green Recovery: A Program to Create Good Jobs and Start Building a Low-carbon Economy.* Washington, DC, CAP; and Union of Concerned Scientists [UCS]. 2008. "US scientists' and economists' call for swift and deep cuts in greenhouse gas emissions." Cambridge, MA, UCS. Available at www.ucsusa.org/global_warming.html.

The US government could eventually do more than its current commitment to reducing carbon dependency, however. The US$78.5 billion in low-carbon initiatives in the ARRA comprises only 10 percent of the total fiscal stimulus package and just under 0.6 percent of US

GDP (see box 1.1).[17] With the funds generated from cap-and-trade permit auctions and the removal of fossil fuel and other perverse energy incentives, the United States could easily expand its commitment to low-carbon investments to an amount equivalent to 1 percent of GDP (approximately US$140 billion), thereby enhancing the employment creation effects, stimulating complementary private investment in dynamic economic sectors and reducing further the carbon dependency of the economy.

Box 2.5 indicates that, with its "triple-twenty" policy, the European Union (EU) is making its own tentative steps towards integrating a low-carbon strategy with economic recovery efforts. The combined strategy received a boost with the European Economic Recovery Plan, launched in March 2009, which included around US$23 billion – or nearly 60 percent of the stimulus package – devoted to low-carbon initiatives at the EU level (see box 1.1). Most of the latter are proposals aimed at supporting more efficient power generation from fossil fuels and encouraging renewable energy development (including subsidies for wind-generated electricity), and tax incentives for encouraging energy efficiency in buildings.[18] Individual EU governments, notably those of Austria, Belgium, France, Germany, Italy, Poland, Spain, Sweden and the United Kingdom, have also included low-carbon initiatives as part of their economy recovery stimulus packages. An important non-EU country in Europe, Norway, has also adopted measures to reduce carbon dependency in its stimulus spending (see box 1.1). For example, Norway has allocated 31 percent of its fiscal stimulus in response to the current recession to fostering low-carbon investments, France 21 percent, Germany 13 percent and the United Kingdom nearly 11 percent (see figure 1.3).

---

[17] Based on 2007 estimated US GDP in PPP terms of $13,780 billion, from the CIA's "The world factbook." Available at www.cia.gov/library/publications/the-world-factbook/rankorder/2001rank.html.

[18] See Robins, Clover and Singh 2009: 26–8 (ch. 1, fn 10).

Box 2.5 The triple-twenty strategy and economic recovery in the European Union

In November 2008 the European Commission announced its "triple-twenty" targets as part of its Second Strategic Energy Review. The goals include a commitment to reduce the greenhouse gas emissions in the European Union 20 percent below 1990 levels by 2020, increasing the share of renewable sources in total energy consumption by 20 percent and improving energy efficiency by 20 percent. The Commission sees this triple-twenty agenda as being the essential first steps in the transition to a low-carbon EU economy by 2050, as well as securing the future energy security of the European Union. The hallmarks of the plan are likely to include improvements in the EU legislation on the energy performance and design of buildings and on energy labeling, and large-scale investments in energy efficiency, renewable energy supplies (which currently comprise 9 percent of EU energy consumption) and the clean use of fossil fuels.

To fulfill its triple-twenty agenda, the European Union will need to develop further a complementary carbon pricing policy. Such a policy already exists in the European Union, which was the first region to set up a broad carbon market in the form of the EU Emissions Trading System, which started functioning in January 2005. The initial goals of the ETS have generally been met: a European-wide carbon price has been established; businesses have begun incorporating this price in their decisions; and the market infrastructure for multilateral trading in carbon has been set up. To achieve the triple-twenty goals, however, the existing ETS will need to be expanded. Future allocation scenarios analyzed by Damien Demailly and Philippe Quirion find that the most cost-effective options for the ETS appear either to be the auctioning of permits, possibly combined with border tax adjustments to maintain the competitiveness of some European industries, or, alternatively, output-based allocation of permits in sectors exposed to international competition and auctioning in electricity generation.

There are also likely to be important synergies in emission reductions and economic gains across the European Union's triple-twenty targets. The ETS is expected to generate US$68.5 billion in permit revenues per year in the next implementation phase, and a substantial amount of these revenues could be invested in energy conservation and supporting the development of renewable energy. Loreta Stankeviciute and colleagues find that the Commission's decision to increase energy efficiency and renewable energy supply by 20 percent by 2020 would also increase greenhouse gas emissions reductions in the transport and building sectors of the EU economy, thus reducing the costs from more stringent emission reductions from the carbon-intensive sectors, such as electricity and cement. In addition, an expanded ETS might also mean more opportunities for global trade in carbon, through an expanded Clean Development Mechanism and Joint Implementation (JI) scheme. If the benefits of importing CDM credits are included in a future ETS scenario, then future EU carbon prices and compliance cost reductions appear to be significantly lower. Similarly, Christoph Erdmenger and colleagues show that more stringent emissions trading combined with measures to improve energy efficiency and renewable energy supply can achieve the goal of a 40 percent reduction in 1990 levels of CO_2 emissions by 2020 for Germany, currently one of the world's major sources of GHGs. The average cost of these combined measures is €50 per tonne of CO_2 avoided, or an additional monthly expenditure per German household of €25. Encouraging such rapid renewable energy supply across Germany and the rest of the European Union may also require modifying electricity pricing policy. Doerte Fouquet and Thomas Johansson show that a feed-in tariff system, in which producers of renewable energy electricity receive a fixed premium in addition to the electricity market price, shows the most promise.

The employment impacts of an immediate "green recovery" investment program to expand energy conservation and renewable energy supply in the European Union are substantial. As the table below indicates, in these two areas the larger the investment and the sooner that the programs can be implemented, the more jobs can be created quickly. The EU renewable energy sector is already economically significant worldwide. EU wind turbine manufacturers currently account for some 80 percent of the global market share, and the European Union has overtaken Japan as the world's leading producer of photovoltaic cells. It is estimated that skilled jobs account for about a third of net employment growth in the EU renewable energy industry.

European job creation by sector

Sector	Scenario	Employment effects
Renewable energy (wind, solar, biofuels)	20 percent expansion of renewable energy by 2020.	950,000 new net jobs by 2010 and 1.4 million by 2020.
Renewable energy (wind, solar, biofuels)	Advanced renewable strategy.	1.7 million new net jobs by 2010 and 2.5 million by 2020.
Retrofitting residential buildings	Retrofit buildings to reduce CO_2 emissions 75 percent by 2050.	1.38 million new jobs.
Retrofitting residential buildings	Retrofit buildings to reduce CO_2 emissions 75 percent by 2030.	2.59 million new jobs.

Source: Renner, Michael, Sean Sweeney and Jill Kubit. 2008. *Green Jobs: Towards Decent Work in a Sustainable, Low-carbon World.* Geneva, UNEP.

An additional advantage of an EU-wide residential building retrofitting program is that it is likely to have substantial employment impacts across all countries in the European Union. For example, in Germany, for every US$1.4 billion invested in retrofitting residential buildings, an estimated additional 25,000 jobs are created. A program for retrofitting all houses in ten European new member states – Cyprus, the Czech Republic, Estonia, Hungary, Latvia, Lithuania, Malta, Poland, Slovakia and Slovenia – would cost up to US$6.4 billion per year and lead to 180,000 new jobs.

Sources: European Commission. 2008. "EU energy security and solidarity action plan: 2nd strategic energy review." Memo/08/703. Brussels, European Commission. Available at http://ec.europa.eu/energy/strategies/2008/2008_11_ser2_en.htm; Convery, Frank J. 2009. "Origins and development of the EU ETS." *Environmental and Resource Economics* 43: 391–412; Demailly, Damien, and Philippe Quirion. 2008. *Changing the Allocation Rules in the EU ETS: Impact on Competitiveness and Economic Efficiency.* Working Paper no. 89. Milan, Fondazione Eni Enrico Mattei [FEEM]; Ellerman, A. Danny, and Paul L. Joskow. 2008. *The European Union's Emissions Trading System in Perspective.* Arlington, VA, Pew Center on Global Climate Change; Erdmenger, Christoph, Harry Lehmann, Klaus Müschen, Jens Tambke, Segastian Mayr and Kai Kuhnhenn. 2009. "A climate protection strategy for Germany: 40% reduction of CO_2 emissions by 2020 compared to 1990." *Energy Policy* 37 (1): 158–65; Fouquet, Doerte, and Thomas B. Johansson. 2008. "European renewable energy policy at crossroads: focus on electricity support mechanisms." *Energy Policy* 36 (11): 4079–92; Renner, Michael, Sean Sweeney and Jill Kubit. 2008. *Green Jobs: Towards Decent Work in a Sustainable, Low-carbon World.* Geneva, UNEP; and Stankeviciute, Loreta, Alban Kitous and Patrick Criqui. 2008. "The fundamentals of the future international emissions trading system." *Energy Policy* 36 (11): 4272–86.

As in the United States, though, more could be done in Europe to combine stimulus policies aimed at immediate economic recovery and job creation with a medium-term strategy for a transition to a low-carbon economy. A critical step in this transition is for the European Union to expand and improve its cap-and-trade Emission Trading System (ETS) to reduce greenhouse gas emissions while making substantial investments over the next year or two in energy efficiency, renewable energy supplies and the clean use of fossil fuels.[19] During

[19] On the origins and development of, and possible reforms to, the ETS, see Convery, Frank J. 2009. "Origins and development of the EU ETS." *Environmental and Resource Economics* 43 (3): 391–412.

the next decade there are likely to be important synergies in emission reductions and economic gains across all EU members if these measures are pursued. An immediate and large-scale investment program to expand energy conservation and renewable energy supply is likely to create at least 1 to 2 million new, full-time jobs. Similarly to the United States, the European Union could implement a green recovery program entailing around US$140 billion in low-carbon investments and incentives, which would be equivalent to around 1 percent of EU GDP.[20] Such investments would add significantly to current EU proposals to spend US$23 billion in green stimulus measures devoted to low-carbon initiatives (see box 1.1). A large part of the financing of any European green recovery program could be met through the revenues generated through an expanded ETS, however. In the next implementation phase, for instance, the ETS is anticipated to earn over US$68 billion in annual revenues for the European Union.

Individual EU governments could also do more to expand low-carbon initiatives. For example, as discussed in chapter 1, the governments of key European countries, such as France, Germany, Sweden and the United Kingdom, are spending much less on low-carbon and environmental investments than the major Asia-Pacific economies, Australia, Japan and South Korea (see figure 1.2). With the exception of Sweden, the governments of most European states are spending much less than 1 percent of their GDP on initiatives to reduce carbon dependency (see figure 2.1).

The examples of China, the United States and the European Union, as well as the Green New Deal enacted by South Korea, indicate that large-scale investment through a green recovery program would not only be an important step in the transition to a low-carbon economy but would also stimulate new economic sectors, increase the demand for skilled work, create jobs and thus boost overall economic recovery and sustain growth. A US$140 billion program

[20] Based on 2007 estimated European Union GDP in PPP terms of $14,430 billion, from the CIA's "The world factbook." Available at www.cia.gov/library/publications/the-world-factbook/rankorder/2001rank.html.

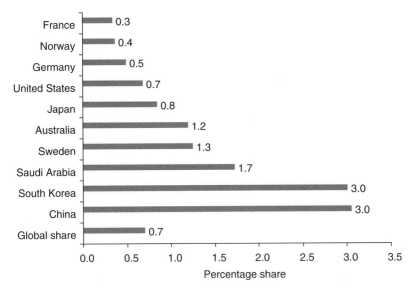

FIGURE 2.1 Green stimulus as a share of GDP
Notes: Based on box 1.1. The figure displays the top ten economies by total amount of green stimulus spending as a percentage of GDP.

implemented over the next two years in both the United States and the European Union – equivalent to about 1 percent of GDP in both economies – would be an essential part of such a Global Green New Deal. The energy conservation and green building investments that form part of South Korea's Green New Deal amount to 0.5 percent of that country's GDP, and the full low-carbon strategy accounts for 1.2 percent (see chapter 5). A similar green recovery stimulus, of approximately the same proportionate magnitude, has been adopted by Australia, and the spending by Japan's government on low-carbon initiatives now amounts to around 0.8 percent of its GDP (see box 1.1). Other high-income economies, especially members of the G20, should adopt similar investment strategies for reducing the carbon dependency of their economies. In China, as well as other large emerging market economies, it is difficult to estimate how much should be invested in an immediate green recovery program, but it is clear from the example of China in box 2.3 that a substantial economy-wide investment in energy efficiency and increasing clean energy supply options would yield substantial benefits in terms of sectoral growth, economic stimulus and employment creation. Already, as shown in box 1.1, the government of China has spent US$175 billion, equivalent to 2.5% of its GDP, on promoting low-carbon initiatives. Other large emerging market economies, especially members of the G20, should follow the lead of China and South Korea and invest at least 1 percent of their GDP over the next two to three years in reducing carbon dependency.

The examples of China, the United States and the European Union also illustrate the importance of adopting a complementary carbon pricing policy.

Europe is already looking beyond the current ETS to implementation of the next phase; in the United States, a comprehensive cap-and-trade system for greenhouse gas emissions is also the expected outcome. In China, a carbon tax is the more likely and feasible option. These various examples suggest that there are a wide range of possible models for a carbon pricing policy for other high-income OECD and emerging market economies to choose from. Both cap-and-trade and carbon tax policies will generate sizable revenues, which could be used for financing a number of investments, including increasing energy conservation and renewable energy supply, reducing poverty and inequality, mitigating distributional impacts and the development of clean energy technologies. Additional revenues could be recycled from the use of other economic instruments, emission taxes and the removal of distortional fossil fuel subsidies. The potential in these economies for ending or reducing fossil fuel subsidies and investing the savings in large-scale investments in clean energy and energy conservation as part of a longer-term transition to a low-carbon development path is significant.

The removal of fossil fuel subsidies may be a particularly important component of any carbon pricing policy for some economies. Globally, around US$300 billion (equivalent to 0.7 percent of

world GDP) is spent annually on such subsidies.[21] The vast majority of fossil fuel subsidies are used to lower artificially the prices
of coal, electricity, natural gas and oil products. Contrary to widely
held views, most of these subsidies do not benefit the poor but the
wealthy; nor do they offer widespread economic benefits. Cancelling
these global subsidies would on its own reduce greenhouse gas emissions globally by as much as 6 percent and add 0.1 percentage points
to global GDP. The financial savings on these subsidies could be
redirected towards investments in clean energy research and development (R&D), renewable energy development and energy conservation, which would further boost economic growth and employment
opportunities.

As indicated in box 2.4, removal of the US$6 billion fossil fuel
subsidies in the United States would provide an additional source
of funding for a green recovery program to be implemented over
the next two years. Generally, however, the scope for removing fossil fuel and comparable energy subsidies is greater in non-OECD
than in OECD economies. Energy subsidies in high-income OECD
economies amount to about US$80 billion annually, but twenty
non-OECD countries account for US$220 billion in such subsid-
ies. Russia has US$40 billion in energy subsidies annually, mostly
for lowering natural gas prices, whereas Iran's energy subsidies
are around US$37 billion. China, Saudi Arabia, India, Indonesia,
Ukraine and Egypt have subsidies in excess of US$10 billion per
year. Venezuela, Kazakhstan, Argentina and Pakistan have subsidies between US$5 and 10 billion annually, and South Africa,
Malaysia, Thailand, Nigeria and Vietnam have subsidies between
US$1 and 5 billion per year.

The removal of major subsidies, such as those on fossil fuels,
is always a difficult political step for individual governments. More
than two-thirds of the US$300 billion annual fossil fuel subsidies
globally occur in countries that are members of the G20 economic

[21] UNEP. 2008. *Reforming Energy Subsidies: Opportunities to Contribute to the
Climate Change Agenda.* Geneva, UNEP.

forum. If the G20 could negotiate and coordinate the phased removal of such subsidies, then it would make their elimination more likely and feasible.

Initiating the reduction in the carbon dependency of all middle- and low-income economies must be an important objective of any Global Green New Deal. As indicated in box 2.1, by 2030 developing economies are expected on current trends to produce over a half of global greenhouse gas emissions. China alone will account for half the emissions of the developing economies, and other large emerging and transition economies will account for much of the rest. The need to provide low-carbon economic development opportunities for low-income economies in the near future is still of paramount importance, however.

As discussed earlier, policies similar to those advanced in China to promote energy efficiency and conservation, increase clean energy supply options and implement carbon pricing policies and other economic instruments (see box 2.3) could be applied in many low-income economies. There is widespread scope for such policies to be implemented across Asia, for example, including its low-income economies.[22] Eliminating fossil fuel subsidies to finance such investments is also potentially an important source of financing for renewable energy and energy-saving investments not only in large emerging market economies but also in low-income economies in which such subsidies are prevalent. In addition, as outlined in box 2.6, energy sector reforms in developing countries, such as Botswana, Ghana, Honduras, India, Indonesia, Nepal and Senegal, have proved to be effective in leading a transition to more efficient and cleaner fuels, which particularly benefit poor households.

---

[22] See, for example, Carmody and Ritchie 2007 (fn 13); Renner, Sweeney and Kubit 2008 (fn 13); UN ESCAP 2008 (fn 7); and Zhang 2008 (fn 13).

Box 2.6 Energy sector reforms and improved services to the poor in developing economies

Botswana, Ghana, Honduras and Senegal have undertaken a number of energy sector reforms that have affected the access of the poor to important fuels, including electricity, petroleum products such as kerosene and candles, charcoal and fuelwood.

All four countries have implemented some electricity sector reforms, including subsidies, stepped or baseline tariff pricing, changes in technology, price setting, loan schemes and community involvement. Senegal, Ghana and Honduras introduced stepped tariffs for low-use consumers, with the aim of increasing access by poor households. Botswana opted instead to invest in a rural electrification programme for deliveries to the poor with subsidized payments. The result was a fivefold rise in rural connections between 1996 and 2003. The reforms and concessionary pricing in Senegal, Ghana and Honduras also increased access to electricity by the poor, but at a slower rate. Thus households in all four countries switched from the use of wood to electricity.

The four countries also allowed private companies to take over the import, distribution and sale of petroleum products. Products such as kerosene and gas became more available to households that would otherwise rely on charcoal and fuelwood for cooking, heating and lighting. Since the 1970s Senegal has also subsidized the acquisition of small butane gas stoves by the rural poor as a substitute for their use of charcoal and wood as cooking fuels. From 1999 to 2001, after 85 percent of the households of all income groups, including the poorest, had converted to gas stoves for cooking, the government reduced the subsidy by 80 percent. Currently, 86 percent of households in the lowest income quintile in Senegal use gas for cooking. Households in Botswana, Ghana and Honduras have also increasingly switched to gas for cooking, although it is much more widely used in urban areas than rural ones.

Because Ghana still has extensive forests and woodlands, the government has allocated some of these forests as fuel plantations and deregulated the private charcoal industry as a means of encouraging the use of charcoal instead of fuelwood for cooking and heating. As a result, from 2001 to 2004 the use of wood declined while charcoal use increased in both rural and urban areas.

Other developing economies are also adopting innovative energy sector reforms to target increased access to energy services by the poor. For example, India is promoting the provision of decentralized technologies by private energy enterprises. Nepal is encouraging the selling of biogas equipment by private companies. Indonesia has developed a public–private partnership initiative so as to improve access to electricity for remote rural communities.

The lessons of the energy sector reform in these developing countries indicate that, if the reforms improve the efficiency of a sector, then both the entire economy as well as the poor will benefit from improved access to energy services, lower costs and an increased quality of supply. In addition, policies targeted at benefiting the poor have also encouraged the more widespread adoption of more efficient and cleaner fuels. Thus, increasing the access of the poor to energy services and improving overall energy efficiency are not incompatible goals in developing economies.

Sources: Prasad, Gisela. 2008. "Energy sector reform, energy transitions and the poor in Africa." *Energy Policy* 36 (8): 2806–1; and UN ESCAP. 2008. *Energy Security and Sustainable Development in Asia and the Pacific.* UN ESCAP, Bangkok

The economic and employment gains for developing economies of such policies could be significant. For example, the IEA estimates that, for each US dollar invested in improving the energy efficiency of electricity generation, more than US$3 in investment costs can be saved in low- and middle-income countries, because present efficiency levels are much lower in these economies.[23] Small hydropower,

[23] As quoted in UN ESCAP 2008 (see fn 13).

biomass and solar photovoltaics already provides electricity, heat, water pumping and other power for tens of millions of people in the rural areas of developing countries. Some 25 million households depend on biogas for cooking and lighting, and 2.5 million households use solar lighting systems. Developing economies currently account for around 40 percent of existing global renewable resource capacity, 70 percent of solar water heating capacity and 45 percent of biofuels production.[24] The expansion of these sectors will therefore be important not only to increase the availability of affordable and sustainable energy services for the world's poor but also to provide much-needed employment opportunities in developing economies.[25]

REDUCING ENERGY POVERTY

Such provision of affordable and sustainable energy services is an essential component of the GGND for reducing energy poverty worldwide. Billions of people in developing economies either have no access to modern energy services or pay high prices for erratic and unreliable services.

As illustrated in box 2.7, Grameen Shakti of Bangladesh is leading the way with the dissemination of three renewable energy technologies – PV solar home systems, biogas facilities and improved cooking stoves – in rural areas. Over 205,000 homes have already been installed with PV solar systems, 6,000 biogas plants have been set up and more than 20,000 improved stoves have been disseminated.

[24] REN21. 2008. *Renewables 2007: Global Status Report*. Paris, REN21 Secretariat, and Washington, DC, Worldwatch Institute.

[25] The lack of data makes it very difficult to estimate the employment potential of increasing renewable energy supply options in the developing world. For example, as reported by Renner, Sweeney and Kubit 2008 (see fn 13), the renewable energy sector accounts currently for more than 2.3 million jobs worldwide. These figures include employment for only a handful of developing economies, though, such as China (943,200 workers in all renewable energy sectors), India (some 10,000 workers in wind power) and Brazil (around 500,000 workers in biofuels energy). Nevertheless, the employment potential across the developing world is significant, since the above statistics suggest that these three developing economies account already for over 65 percent of renewable energy employment worldwide.

This has led to the creation of some 20,000 jobs, the training of over 1,000 renewable energy technicians, and numerous other employment opportunities through small-scale training. By 2015 the goal is to reach 7.5 million households with PV solar systems, establish 500,000 biogas units and provide 2 million stoves, with a direct employment potential of at least 100,000 jobs and the training of 10,000 technicians.

Box 2.7 Grameen Shakti and renewable energy use by the poor in Bangladesh

Through its innovative micro-credit scheme, Grameen Shakti in Bangladesh has been embarking on an ambitious program to provide a range of affordable renewable energy technologies to rural households. Already the company has installed over 205,000 homes across Bangladesh with photovoltaic solar systems capable of powering lights and small-scale electronic appliances (e.g. refrigerators, televisions, cellphones, computers and radios). Over 8,000 PV solar systems are being installed per month, and demand for the systems is increasing exponentially. The goal is to install 2 million PV solar systems in homes by 2011, and 7.5 million by 2015, which would reach a half of the Bangladeshi population.

Across Bangladesh, Grameen Shakti has also installed 6,000 biogas plants, which convert animal dung and organic litter into pollution-free biogas and slurry. The biogas can be used for cooking food, for lighting and for producing electricity through home generators. The slurry is used as organic fertilizer and as food in fish farming. More than thirty large-scale plants provide electricity directly to households. Grameen Shakti has set itself the goal of establishing 500,000 biogas plants by 2015. In the long run, with the rising cost of kerosene and other conventional fuels, scarcity of wood and higher chemical fertilizers, at least 4 million biogas plants could be constructed in Bangladesh.

Grameen Shakti has also disseminated over 20,000 improved cooking stoves, and has the goal of providing 1 million stoves by 2010 covering 35,000 villages. The longer-term market potential is for 2 million stoves by 2015. By replacing traditional stoves, the improved cooking stoves hope to reduce fuelwood depletion and protect women and young children from indoor pollution.

The employment and other economic opportunities of the program are far-reaching. At least 20,000 jobs have been created already with the current uptake of these three renewable energy technologies across Bangladesh. Around 1,000 women have been trained as PV solar or improved stove technicians, and many trainees have gone on to set up their own renewable energy businesses. Thirty-three Grameen Technology Centers have been established in rural areas to carry out training and manufacturing. Through these centers, more than 45,000 rural women have learned to take care of the PV solar systems installed in their homes, and at least 10,000 schoolchildren have learned about the new renewable energy technologies. Over 1,000 local masons have been trained as part of the biogas plant construction program, and 1,000 demonstration farm plots have been established to popularize the use of slurry as organic fertilizer. Another 1,000 or so improved cooking stove technicians have been trained, and around thirty-five manufacturing units have been set up through seed capital and technical assistance. The goals are to create at least 100,000 direct jobs by 2015, mainly for women, through the renewable energy technology program and to train at least 10,000 technicians.

Source: Barau, Dipal. 2008. "Bringing green energy, health, income and green jobs to Bangladesh." Paper presented at preparatory meeting, International Advisory Board to the International Climate Protection Initiative of the German Federal Ministry for the Environment, Nature Conservation and Nuclear Safety. Poznan, Poland, December 7.

Access to modern energy services not only reduces poverty but also contributes to economic growth, by improving productivity, facilitating local income generation and reducing unit energy costs. The use of more efficient fuels can reduce the large share of household income spent on cooking, lighting and heating, thus leading to greater expenditures on food, education, health services and other basic needs. Low modern energy service use is also correlated with high infant mortality, illiteracy and fertility, and with low life expectancy.

To achieve the objective of improving the access of the world's poor to modern energy services and therefore promoting growth and development in the poorest economies, a report for the UNDP and the World Bank advocates three key goals: increasing access to modern fuels and cleaner biomass systems for cooking and heating; ensuring access to electricity in all urban and peri-urban areas; and providing access to mechanical power and electricity at centralized points in rural areas.[26] The report also suggests, however, that such efforts in developing economies will need institutional support and capacity building from the international community to ensure that these economies have the skills and technology needed to support the development and expansion of modern energy services. As discussed in chapter 4, such skills, technology and finance shortfalls are some of the major challenges facing developing economies in implementing a low-carbon strategy for reducing energy poverty.

IMPROVING THE SUSTAINABILITY OF TRANSPORTATION

Globally, the transportation sector accounts for over a quarter of total world energy use and 14 percent of total greenhouse gas emissions.[27] In high-income economies, transportation's share of GHG emissions is even higher; for example, it stands at 26 percent in the United States and nearly 19 percent in the European Union. The highest rates of growth in emissions from transportation are occurring in the Middle

---

[26] Modi *et al.* 2005 (see ch. 1, fn 23).

[27] Barker, T., I. Bashmakov, L. Bernstein, J. E. Bogner, P. R. Bosch, R. Dave, O. R. Davidson, B. S. Fisher, S. Gupta, K. Halsnæs, G.J. Heij, S. Kahn Ribeiro, S. Kobayashi, M. D. Levine, D. L. Martino, O. Masera, B. Metz, L. A. Meyer, G.-J. Nabuurs, A. Najam, N. Nakicenovic, H.-H. Rogner, J. Roy, J. Sathaye, R. Schock, P. Shukla, R. E. H. Sims, P. Smith, D. A. Tirpak, D. Urge-Vorsatz and D. Zhou. 2007. "Technical summary." In B. Metz, O. R. Davidson, P. R. Bosch, R. Dave and L. A. Meyer (eds.). *Climate Change 2007: Mitigation of Climate Change.* Cambridge, Cambridge University Press: 25–94.

East and North Africa (4.0 percent annual average growth from 1990 to 2005), Asia (3.9 percent), sub-Saharan Africa (3.5 pecent) and Latin America and the Caribbean (3 percent).[28] Worldwide, the transport sector is responsible for the fastest-growing increase in GHG emissions of all economic sectors, and road transport currently accounts for 74 percent of all emissions from transport.

Unless there is a major shift away from current patterns of energy use, world transportation energy use is expected to grow at a rate of 2 percent per year, such that energy use and GHG emissions will have risen about 80 percent above 2002 levels by 2030.[29]

Improving the sustainability of transportation is also essential for other environmental and economic reasons. Transport is an important infrastructure sector in modern economies and can act as an important stimulus to growth. Transportation networks are essential to the daily functioning of cities, and, at the same time, population growth, urbanization and industrial activity are the main drivers for the growth of the transport sector, its increased energy use and its growing share of global GHG emissions, especially in rapidly developing economies. It is estimated that the transport sector in urban metropolitan areas accounts for a third or more of total GHG emissions by cities.[30] In addition, air pollution from transport has become one of the worst environmental and health hazards in the urban areas of developing countries, particularly on account of the high concentrations of urban populations, rapid rates of urbanization and inefficient transport systems. Finally, the poor in urban areas are adversely affected by a lack of access to public transportation, the high cost of motorized transport and high accident rates arising from unreliable road transport.

---

[28] These data on greenhouse gas emissions from transportation are from CAIT, version 6.0, 2008.

[29] Barker, Bashmakov, Bernstein *et al.* 2007 (see fn 27).

[30] World Bank. 2006. *Promoting Global Environmental Priorities in the Urban Transport Sector: Experience from World Bank Group – Global Environmental Facility Projects.* Washington, DC, World Bank.

Creating a more sustainable global transport system is also about enhancing the efficiency, growth and job potential of transport networks. There are several reasons why the current global transport system, with its increasing overreliance on motorized and privately owned road transport, is failing on all three counts.

First, such a system has stressed the benefits of mobility over accessibility. This has resulted in unexpected consequences for urban development, land use planning and employment opportunities. For example, in the United States, the rapid expansion of the highway system between 1950 and 1990 contributed significantly to the population decline of major cities.[31] Unfortunately, the US model has become the model for global transport systems, especially as per capita income rises and automobile use increases. This auto-oriented urban structure, rather than improving the accessibility of jobs, may have worsened it. For example, a study comparing Boston, Los Angeles and Tokyo shows that job accessibility is significantly lower in all three cities for public transit users than for automobile users, but accessibility for public transit users in the US cities is much lower than in Tokyo. In other words, in modern metropolitan areas, lack of access to a private vehicle reduces employment opportunities, but this is particularly true as countries follow the US transportation example and become more auto-oriented.[32]

Second, the bias in the current global transport system towards greater motorized vehicle use, road transport and increased energy use is further exacerbated by sizable transportation market distortions, including the "underpricing" of motorized travel, current urban and land use planning practices that encourage automobile use, and distortions in public investment in favor of road transport over other modes of travel. These distortions lead to additional economic

[31] Baum-Snow, Nathaniel. 2007. "Did highways cause suburbanization?" *Quarterly Journal of Economics* 122 (2): 775–805.
[32] Kawabata, Mizuki, and Qing Shen. 2006. "Job accessibility as an indicator of auto-oriented urban structure: a comparison of Boston and Los Angeles with Tokyo." *Environment and Planning B: Planning and Design* 33 (1): 115–30.

and social costs, including traffic congestion, higher transportation costs, inefficient energy consumption and an increased incidence of accidents. Most of these latter costs are "external," in that they are imposed on others by vehicle users, and typically comprise about a third of the total costs of automobile use.[33] In the United States, such costs are approaching US$50 billion a year.[34] The economic consequences are often cumulative and far-reaching. In the case of congestion, for example, there are multiple economic effects. A World Bank report finds that the trend towards increased per capita vehicle use in developing economies is leading rapidly to more road congestion, which in turn increases travel time for surface public transport such as buses. The result is more auto and taxi use, however, adding to the congestion problem.[35] In large US metropolitan areas, vehicle congestion has reached such significant proportions that it is impacting employment growth. Estimates suggest that a 10 percent increase in congestion, for a city with travel delays comparable to that of Los Angeles, reduces long-run employment growth by 4 percent.[36] As current trends in global urbanization and traffic congestion continue, the reductions in employment growth in major cities could be substantial. The billions of dollars that policymakers spend annually on expanding the road network are becoming less effective in decreasing congestion. For example, in the United States, every dollar spent on highways reduces the congestion costs to motorists, trucking operations and shipping firms by only eleven cents.[37]

Third, the current global transport system, which encourages more private motorized vehicle use, also disadvantages the poor. In Mumbai, India, over 44 percent of all commuters walk to work, and

[33] Litman, Todd. 2006. "Transportation market distortions." *Berkeley Planning Journal* 19: 19–36.
[34] Winston, Clifford, and Ashley Langer. 2006. "The effect of government highway spending on road users' congestion costs." *Journal of Urban Economics* 60 (3): 463–83.
[35] World Bank 2006 (see fn 30).
[36] Hymel, Kent. 2009. "Does traffic congestion reduce employment growth?" *Journal of Urban Economics* 65 (2): 127–35.
[37] Winston and Langer 2006 (see fn 34).

63 percent of the poor walk to work. The poor who rely on transport generally use public transit: 21 percent of the poor in the urban center take the bus to work and 25 percent of the poor in the suburbs take rail to work.[38] Throughout the developing world, at low levels of income people generally take public transit, use some form of non-motorized transport or simply walk. At a middle income level, there is increased reliance on small motorized transport, such as jitneys, scooters or motorcycles. It is only at high income levels that private car vehicle use emerges. It is the low- and middle-income households that spend the most on transportation, however: up to 30 percent of their income in urban areas.[39] Similarly, in Africa, the poorest urban households pay as much as a quarter of their income for transport.[40] As a result, it is the poor who suffer disproportionately from higher transportation costs. For example, in four Asian developing economies, as fuel prices rose between 2002 and 2005 poor households paid 120 percent more for transportation.[41] In rich countries, such as the United States, the poor tend to concentrate in city centers, spend a higher proportion of their income on transportation expenditures and are highly reliant on public transit.[42] Thus, poor households are vulnerable to the costs and availability of public transportation systems, which are often underfunded and limited; consequently, access to public transit has a significant bearing on rates of labor participation and the employment of inner city residents.[43]

A Global Green New Deal should aim to improve the sustainability of transportation systems worldwide, including better access

[38] Baker, Judy, Rakhi Basu, Maureen Cropper, Somik Lall and Akie Tkeuchi. 2005. *Urban Poverty and Transport: The Case of Mumbai.* Policy Research Working Paper no. 3693. Washington, DC, World Bank.

[39] Sperling, Daniel, and Deborah Salon. 2002. *Transportation in Developing Countries: An Overview of Greenhouse Gas Reduction Strategies.* Arlington, VA, Pew Center on Global Climate Change.

[40] Renner, Sweeney and Kubit 2008 (see fn 13).

[41] UN ESCAP 2008 (see fn 7).

[42] Glaeser, Edward L., Matthew E. Kahn and Jordan Rappaport. 2008. "Why do the poor live in cities? The role of public transportation." *Journal of Urban Economics* 63 (1): 1–24.

[43] Sanchez, Thomas W. 1999. "The connection between public transit and employment." *Journal of the American Planning Association* 65 (3): 284–96.

to transport for the poor, and at the same time boost short-run economic recovery and create millions of jobs.

Achieving these multiple goals is possible through progress in five main areas:

- developing the next generation of fuel-efficient cars, low-carbon biofuels and the delivery system infrastructure for the new fuels and cars;
- encouraging modal shifts in transportation systems from road transport to rail and public transit;
- reducing the miles traveled in motorized vehicles – through smart transport, urban and land use planning;
- improving the accessibility of affordable transport for the poor; and
- removing transport market distortions and implementing, where appropriate, market-based instruments and regulations to improve the sustainability of transport systems.

The next section provides examples of various measures that could be implemented by national governments of all economies, and which would also stimulate new economic sectors, increase the demand for skilled work and create jobs, thereby boosting overall economic recovery and sustaining growth.

ACTIONS TO MAKE TRANSPORT MORE SUSTAINABLE

One of the hallmarks of the current worldwide recession is the slump in global automobile sales. In late 2008 car sales were 30 percent down over the previous year, and the average annual rate of decline is expected to be at least 8 percent in 2009.[44] Two of the three big auto manufacturers in the United States, General Motors and Chrysler, entered bankruptcy, and the third, Ford, has received a loan bailout from the US government. Toyota has predicted its first fiscal year operating loss in its seventy years of operation, and Nissan has reported a decline in global production of more than a third. As the recession deepens, the crisis in the global auto industry is expected to worsen, given that, historically, employment and income growth have been the key determinants of vehicle sales.

[44] Gomes, Carlos. 2009. *Global Auto Report*, January 8. Toronto, Scotiabank Group.

Attempts to revive the world economy go hand in hand with the recovery of the global automobile industry. With the industry facing falling sales, especially for its less fuel-intensive passenger vehicles, and becoming more dependent on financial loans and other support from national governments, now is the ideal time to combine a recovery program for the auto industry with the necessary incentives and restructuring to develop the next generation of fuel-efficient vehicles and the biofuels for their use.

As indicated in box 2.8, the employment implications of developing more fuel-efficient vehicles for the global automobile industry could be significant. If the entire worldwide industry moved to similar rates of employment to Japan's auto makers in producing vehicles with cleaner technology, then over 3.8 million jobs could be directly related to the production of vehicles with high fuel efficiency, hybrid and alternative fuel use and low-emission technologies. In addition, the ratio of indirect to direct jobs currently ranges from 4:1 (Japan) to 6.5:1 (United States). If the ratio were 5:1 worldwide, then up to 19 million additional ancillary jobs in fuel refining and distribution, sales, repairs and services could be created by developing cleaner vehicle technology. Of course, there would also be significant job displacement as traditional vehicle manufacture declines. In the United States, though, it is estimated that just increasing fuel economy standards could expand fuel-efficient vehicle production and create directly up to 350,000 new jobs net, mostly in the states worst affected by the current crisis in the global automobile industry: Michigan, Ohio, California and Indiana.

Box 2.8 Fuel-efficient vehicles and employment

Employment in the global automobile manufacturing industry, including parts and accessories production, is estimated to be around 8.4 million. Most of this employment is concentrated in the major auto-producing economies: the United States, Europe, Japan and South Korea. Some large emerging market economies also have an expanding car manufacturing industry and employment, such as China (1.6 million workers), Russia (755,000), Brazil (289,000), India (270,000) and Thailand (182,000). The indirect employment of the global car industry, including fuel refining and distribution, sales, repairs and services, is even larger, however. For example, in the United States such indirect jobs total 6.5 million, and in Japan 4 million.

It is difficult to estimate the number of direct manufacturing jobs involved in the production of vehicles with high fuel efficiency, hybrid and alternative fuel use (including electric), low emissions and other cleaner technologies. Estimates range from about 800,000 to a quarter of a million employees globally, or only about 3 to 10 percent of the total global auto-related workforce. In comparison, in Japan 434,000 workers are employed in the production of hybrid and low-emission vehicles, or nearly 46 percent of a total automobile manufacturing workforce of 952,000. If the same proportion of workers in the global manufacturing industry were employed in producing cleaner vehicles, then this activity would account for over 3.8 million jobs worldwide. As part of its Green New Deal, South Korea expects to invest nearly US$1.5 billion in fuel-efficient vehicles and clean fuel, creating over 14,000 new jobs (see chapter 5).

Developing economies would also benefit from this job creation. Since June 2007 Thailand has granted a range of tax incentives to manufacturers of "eco-cars" that have a limited engine size, obtain at least forty-seven miles per gallon of fuel and generate 120 grams of CO_2 per kilometer driven, and meet European emission standards. The cars will not only be sold in the domestic market but are also aimed at other Asian countries, Australia and Africa. Although it is too early to know the implications for net job creation in Thailand, it is anticipated that the eco-car initiative has the potential to attain a large share of the country's current 182,000 jobs in auto manufacturing. Similarly, studies for China show that the country could move to cleaner vehicle technology by introducing a package of investment and incentive policies that strengthen vehicle emission standards, advance fuel quality and promote hybrid and alternative fuel vehicles. If such an approach were adopted, a much larger proportion of the 1.6 million Chinese auto jobs would be accounted for by these technologies.

Given the structural change and job displacement that would occur in the automobile industry from a massive switch to fuel-efficient vehicle production, the relevant estimate is the creation of new net employment. A study for the United States shows that increases in the corporate average fuel economy standards for vehicles could create between 73,000 and 350,000 new net jobs as well as reducing US annual oil consumption and greenhouse gas emissions. Most of the net employment creation would occur in the traditional automobile manufacturing states that are currently experiencing the worst job losses under the current crisis in the global car industry: Michigan, Ohio, California and Indiana.

Sources: Bezdek, Roger H., and Robert M. Wendling. 2005. "Potential long-term impacts of changes in US vehicle fuel efficiency standards." *Energy Policy* 33 (3): 407–19; Renner, Michael, Sean Sweeney and Jill Kubit. 2008. *Green Jobs: Towards Decent Work in a Sustainable, Low-carbon World.* Geneva, UNEP; and Zhao, Jimin. 2006. "Whither the car? China's automobile industry and cleaner vehicle technologies." *Development and Change* 37 (1): 121–44.

Developing the next generation of low-carbon biofuels and a national delivery system will be an important complement to the expansion of fuel-efficient vehicles in the global automobile industry (see box 2.9). Interest in biofuels for motorized vehicles has increased worldwide because of concerns over energy security and reducing greenhouse gas emissions and the need to increase and diversify agricultural and export income. The employment potential could be substantial. Already, at least 1.2 million jobs are involved worldwide in biofuel production, and, given the high labor intensity of biofuels, the expansion of global production could easily yield 10 million jobs or more.

Box 2.9 Biofuels: economic potential or environmental scourge?

Concerns about energy security and greenhouse gas emissions and the desire to increase agricultural and export income have led to the rapid expansion of biofuel production globally. For example, from 2004 to 2007 global ethanol production leapt from 10.8 billion gallons to 13.1 billion gallons, an increase of nearly 25 percent. Although nearly 88 percent of this output comes from two countries, the United States and Brazil, increasingly other countries, including many developing economies and regions, are investing in biofuel production. Currently, nearly 1.2 million jobs globally are estimated to come from such production, but this may underestimate the total employment impact of the sector, since the global estimate is based on five countries: Brazil (some 500,000 workers), the United States (312,200), China (266,000), Germany (95,400) and Spain (10,350). The future employment and economic potential of the industry looks even stronger, especially in developing economies. For example, Colombia is expected to add 170,000 jobs in its sugar ethanol industry over the next several years, Venezuela might create a million jobs through a similar ethanol program, Nigeria's biofuels expansion from cassava and sugar cane could generate 200,000 jobs, and across sub-Saharan Africa as many as 700,000 to a million new jobs could be created through increased ethanol production. Because on average biofuels require about 100 times more workers per joule of energy content produced compared to fossil fuels, it is thought that future net job creation from expanded global biofuel production could reach 10 million.

World ethanol fuel production, 2007

Country	Millions of gallons
United States	6,498.6
Brazil	5,019.2
European Union	570.3
China	486.0
Canada	211.3

Table (*cont.*)

Country	Millions of gallons
Thailand	79.2
Colombia	74.9
India	52.8
Central America	39.6
Australia	26.4
Turkey	15.8
Pakistan	9.2
Peru	7.9
Argentina	5.2
Paraguay	4.7
World total	13,101.7

Source: Renewable Fuels Association, ethanol industry statistics, available at www.ethanolrfa.org/industry/ statistics.

Complaints about the environmental and economic impacts of first-generation biofuel production are also mounting, however. In many regions, the main biofuel feedstocks, such as sugar cane, corn (maize) and oil palm, have exacerbated existing problems of deforestation, water use, biodiversity loss and air and water pollution. The rapid increase in corn-based ethanol production in the United States may have contributed to problems of food and feed shortage and rising prices. Large-scale plantation monoculture of oil palm and sugar cane may be contributing to tropical forest conversion and the displacement of small-scale farmers and indigenous people in the developing world. Working conditions on some plantations and processing factories may also be less than ideal, and may involve the exploitation of under-age workers, and even forced labor. Finally, there are concerns that the fuel efficiency of current biofuel crops, especially corn-based and rapeseed ethanol, is too low.

Further development and production of global biofuels must focus on minimizing these economic, environmental and social costs. The development of second-generation feedstocks and converting more of the energy in cellulose plant material are promising starting points. For example, of the current feedstock, only palm oil, sugar cane and sugar beets yield sufficiently high amounts of gasoline-equivalent fuel on a per hectare basis. New feedstocks that have the potential for even higher per hectare fuel yields include algae, castor oil, crop wastes, jatropha, lignin, perennial grasses, short-rotation woody crops and forest industry wastes. These new feedstocks have the potential to reduce land and water use conflicts and produce economic and employment benefits if they can become cost-effective, and also create less pressure on agricultural and forest lands, water supplies and input use. Brazil has employed the crop waste from sugar cane (bagasse) to generate heat and electricity, and is currently exploring using both bagasse and the sugar crop to boost fuel yields per hectare. The US government is putting up US$18 million in connection with the research, development and demonstration of the fuel potential of many second-generation stocks. In the developing world, the increased use of jatropha and castor oil is already being developed. These and other oil seed crops may improve job creation prospects because they need to be harvested manually. In Mali, jatropoha-based biofuel will replace imported diesel and generate local employment opportunities. In India, it is estimated that a jatropha farm could provide 313 person-days per hectare of employment in the first year of planting and fifty person-days per ha thereafter. Brazil estimates that harvesting castor oil could provide 0.3 jobs per ha and jatropha 0.25 jobs per ha, compared to 0.2 for oil palm and 0.07 for soybeans.

In addition, labor and environmental regulations on biofuel production, harvesting and processing need to be adopted and enforced worldwide. ILO recommendations on under-aged labor use and working conditions and practices need to be adopted and strictly adhered to. In addition, biofuel projects, especially large-scale plantations, need to be vetted for their potential impacts on land and water use, deforestation, displacing other forms of agricultural production and affecting the livelihoods of small farmers and indigenous populations.

Sources: Goldemberg, José, Suani Teixeira Coelho and Patricia Guardabassi. 2008. "The sustainability of ethanol production from sugarcane." *Energy Policy* 36 (6): 2086–97; Peña, Naomi. 2008. *Biofuels for Transportation: A Climate Perspective.* Arlington, VA, Pew Center on Global Climate Change; Renewable Fuels Association, ethanol industry statistics, available at www.ethanolrfa.org/industry/statistics; and Renner, Michael, Sean Sweeney and Jill Kubit. 2008. *Green Jobs: Towards Decent Work in a Sustainable, Low-carbon World.* Geneva, UNEP.

There are major concerns about the negative consequences of increased biofuel production worldwide, however, including the competing demands for land and water, deforestation and pollution, the displacement of small farmers and indigenous people, poor working conditions and labor practices, and the impacts on global food and feed prices. The development of second-generation feedstock that could yield higher-gasoline-equivalent fuel productivity, such as algae, castor oil, crop wastes, jatropha, lignin, perennial grasses, short-rotation woody crops and forest industry wastes, may reduce some of these problems and also create more opportunities for employment (see box 2.9). Such developments need to be complemented by the adoption and enforcement of labor and environmental regulations worldwide to improve working practices and conditions and to reduce impacts on land and water use, deforestation and the displacement of other agricultural activity, small farmers and indigenous populations.

Developing a more sustainable transportation strategy should also emphasize public and rail transport, which are less carbon- and energy-intensive than private motorized vehicle travel, and which also have the potential to create jobs.

Investments in urban public transit and rail networks to transport passengers and freight not only create jobs directly in the employment of transit and railway operators and workers but also have strong multiplier effects on job creation, by providing basic infrastructure investments that boost a wide range of construction, engineering and manufacturing jobs at all different skill levels (see box 2.10). Public urban transit systems have significant direct employment impacts globally, accounting for 367,000 workers in the United States and 900,000 in the European Union alone. Investment in public urban transit also has major secondary employment effects. In Europe, public transit investments have a multiplier effect of 2.0 to 2.5 indirect jobs created, but in countries that invest heavily in public transport, such as Switzerland, the multiplier effect rises to 4.1. In addition, the induced employment effect of reducing the costs of transport to the urban poor and improving their mobility may also be significant. Investments in pubic and rail transport, along with land use and urban planning to improve non-motorized transport such as bicycling and walking, may also lead to a "modal shift" in densely populated areas away from vehicular use to these other forms of transport. The result may be not just reduced pollution and greenhouse gas emissions but also net job creation.

Box 2.10 Public and rail transport and employment

Public urban transit systems have significant direct employment impacts globally, accounting for 367,000 workers in the United States and 900,000 in the European Union alone. In developing countries, such as China, Egypt, Ghana, India, Indonesia, Iran, Mexico, South Africa and South Korea, the expansion of compressed natural gas (CNG) buses and bus rapid transit (BRT) systems is reducing urban air pollution and creating new manufacturing and operating employment. For example, in New Delhi, India, the introduction of CNG buses is expected to add 18,000 new jobs.

Investment in public urban transit has also had major secondary employment effects. In Europe, public transit investments have a multiplier effect of 2.0 to 2.5 indirect jobs created, but in countries that invest heavily in public transport, such as Switzerland, the multiplier effect rises to 4.1. Investments in public transit can also induce employment by making transport more affordable for the poor. For example, in major cities in the United States, access to public transit is a significant factor in connection with rates of labor participation and the employment of poor inner-city residents. In Mumbai, India, the availability of public transport is a critical factor in the mobility of the poor and their access to job opportunities. This is particularly true for the poor living on the fringes of the urban center, who are isolated by long commuting distances that prevent the use of non-motorized vehicles or walking.

Investments in rail systems will not only provide an alternative to road vehicles for moving passengers and freight but also create substantial employment. For example, in the United States, a ten-year federal investment program in new high-speed rail systems and their maintenance is estimated to have the employment potential of nearly 250,000 new jobs. As part of its Green New Deal, South Korea expects to generate over 138,000 new jobs through mass transit and railroad investments (see chapter 5). In Europe, the lack of investment in its existing rail systems is contributing to a decline in the workforce. Railway transport still accounts for around 900,000 jobs, but employment has fallen steadily in recent decades, including a 14 percent decline from 2000 to 2004. Employment in the manufacture of railway and tramway locomotives has also fallen significantly, to just 140,000 workers. In developing economies, railways remain an important source of transport of passengers and freight, but unless more investment is forthcoming the employment potential is lessening. For example, from 1992 to 2002 in China employment in the railways fell from 3.4 to 1.8 million, while in India it fell from 1.7 to 1.5 million. The neglect of rail investments in Africa is also reducing employment, in addition to worsening the continent's transportation problems.

Investments that provide alternatives to car use reduce pollution and greenhouse gas emissions as well as create employment. A study in Germany finds that such investments financed partially by higher gasoline taxes would double public and rail transport, increase bicycle use by 72 percent and decrease distances traveled by car by 8 percent – and create 208,000 additional net jobs. A similar UK study estimates a 70 to 80 percent increase in railway and bus use as well as more bicycling and walking, while reducing reliance on car use. The resulting employment effect was a net increase of 87,000 to 122,000 new jobs.

Sources: Baker, Judy, Rakhi Basu, Maureen Cropper, Somik Lall and Akie Tkeuchi. 2005. *Urban Poverty and Transport: The Case of Mumbai.* Policy Research Working Paper no. 3693. Washington, DC, World Bank; Renner, Michael, Sean Sweeney and Jill Kubit. 2008. *Green Jobs: Towards Decent Work in a Sustainable, Low-carbon World.* Geneva, UNEP; Sanchez, Thomas W. 1999. "The connection between public transit and employment." *Journal of the American Planning Association* 65 (3): 284–96; and World Bank. 2006. *Promoting Global Environmental Priorities in the Urban Transport Sector: Experience from World Bank Group – Global Environmental Facility Projects.* Washington, DC, World Bank.

The employment and economic gains of public and rail investments can be enhanced in the short run by targeting them carefully. For example, the low-carbon strategy advocated for the United States and outlined in box 2.4 suggests that the following investments in the country's mass transit system could be implemented immediately:

- expanding existing bus and subway services in urban areas;
- lowering public transportation fares;
- expanding federal support for state and municipal transit operation and maintenance budgets;
- increasing federal subsidies for employer-based mass transit incentives; and
- funding critical mass transit programs currently bottlenecked for lack of federal financing.[45]

A similar set of short-term policies to enhance economic recovery, create employment and improve the sustainability of transportation systems could be adopted by the European Union and other high-income economies. In developing economies, priority has to be placed on investments that develop safe, reliable and affordable urban transport systems, based on fuel-efficient systems such as compressed natural gas buses and bus rapid transit systems. The

[45] Pollin *et al.* 2008 (see part II introd., fn 6).

expansion and maintenance of and improvements in railway networks for passengers and freight should also be an important goal.

Enhancing the economic, environmental and employment gains from a sustainable transportation strategy will require the removal of transport market distortions and the implementation of market-based instruments and regulations (see box 2.11). The removal of market and planning distortions would help minimize economic waste, reduce pollution and congestion, foster greater transport choice and facilitate sustainable transport strategies that would boost economic recovery and employment. Fiscal policies, such as fuel and vehicle taxes, new vehicle incentives, road fees, user fees, vehicle insurance and fleet vehicle incentives, can have powerful impacts on encouraging the introduction of cleaner, fuel-efficient vehicles. Combining these policies with regulatory measures, such as more stringent greenhouse gas and fuel economy standards, may produce the most important shifts in vehicle demand and use. Such policies are proving increasingly attractive not only to high-income OECD economies but also to large emerging market economies, such as China and India.

Box 2.11 Market reforms and fiscal policies for sustainable transportation

The overwhelming evidence is that transport market distortions, including the "underpricing" of motorized travel, current urban and land use planning practices that encourage automobile use, and distortions in public investment in favor of road transport over other modes of travel, are systematically biasing the development of transportation networks worldwide to favor road transportation and excessive motor vehicle use. Removal of these distortions would help cut the level of economic waste, reduce pollution and congestion, foster greater transport choice and facilitate sustainable transport strategies that would boost economic recovery and employment (see boxes 2.8 to 2.10). The key areas in which transport market and planning reforms could be implemented by all national governments are indicated in the following table.

Potential reforms of transportation market and planning distortions

	Description	Potential reforms
Consumer options and information	Markets often offer limited alternatives to motorized vehicle transport.	Recognize the value of alternative modes of transport and more accessible development in planning decisions.
Underpricing	Many vehicle costs are fixed or external; fixed costs lead to more vehicle use, and external costs are not borne by motorists.	Where feasible, convert fixed costs to variable charges and charge motorists directly for the costs they impose.
Transport planning	Transportation planning and investment practices favor road transport expansion even when other solutions are more cost-effective.	Incorporate full costs of road transport and use, including external costs, and apply least-cost planning so alternative modes and management strategies are funded if they are cost-effective.
Land use policies	Current land use planning policies encourage lower-density auto-oriented development.	Apply smart growth policy reforms that support more multi-modal, accessible land use development.

Source: Based on Litman, Todd. 2006. "Transportation market distortions." *Berkeley Planning Journal* 19: 19–36.

To tackle the persistent problem of the "underpricing" of road transport relative to alternative modes of travel, as well as to encourage the development of more fuel-efficient vehicles, a number of fiscal policies and market-based instruments could be adopted. Some countries have already employed such instruments as part of their efforts to tackle some of the key external costs imposed by motorized vehicle use and to encourage more fuel-efficient transport. The following table lists various fiscal policies and gives examples of "best practice" uses of these instruments by specific countries.

Fiscal policies can have lasting impacts on fuel consumption, pollution and the development of fuel-efficient vehicles. For example, a study by Thomas Sterner shows that, if all OECD countries adopted fuel taxes equivalent to those adopted by countries with the highest rates, then total vehicle fuel consumption in the OECD would be 36 percent less and carbon emissions reduced by half. Governments can also promote fuel efficiency in motorized vehicles through greenhouse gas and fuel economy standards. The European Union has a target standard of 130 grams of CO_2 per kilometer driven for certain types of new vehicles, and Japan will phase in by 2015 the toughest standards of 125 grams of CO_2 per kilometer driven for all new passenger vehicles. A mix of fiscal policies and fuel economy standards may be the most effective means of introducing cleaner and more fuel-efficient cars. In addition, regulations could be made more cost-effective by introducing tradable fuel economy credits or "feebate" schemes, which would award rebates if standards are exceeded but charge fees for under-compliance. For example, a mixture of regulatory standards, fiscal policies and technological change has allowed California over the last fifteen years to achieve a remarkable "greening" of its vehicle fleet and rapid improvements in air quality, despite the continuing fast-paced growth of its urban areas. Such policies are proving attractive to large emerging market economies. China is gradually increasing its fuel economy standards and adopting more fiscal policy measures, especially vehicle and fuel

International best practices in fiscal policies for sustainable transportation

Fuel tax	Gasoline/diesel tax (Poland); carbon tax (Sweden).
Vehicle tax	Annual vehicle attribute taxes and fees (European Union); tax and fee reductions or exemptions for new clean, fuel-efficient cars (Denmark, Germany, Japan); annual fees for CO_2 and smog externalities (Denmark; United Kingdom).
New vehicle incentives	Clean car rebates (Japan, United States); "gas guzzler" tax (United States); "feebate": variable purchase tax with fuel consumption (Austria).
Road fees	Road pricing/high occupancy toll lanes (California, US); congestion pricing (London, UK); full externality-based road pricing (Singapore).
User fees	Parking fees (California, US); in-lieu fees for parking (Canada, Germany, Iceland, South Africa); parking demand management (United States).
Vehicle insurance	Fines for lack of mandatory insurance (United Kingdom, United States); insurance-specific auto tax (France); pay-as-you-drive and pay-as-you-pump insurance (United Kingdom, United States).
Fleet vehicle incentives	Cost-effective, clean and fuel-efficient public fleets (Canada); incentives for clean, fuel-efficient company cars (United Kingdom).

Source: Adapted from Gordon, Deborah. 2005. "Fiscal policies for sustainable transportation: international best practices." In Energy Foundation (ed.). *Studies on International Fiscal Policies for Sustainable Transportation.* San Francisco, Energy Foundation: 1–80.

taxes, to introduce more fuel-efficient vehicles. India, too, has started phasing in such policies.

Sources: An, Feng, Deborah Gordon, Hui He, Drew Kodjak and Daniel Rutherford. 2007. *Passenger Vehicle Greenhouse Gas and Fuel Economy Standards: A Global Update.* Washington, DC, International Council on Clean Transportation; Fischer, Carolyn. 2008. "Comparing flexibility mechanisms for fuel economy standards." *Energy Policy* 36 (8): 3116–24; Gordon, Deborah. 2005. "Fiscal policies for sustainable transportation: international best practices." In Energy Foundation (ed.). *Studies on International Fiscal Policies for Sustainable Transportation.* San Francisco, Energy Foundation: 1–80; Huang, Yongh. 2005. "Leveraging the Chinese tax system to promote clean vehicles." In Energy Foundation (ed.). *Studies on International Fiscal Policies for Sustainable Transportation.* San Francisco, Energy Foundation: 90–7; Kahn, Matthew E., and Joel Schwartz. 2008. "Urban air pollution progress despite sprawl: the 'greening' of the vehicle fleet." *Journal of Urban Economics* 63 (3): 775–87; Litman, Todd. 2006. "Transportation market distortions." *Berkeley Planning Journal* 19: 19–36; Minato, Jari. 2005. "Clean vehicle promotion policies in Japan." In Energy Foundation (ed.). *Studies on International Fiscal Policies for Sustainable Transportation.* San Francisco, Energy Foundation: 81–9; Sterner, Thomas. 2007. "Fuel taxes: an important instrument for climate policy." *Energy Policy* 35 (6): 3194–202; and Zhang, ZhongXiang. 2008. "Asian energy and environmental policy: promoting growth while preserving the environment." *Energy Policy* 36 (10): 3905–24.

SUMMARY AND CONCLUSION

Reducing the carbon dependency of the world economy is increasingly seen as a means of addressing the twin global objectives of energy security and climate change mitigation simultaneously. Transitioning to a low-carbon world economy is also imperative for improving the human development prospects of the world's poor, especially combating the worldwide problem of energy poverty. Policies to improve energy efficiency and expand clean energy supply options, if implemented correctly, can create a substantial number of jobs and boost important economic sectors in the short term. Promoting such initiatives through public and private investment is critical for a GGND and for jump-starting the transition to a low-carbon economy. The examples of low-carbon strategies for China, the United States and the European Union discussed in this chapter also illustrate the importance of adopting a complementary carbon pricing policy. An important component of any low-carbon strategy implemented under a GGND should be policy actions to improve the sustainability of transport, including improving the accessibility of transport to the poor worldwide. Ensuring that the economic recovery of the worldwide automobile industry is "green" requires encouraging the development of fuel-efficient vehicles and the next generation of biofuels for these vehicles. Public and rail transport are less carbon- and energy-intensive than private motorized vehicle travel, and they also have the potential for creating jobs.

The low-carbon, "green recovery" strategies advocated in this chapter, including the additional policies and investments for sustainable transport, suggest that publicly funded programs, initiatives and spending equivalent to about 1 percent of GDP by the major economies comprising the G20 would have a substantial impact on reducing carbon dependency while providing an immediate boost to economic recovery and job creation. As part of its Green New Deal, South Korea has already adopted this target, spending over 1.2 percent of its GDP on investments for railroads and mass transit, and clean fuels, energy conservation and environmentally friendly buildings that will also create 334,000 jobs (see chapter 5). The Chinese government is already committed spending to low-carbon initiatives equivalent to 2.5 percent of that country's GDP (see box 1.1).

As outlined in this chapter, much of the financing of the proposed low-carbon measures could come from removing and reallocating perverse energy and transport subsidies and other market distortions, as well as from complementary carbon pricing policies, such as the revenues from cap-and-trade or any additional taxes. It seems reasonable, therefore, to recommend that high-income economies aim for the 1 percent of GDP target for implementing a low-carbon strategy as part of the GGND. Large emerging market economies, such as China (as discussed in the example in this chapter), could also aim to spend at least 1 percent of their GDP on the national actions proposed for reducing carbon dependency.

Given that the G20 economies jointly account for about 90 percent of the world economy, if all of them adopted the 1 percent of GDP target, the total amount spent would amount to about one-quarter of the nearly US$3 trillion in G20 stimulus investments to date (see box 1.1). If the G20 economies coordinated the timing and implementation of these investments globally, the overall impact on moving the world economy to a low-carbon recovery path would be boosted. As discussed in this chapter, there would probably be substantial impacts in terms of employment creation and the recovery of key economic sectors. Developing economies should also implement many of the low-carbon measures discussed in this chapter, especially those that improve the access of the poor to transportation, although it is difficult to determine how much these economies should spend on these activities.

3   Reducing ecological scarcity

The previous chapter looked in detail at measures aimed towards creating low-carbon economies as part of an overall Global Green New Deal that can stimulate economic recovery and create employment over the next one to two years while putting the world on a more economically and environmentally sustainable development path. Such a strategy should be a priority for all countries – high-income OECD economies, large emerging market economies and low-income economies.

Although a low-carbon strategy is important to a GGND, this chapter addresses another critical area: the reduction of ecological scarcity, which is crucial to the aim of eliminating poverty worldwide. Such an objective is essential. A GGND cannot be truly global in scope unless it addresses all the pressing needs of the world economy. As emphasized in part I, the issue of extreme world poverty is an ongoing problem that needs to be urgently addressed.

Accordingly, a principal objective of a GGND is that it must also contribute to achieving the Millennium Development Goals for developing countries, so that by 2025 the goal of ending extreme global poverty is attainable. This chapter establishes the link between ecological scarcity and the livelihoods of the poor. It then outlines several ways in which national actions can improve these livelihoods while making progress towards reducing ecological damage, improving natural resource management and managing global water scarcity.

ECOLOGICAL SCARCITY AND POVERTY
Ecological scarcity is the loss of myriad ecosystem benefits, or "services," as these systems are exploited for human use and economic activity.[1]

---

[1] Barbier, Edward B. 1989. *Economics, Natural Resource Scarcity and Development: Conventional and Alternative Views.* London, Earthscan, 96–7.

As noted in part I, this scarcity problem is becoming ever more acute on a global scale, and is manifesting itself in the loss of many vital ecosystem services. The world's ecosystems and freshwater sources will continue to be endangered by a world economic recovery that ignores environmental degradation. Over the past fifty years ecosystems have been modified more rapidly and extensively than in any comparable period in human history, largely to meet the fast-growing demand for food, freshwater, timber, fiber and fuel. The result has been a substantial and largely irreversible loss of biological diversity. Approximately fifteen out of twenty-four major global ecosystem services have been degraded or used unsustainably, including freshwater, capture fisheries, air and water purification, and the regulation of regional and local climate, natural hazards and pests.[2]

Poor people in developing countries are especially vulnerable to the resulting loss in critical ecological services.[3] Nearly 1.3 billion people in developing economies – over a fifth of the world's population – live on lands prone to degradation and water stress, and in upland areas, forest systems, drylands and similar fragile environments (see box 1.2). Almost a half of this population (631 million people) consists of the rural poor.[4] For the world's poor, global water scarcity manifests itself as a water poverty problem. One in five people in the developing world lacks access to sufficient clean water, and about half the developing world's population, or 2.6 billion people, do not have access to basic sanitation. More than 660 million of the people without sanitation live on less than US$2 a day, and more than 385 million survive on less than US$1 a day.[5]

As the world economic crisis deepens and expands, it affects the livelihoods of the poor, who are the ones most vulnerable to the economic consequences; increasing ecological scarcity adds further to their economic vulnerability.

[2] MA 2005 (see ch. 1, fn 14).
[3] OECD 2008; UNDP 2008; Sukhdev 2008 (see ch. 1, fn 15, for all three).
[4] World Bank 2002; Comprehensive Assessment of Water Management in Agriculture 2007 (see ch. 1, fn 16, for both).
[5] UNDP 2006 (see ch. 1, fn 20).

A GGND must therefore also tackle urgently the problem of extreme world poverty caused by rising ecological scarcity, as well as implementing measures that more directly reduce the vulnerability of the world's poor.

This chapter outlines several ways in which the vulnerability of the poor can be ameliorated, through specific national actions in three main areas in developing economies:

- Policies, investments and reforms to enhance the sustainable and efficient use of natural resources and production processes dependent on them, and to ensure that the sufficient financial returns generated from these activities are reinvested in the industrial activities, infrastructure, health services, education and skills necessary for long-term economic development.
- Targeting investments and other policy measures for improving the livelihoods of the rural poor, especially those living in fragile environments.
- Protecting and improving the provision of ecosystem services on which the extreme poor depend.

If a Global Green New Deal is to have a lasting impact on reducing worldwide poverty and at the same time ensure that the ensuing global economic recovery is sustainable, however, then the GGND must also include policy measures to address another looming global ecological scarcity problem: the emerging water crisis.

There are two aspects of this emerging water crisis: the worldwide scarcity of freshwater supplies relative to increasing demand, and the lack of clean water and sanitation available for millions of the poor in developing regions. This chapter also outlines how a GGND must improve water management worldwide in order to meet these two challenges.

IMPROVING THE SUSTAINABILITY OF PRIMARY PRODUCTION

Improving the sustainability of primary production in developing economies is an important means to achieving the goal of reducing worldwide poverty.

Most developing countries, and certainly the majority of the populations living within them, are directly dependent on the exploitation of natural resources. For many of these economies, primary product exports account for the vast majority of their export earnings, and one or two primary commodities make up the bulk of exports.[6] On average across these countries, agricultural value added accounts for around 40 percent of their GDP, and nearly 80 percent of the labor force is engaged in agricultural or resource-based activities.[7] By 2025 the rural population of the developing world will have increased to almost 3.2 billion individuals.[8]

Many of these rural people in developing countries depend directly on the exploitation of natural resources and the environment for agriculture, livestock raising, fishing, basic materials and fuel – to meet their own subsistence requirements and to sell in markets for cash income. The lack of water supply, sanitation and other infrastructure services suggests that the increased public provision of such basic services is highly valued by many households. Rapid land use change has meant that many natural environments and habitats are disappearing quickly, with the result that critical ecological services are being disrupted or lost, including freshwater, fisheries and other vital benefits. The demise of key ecosystems of the developing world includes mangroves (some 35 percent either lost or degraded), coral reefs (30 percent) and tropical forests (30 percent).[9]

As noted above, the livelihoods of one-quarter of the population in developing countries – almost 1.3 billion – are particularly

---

[6] Barbier, Edward B. 2005. *Natural Resources and Economic Development.* Cambridge, Cambridge University Press.

[7] World Bank 2008 (see ch. 1, fn 41).

[8] UN. "World urbanization prospects: the 2007 revision, executive summary." Available at http://esa.un.org/unup.

[9] See, for example, Houghton, R. A. 1995. "Land-use change and the carbon cycle." *Global Change Biology* 1 (4): 257–87; MA 2005 (see ch. 1, fn 14); Sukhdev 2008 (see ch. 1, fn 15); UNEP. 2006. *Marine and Coastal Ecosystems and Human Well-being: A Synthesis Report Based on the Findings of the Millennium Ecosystem Assessment.* Nairobi, UNEP; and Valiela, I., J. L. Bowen and J. K. York. 2001. "Mangrove forests: one of the world's threatened major tropical environments." *BioScience* 51 (10): 807–15.

vulnerable to ecological disruption, and they account for many of the world's extreme poor who live on less than US$2 per day (see also box 1.2). These populations live in regions with no access to irrigation systems, farm poor soils or land with steep slopes, and inhabit fragile forest systems. By 2015, despite a decline in the share of the world population living in extreme poverty, there are still likely to be nearly 3 billion people living on less than US$2 a day. As indicated in box 3.1, many low- and middle-income economies fall into a persistent pattern of resource use characterized by chronic resource dependency, the concentration of large segments of the population in fragile environments, and rural poverty.

Box 3.1 Low- and middle-income economies and patterns of resource use

Many low- and middle-income economies fall into a persistent pattern of resource use that displays a chronic state of resource dependency, the concentration of large segments of the population in fragile environments, and rural poverty. The table on p. 102 reveals this pattern by taking seventy-one developing economies that have at least 20 percent of their total populations living in marginal areas (following the definition in box 1.2) and grouping them by the degree of resource dependency of the economy, as measured by the share of primary commodities in total exports. The figure in parentheses by each country also indicates the share of the rural population living below the national rural poverty line.

Fifty-five of these developing economies have a primary product export share of 50 percent or more, and could therefore be considered highly resource-dependent. All these economies also exhibit a high incidence of rural poverty – i.e. at least 20 percent or more of their rural population is poor. The sixteen countries that have a large share of their populations on rural lands but are less resource-dependent (with a primary product export share of less than 50 percent) still have a high incidence of rural poverty. Only two, Jordan and Tunisia, have rural poverty rates below 20 percent.

Resource dependency and the share of population on fragile land

	Share of population on fragile land > 50%	Share of population on fragile land 30–50%	Share of population on fragile land 20–30%
Primary product export share > 90%	Burkina Faso (52.4) Chad (67.0) Congo, Democratic Republic (n.a.) Laos (41.0) Mali (75.9) Niger (66.0) Papua New Guinea (41.3) Somalia (n.a.) Sudan (n.a.) Yemen (45.0)	Algeria (30.3) Angola (n.a.) Benin (33.0) Botswana (n.a.) Cameroon (49.9) Comoros (n.a.) Equatorial Guinea (n.a.) Ethiopia (45.0) Gambia (63.0) Guyana (n.a.) Iran (n.a.) Mauritania (61.2) Nigeria (36.4) Rwanda (65.7) Uganda (41.7)	Ecuador (69.0) Congo, Republic (n.a.) Liberia (n.a.) Zambia (78.0)
Primary product export share 50–90%	Egypt (23.3) Zimbabwe (48.0)	Central African Republic (n.a.) Chad (67.0) Guatemala (74.5) Guinea (n.a.) Kenya (53.0) Morocco (27.2)	Bolivia (83.5) Burundi (64.6) Côte d'Ivoire (n.a.) El Salvador (49.8) Ghana (39.2) Guinea-Bissau (n.a.) Honduras (70.4) Indonesia (34.4)

Table (*cont.*)

	Share of population on fragile land > 50%	Share of population on fragile land 30–50%	Share of population on fragile land 20–30%
		Senegal (40.4)	Madagascar (76.7)
		Sierra Leone (79.0)	Mozambique (55.3)
		Syria (n.a.)	Myanmar (n.a.)
		Tanzania (38.7)	Panama (64.9)
			Peru (72.1)
			Togo (NA)
Primary		Costa Rica (28.3)	China (46.0)
product		Haiti (66.0)	Dominican
export share		Lesotho (53.9)	Republic (55.7)
< 50%		Nepal (34.6)	India (30.2)
		Pakistan (35.9)	Jamaica (25.1)
		South Africa (n.a.)	Jordan (18.7)
			Malaysia (n.a.)
			Mexico (27.9)
			Sri Lanka (79.0)
		Tunisia (13.9)	Vietnam (35.6)

Notes: Primary commodity export share is the average export share 1990–9 for low- and middle-income countries, from Barbier, Edward B. 2005. *Natural Resources and Economic Development.* Cambridge, Cambridge University Press. Share of population on fragile land is from World Bank. 2002. *World Development Report 2003.* Washington, DC, World Bank. Figure in parenthesis is the percentage of the rural population living below the national rural poverty line, from World Bank. 2008. *World Development Indicators 2008.* Washington, DC, World Bank.

> The concentration of populations in fragile environments and resource dependency seem to be correlated. All but four of the fifty-five highly resource-dependent economies have at least 30 percent of their populations located in marginal rural areas. Ten of these economies have at least 50 percent of their populations concentrated in fragile environments. In contrast, none of the sixteen less resource-dependent economies have 50 percent or more of their populations located on marginal lands.

Improving the sustainability of primary production in developing countries would therefore allow resource-dependent developing economies to achieve multiple development objectives.

For the foreseeable future, however, primary product exports will remain the main source of export earnings and savings to facilitate the foreign direct investment, domestic private and public investment and international borrowing necessary for financing sustained economic development. Sustainable income from primary production is not only essential for generating the necessary savings and revenues in the long run but also important to ensure that sufficient financial flows are available for investment in the physical capital, infrastructure, skills, health services and educational opportunities necessary for long-term development.

Encouraging more primary production from a country's natural resource endowment is not truly sustainable unless it also alleviates the persistence of widespread poverty, especially rural poverty, and improves the economic livelihoods of the large numbers of people concentrated in fragile, resource-poor environments. Too often in developing economies the main export-oriented primary production activities are isolated enclaves that have little in the way of forward and backward linkages with the rest of the economy. The income and employment benefits are limited to those producers, workers and entrepreneurs fortunate enough to participate in the sector, but the vast majority of rural households, low-skilled workers and traditional industries in the economy hardly benefit. Moreover, the economy often specializes in producing a handful of, or even just one or two, main primary product exports. Any processing activities are vertically integrated with the primary production but not necessarily horizontally linked to the rest of the economy.

Although the large returns from investments to expand export-oriented primary production attract wealthy investors, the downside is that many developing country governments have encouraged such investors too much by sector-specific and/or economy-wide policies that routinely distort markets and incentives in their favor. The result is often the encouragement of the wasteful use of natural resources, more costly but less efficient production activities and persistent problems of corruption and poor governance.[10]

A Global Green New Deal should aim to improve the sustainability of primary production activities worldwide, and at the same time contribute to the goal of reducing materially extreme world poverty.

The next section provides examples of the type of national actions that can be adopted by developing country governments to achieve this objective of improving the overall sustainability of primary production, natural resource management and economic development.

CREATING MORE SUSTAINABLE RESOURCE-DEPENDENT ECONOMIES

Because developing countries differ widely in their natural resource endowments and primary production activities, and even their level

[10] See, for example, Ascher, William. 1999. *Why Governments Waste Natural Resources: Policy Failures in Developing Countries*. Baltimore, Johns Hopkins University Press; Auty, Richard M. (ed.). 2001. *Resource Abundance and Economic Growth*. Oxford, Oxford University Press; Auty, Richard M. 2007. "Natural resources, capital accumulation and the resource curse." *Ecological Economics* 61 (4): 600–10; Barbier 2005 (see fn 6); Gylfason, Thorvaldur. 2001. "Nature, power, and growth." *Scottish Journal of Political Economy* 48 (5): 558–88; Isham, Jonathon, Michael Woolcock, Lant Pritchett and Gwen Busby. 2005. "The varieties of resource experience: natural resource export structures and the political economy of economic growth." *World Bank Economic Review* 19 (2): 141–74; Jensen, Nathan, and Leonard Wantchekon. 2004. "Resource wealth and political regimes in Africa." *Comparative Political Studies* 37 (7): 816–41; Stijns, Jean-Philippe. 2006. "Natural resource abundance and human capital accumulation." *World Development* 34 (6): 1060–83; Torvik, Ragnar. 2002. "Natural resources, rent seeking and welfare." *Journal of Development Economics* 67 (2): 455–70; and Wunder, Sven. 2003. *Oil Wealth and the Fate of the Forest: A Comparative Study of Eight Tropical Countries*. London, Routledge.

of economic development, it is difficult to formulate a prescription of the types of policies, investments and reforms that are required by all countries to improve the sustainable and efficient use of natural resources and production processes dependent on them.

These measures need to ensure that natural resources and their dependent production processes are developed efficiently so as to generate the greatest economic returns from these activities, that the political and legal institutions governing resource management and primary production discourage waste, corruption and illegal activities and that the financial returns from primary production are reinvested in the economy to develop complementary processing and other industrial capacities, enhance human skills, health and education and create a more diversified economy.

To illustrate the specific strategies that resource-dependent developing economies might pursue to achieve these objectives, this section focuses on three economies that have shown a great deal of progress: Malaysia, Thailand and Botswana. All three of these countries have managed to achieve long-term investment rates exceeding 25 percent of GDP and long-run average annual growth rates exceeding 4 percent, which are, respectively, investment and growth rates comparable to those of high-income economies.[11] Malaysia and Thailand represent examples of developing economies that have managed to diversify their economies successfully through the reinvestment of the financial gains from primary production for export. Botswana is an example of a resource-rich economy that has developed favorable institutions and policies for managing its natural wealth and primary production for extensive economy-wide benefits.

Malaysia has implemented a number of policies to improve the economic returns from its primary production activities, mainly

[11] Gylfason 2001 (see fn 10). Indonesia also achieved similarly high rates of investment and per capita GDP growth, but Gylfason concludes that "a broader measure of economic success – including the absence of corruption, for instance – would put Indonesia in less favourable light. Moreover, Indonesia has weathered the crash of 1997–1998 less well than either Malaysia or Thailand."

from the mineral and forest products industries, and has reinvested these returns for the purposes of diversifying the economy (see box 3.2). The result has been a rapid decline in the resource dependency of the economy in recent decades, a widespread improvement in employment, wages and livelihoods, and the expansion of educational and training opportunities. In line with many developing economies, however, Malaysia's fast-paced development has been accompanied by the significant depletion of mineral, timber and other natural resources as well as the conversion of forests into agricultural land. On the whole, though, the development strategy has succeeded in using investible funds from resource use and primary production to finance physical and human capital formation that more than offset the depletion of natural resources.

Box 3.2 Improving the sustainability of primary production: Malaysia

Present-day Malaysia exports processed plantation crops (including tropical timber products) and bases industrial development on export-oriented, labor-intensive manufacturing. As indicated in box 3.1, although 20 to 30 percent of Malaysia's population is still concentrated on fragile land, its share of primary product to total exports has fallen to a third. The decline in Malaysia's resource dependency is particularly remarkable given that primary product export share was 94 percent in 1965 and still 80 percent as recently as 1980/1.

Malaysia's long-run economic growth performance has been strong, reflecting the sustained reinvestment of the economic returns from primary production for export into physical and human capital. Long-term average annual growth in Malaysia has averaged 4.0 percent. Long-term investment in gross fixed capital formation as a share of GDP has averaged 28 percent, which exceeds the world average for high-income economies. Moreover, long-run net investment in Malaysia, adjusted for the depletion of minerals and timber, was positive in all years but one, and net domestic product rose by 2.9

percent per year. Gross primary and secondary school enrollment rates in Malaysia have been considerably higher than in other low- and middle-income countries, and in the case of primary school enrollment the rates match that of higher-income economies. This successful reinvestment of primary production revenues has been the key to the diversification of the Malaysian economy, including the rapid decline in its resource dependency, rising rural wages and the absolute as well as relative fall in the agricultural labor force. Other economy-wide benefits have also occurred, such as an increase in the number of urban and rural households with access to piped, treated water.

As in the case of other low- and middle-income economies, Malaysia's development has been accompanied by significant agricultural land expansion, especially at the expense of tropical forests. Much of the land conversion has been used to boost the production of perennial plantation crops, such as oil palm and rubber. Malaysia is also a major world exporter of tropical timber products, and is the leading world exporter of wood-based panels. Thus considerable investments have occurred in agro-industrial and forest-based industries, with extensive forward and backward linkages to domestic plantation crops and tropical forestry.

With regard to governance, Malaysia ranks comparably with high-income economies in terms of political stability, accountability, government effectiveness, the regulatory framework, the rule of law and the control of corruption. Malaysia has held successful democratic elections and managed relatively smooth transitions in political power. The long-term political stability of Malaysia is particularly remarkable given that the population is ethnically diverse, containing a Malay majority with sizable Chinese and Indian minorities. Overall, Malaysia appears to have the "good governance" necessary for the long-run management of its natural resource wealth and the reinvestment of resource rents to achieve a more diversified and prosperous economy.

Several policies appear to have been especially critical to the successful strategy of reinvesting the returns from developing primary production activities in Malaysia. First, from the 1970s onwards the revenues from the mineral and timber industries amounted to about one-third of gross domestic investment, and the most effective policies were aimed at generating and reinvesting these key revenues. These policies included petroleum-sharing contracts, which both attracted investment from international oil companies to provide essential capital and technology while at the same time ensuring that substantial oil revenues were retained within Malaysia. The establishment of the Permanent Forest Estate in Peninsular Malaysia also enhanced the development of long-term timber management for forest-based industries as well as maintaining a sustained flow of timber revenues. Although substantial tropical deforestation did occur, forest and land use policies were implemented to ensure that deforestation led to the expansion of tree crop plantations for export. Malaysia became a leading innovator and global producer in this industry, thanks in large part to the country's investment in agricultural research. This contrasts with the situation in many other tropical countries, where the end result of deforestation has been unproductive, degraded land. Finally, the substantial reinvestment of primary production revenues from minerals, timber and plantation crop exports was vital to the industrial development of export-oriented, labor-intensive manufacturing, which has in turn led to the diversification of the present-day Malaysian economy. Thus, these policies ensured that the Malaysian economy as a whole succeeded in using investible funds from resource use and primary production to build up stocks of physical and human capital that more than offset the depletion of mineral, timber and other natural resources.

More recently, the successful diversification of the Malaysian economy has created its own "virtuous circle" with regard to reducing land degradation and deforestation, halting the depletion of fisheries and other renewable resources and combating rural poverty. For example, the reduced deforestation and rural poverty in Peninsular Malaysia owe much to the region's rapid economic growth and diversification. Better employment opportunities in labor-intensive manufacturing has spilled over into higher real wages in agriculture and a declining workforce as labor has moved out of rural areas. The result has been less land clearing and less pressure on fragile environments, including coastal and marine ecosystems. Increased rural–urban migration and the absolute decline in the agricultural labor force have been accompanied by rising rural wages and better employment prospects for the rural poor. Finally, the declining pressure on rural resources and land has also enabled Malaysia to implement resource management policies in agriculture and fisheries. For example, the government has implemented land rehabilitation programs for smallholder rice and rubber, which has overcome problems of land fragmentation and improved the economic viability of these smallholdings. In marine fisheries, several policies have been instigated to reduce overfishing in commercial and traditional coastal fisheries by controlling fishing effort and increasing returns.

Not all resource management strategies have been successful in the country, however. In agriculture, some government programs wasted substantial subsidies on attempting to rehabilitate smallholder land that was not economically viable, while at the same time policy-induced rigidities in land markets actually increased the amount of productive land that was idled. Although policies to control overfishing in coastal areas were implemented, deep-sea fishing remained largely open access. In addition, too often resource management strategies in Malaysia have been driven by an emphasis on maximizing physical production rather than on maximizing net economic benefits. This has been exacerbated by the direct involvement of public enterprises in key sectors, such as forestry, petroleum and fishing. The overexploitation of Malaysia's remaining tropical timber reserves in Sabah and Sarawak to feed the forest-based industries in Peninsular Malaysia is a worrisome problem, which has been fueled by long-term policies of log export restrictions and the protection of wood panels and furniture industries, leading to overcapacity and inefficiencies in timber processing. Recently there have been concerns about the expansion of oil palm plantations and their impact in terms of excessive deforestation.

Sources: Auty, Richard M. 2007. "Natural resources, capital accumulation and the resource curse." *Ecological Economics* 61 (4): 600–10; Barbier, Edward B. 1998. "The economics of the tropical timber trade and sustainable forest management." In F. B. Goldsmith (ed.). *Tropical Rain Forest: A Wider Perspective.* London, Chapman and Hall: 199–254; Barbier, Edward B. 2005. *Natural Resources and Economic Development.* Cambridge, Cambridge University Press; Coxhead, Ian, and Sisira Jayasuriya. 2003. *The Open Economy and the Environment: Development, Trade and Resources in Asia.* Northampton, MA, Edward Elgar; Gylfason, Thorvaldur. 2001. "Nature, power, and growth." *Scottish Journal of Political Economy* 48 (5): 558–88; Kaufmann, Daniel, Aart Kraay and Massimo Mastruzzi. 2003. *Governance Matters III: Governance Indicators for 1996–2002.* Policy Research Working Paper no. 3106. Washington, DC, World Bank; Vincent, Jeffrey R., Razali M. Ali and Associates. 1997. *Environment and Development in a Resource-rich Economy: Malaysia under the New Economic Policy.* Cambridge, MA, Harvard University Press; and World Bank. 2008. *World Development Indicators 2008.* Washington, DC, World Bank.

Thailand's approach to diversifying its economy and sustaining growth was initially similar to that of Malaysia (see box 3.3). Thailand's remarkable success with resource-based development has been achieved without the benefit of substantial mineral and timber reserves capable of generating significant economic returns, however. Instead, this development has been accomplished through considerable investments in agro-industrial industries, with extensive forward and backward linkages to domestic plantation crops, food crops and fisheries. The result has been a decline in the agricultural sector relative to the rest of the Thai economy, including a dynamic and labor-intensive manufacturing sector, accompanied by rising rural wages and a fall in the total planted area, which in turn has reduced pressures for land conversion and deforestation. There are problems in some sectors, though, such as the overexpansion of shrimp aquaculture at the expense of coastal mangrove systems, and the lack of a coherent development strategy for poorer upland areas. Overall, however, Thailand has demonstrated that economic diversification and development can be achieved through careful policies and investments in a food export agriculture-based economy and the reinvestment of the resulting economic returns.

Box 3.3 Improving the sustainability of primary production: Thailand

In many ways, Thailand's success resembles that of Malaysia. Since the 1970s Thailand has been a net food exporter with industrial development based on export-oriented labor-intensive manufacturing. As a consequence, resource dependency in the Thai economy has declined steadily; the primary product export share was 95 percent in 1965 and 68 percent in 1980/1, and stands at 30 percent currently. Although 80 percent of the population still lives in rural areas, the share of the rural population living in poverty is only 18 percent. The diversification of the Thai economy and the decline in its resource dependency have been accompanied by rising rural wages and an absolute as well as a relative fall in the agricultural labor force.

Thailand's successful diversification strategy is reflected in its long-run growth and investment patterns. Annual growth in GDP per capita has averaged 4.7 percent over several decades, and the share of gross fixed capital formation in GDP has averaged 28 percent. Both trends exceed world averages and that of high-income economies. In addition, primary and secondary school enrollment rates are above those of low- and middle-income economies and comparable with world rates. Thailand's development has been accompanied by significant agricultural land expansion at the expense of tropical forests, mainly through new land for perennial plantation crops. Thailand's remarkable success with resource-based development has occurred without the benefit of substantial mineral and timber reserves capable of generating significant economic returns, however, being achieved instead through sizable investments in agro-industrial industries, with wide-ranging forward and backward linkages to domestic plantation crops, food crops and fisheries. Good governance appears to have been crucial to the success of this long-term development strategy in Thailand.

In Thailand's economy, traded food production and plantation crops dominate both upland and lowland farming, and so the pressures on upland forests are determined solely by interregional labor migration. Any increase in labor demand in the lowlands results in reduced deforestation, as the total area of upland agriculture declines. The emphasis on agro-industrialization, with forward and backward linkages, and on the reinvestment of rents in labor-intensive manufacturing has therefore generated a "virtuous cycle" of declining land degradation and deforestation, better management of fisheries and other renewable resources and improving rural livelihoods. The key to this process was a profound structural change in the Thai economy, however, reflected in rising prices for non-trade, mainly non-agricultural goods, the growth of non-agricultural investment and rising labor productivity outside the farm sector. The result has been increased employment opportunities in sectors other than agriculture, rising rural wages, declining relative agricultural prices and thus a reduction in farm profits and investment. The overall outcome was a contraction in the agricultural sector relative to the rest of the Thai economy, accompanied by a fall in the total planted area, which in turn reduced pressures for land conversion and deforestation. Meanwhile, the agricultural sector has been forced to become more efficient, commercially oriented and internationally competitive. As a result, substantial interregional migration has occurred from highland to lowland areas to take advantage of the rising rural wages accompanying the commercialization of agriculture on favorable and productive lands, even as total rural employment opportunities and planted area across Thailand have fallen. In addition, the economy-wide trade reforms implemented in Thailand provided further stimulus to labor-intensive manufacturing industries, generated greater employment opportunities outside rural areas and significantly reduced pressures on frontier agricultural soils, forests and watersheds.

In other sectors, such as fisheries, Thailand has also promoted export-oriented industries, particularly shrimp. Since 1979 Thailand has been the world's major shrimp producer, and one-third of all shrimp marketed internationally comes from Thailand. Although shrimp are also caught in coastal fisheries, the vast majority of Thailand's shrimp production now comes from aquaculture. The total value of export earnings for shrimp is around US$1 to US$2 billion annually, and the government has been keen to expand these exports. Thailand has also sought to manage its coastal fisheries through zoning. Since 1972 the 3 kilometer offshore coastal zone in southern Thailand has been reserved for small-scale, traditional marine fisheries. The Gulf of Thailand is divided into four such major zones, and the Andaman Sea (Indian Ocean) comprises a separate, fifth, zone.

Nevertheless, there have been problems with some resource management strategies pursued in Thailand. First, ill-defined property rights for forest areas have contributed to excessive upland deforestation and the rapid conversion of mangroves to shrimp farms in Thailand. Historically, this has been a common problem for all forested areas in Thailand. Although the state, through the Royal Forestry Department, ostensibly owns and controls forest areas, in practice they are de facto open access areas onto which anyone can encroach. Estimates of the amount of mangrove conversion due to shrimp farming vary, but studies suggest that up to 50 to 65 percent of Thailand's mangroves have been lost to shrimp farm conversion since 1975. In provinces close to Bangkok, mangrove areas have been devastated by shrimp farm developments. This has led to substantial losses to local communities dependent on mangrove-based activities and the habitat support provided by the mangroves for coastal fisheries, as well as leaving coastal populations vulnerable to frequent tropical storm events. Second, the build-up of manufacturing and agro-industries coupled with the increasing commercialization of agriculture may lead to better land and water management but is worsening other environmental problems, such as pollution and congestion in cities (particularly Bangkok), industrial and toxic waste, the overuse of pesticides and non-point pollution in agriculture.[12] Finally, the increasing commercialization of agriculture is likely to continue the trends towards the consolidation of land holdings, the adoption of labor-saving innovations and reductions in cropping intensities, which will add to labor substitution and declining employment opportunities in agriculture. Although this may have removed less productive, marginal upland areas from food production, rural employment opportunities in lowland areas are likely to become available less frequently and provide less work for the rural poor from upland areas. In Thailand, there does not appear to be a set of policies targeted at the upland areas to (i) manage the transition from rice and subsistence crop production to a variety of commercially oriented agricultural enterprises, such as maize, horticulture, tree crops, dairy and livestock raising, (ii) promote these enterprises in those upland areas with the most suitable agro-ecological conditions – i.e. areas that are less susceptible to erosion and have favorable microclimates, (iii) provide R&D support to develop adequate post-harvest and marketing facilities, targeted to smallholder production, and to facilitate the integration of these upland enterprises with the economy's agro-industrial development strategy, and (iv) encourage the commercialization of upland agriculture as an alternative source of employment for the rural poor in these areas.

Sources: Barbier, Edward B. 2005. *Natural Resources and Economic Development.* Cambridge, Cambridge University Press; Barbier, Edward B., and S. Sathirathai (eds.). 2004. *Shrimp Farming and Mangrove Loss in Thailand.* Cheltenham, Edward Elgar; Coxhead, Ian, and Sisira Jayasuriya. 2003. *The Open Economy and the Environment: Development, Trade*

---

[12] "Non-point pollution," in this case, means water run-off that has been polluted by fertilizers, pesticides and the residues from other farming activities and which eventually flows into rivers, lakes and other bodies of water.

and Resources in Asia. Northampton, MA, Edward Elgar; Feeny, David. 2002. "The co-evolution of property rights regimes for man, land, and forests in Thailand, 1790–1990." In John F. Richards (ed.). *Land Property and the Environment.* San Francisco, Institute for Contemporary Studies Press: 179–221; Gylfason, Thorvaldur. 2001. "Nature, power, and growth." *Scottish Journal of Political Economy* 48 (5): 558–88; Kaosa-ard, M., and S. S. Pednekar. 1998. *Background Report for the Thai Marine Rehabilitation Plan 1997–2001.* Bangkok, Thailand Development Research Institute Foundation; Kaufmann, Daniel, Aart Kraay and Massimo Mastruzzi. 2003. *Governance Matters III: Governance Indicators for 1996–2002.* Policy Research Working Paper no. 3106. Washington, DC, World Bank; Pingali, Prabhu L. 2001. "Environmental consequences of agricultural commercialization in Asia." *Environment and Development Economics* 6 (4): 483–502; and World Bank. 2008. *World Development Indicators 2008.* Washington, DC, World Bank.

Botswana demonstrates that being an African economy and a country entirely dependent on mineral export earnings are not barriers to achieving substantial and sustained economic progress (see box 3.4). One of the keys to Botswana's success has been the adoption of appropriate and stable economic policies during commodity booms and busts. Such policies include managing the exchange rate to avoid excessive appreciation during boom periods; using windfalls to build up international reserves and government balances that provide a cushion when booms end; avoiding large-scale increases in government expenditure and, instead, targeting investments to public education and infrastructure; and, finally, pursuing an economic diversification strategy that has led to modest increases in labor-intensive manufactures and services. Botswana has also developed complementary legal and political institutions for facilitating the long-term management of the economy, fostering political stability and low corruption and investing in universal education. Botswana's continued success will depend on progress in reducing its overreliance on public sector investment, encouraging the transition of manufacturing from producing nontradable to export goods and developing a successful agricultural strategy aimed at the rural poor and populations living in fragile environments.

Box 3.4 Improving the sustainability of primary production: Botswana

Botswana has remained heavily dependent on mineral export earnings, principally diamonds. Not only are nearly all its exports from primary products, but, in addition, minerals, especially diamonds, account for one-third of GDP and a half of government revenue. Because of its high resource dependency, since the 1970s Botswana has experienced periodic and substantial commodity export booms and windfalls. Since 1965, though, the country has had one of the highest rates of long-term growth in the world, and very high rates of government expenditures on education in relation to GDP. Botswana's long-run share of investment in GDP is equivalent to that of Malaysia and Thailand, and Botswana also has comparably high rates of primary and secondary school enrollment. Thus, unusually for most mineral-dependent economies, Botswana has achieved substantial economic success by reinvesting its resource wealth in physical and human capital.

Botswana's success in managing cycles of commodity booms and busts is attributable largely to its adoption of appropriate and stable economic policies, including managing the exchange rate to avoid excessive appreciation during boom periods, using windfalls to build up international reserves and government balances that provide a cushion when booms end, avoiding large-scale increases in government expenditure and instead targeting investments to public education and infrastructure and pursuing an economic diversification strategy that has led to modest increases in labor-intensive manufactures and services. Such long-term policies for the stable management of the economy are possible only if legal and political institutions function well, however. Botswana has had considerable political stability and a lack of civil conflict that are on par with high-income economies. In addition, the government has an international reputation for "honest public administration," and, overall, Botswana is generally rated the least corrupt country in Africa.

The cornerstone of the government's long-run development policy has been the recovery and reinvestment of resource rents. Over several decades the government has collected, on average, 75 percent of mining rents through taxes and royalties. These mineral revenues have been reinvested in public capital, and public sector investment has accounted for 30 to 50 percent of total gross fixed capital formation in the economy. Although much of this public expenditure has been on infrastructure, such as roads, the expansion of water connections, electricity and communications, there has been an increasing emphasis on investment in education and health, which in recent years has averaged 24 percent of the capital development budget.

Since the mid-1990s the main planning tool for guiding this public investment in Botswana has been the sustainable budget index (SBI). This index is simply the ratio of non-investment spending to recurrent revenues. An SBI value of 1.0 or less has been interpreted to mean that public consumption is sustainable because it is financed entirely out of revenues other than from minerals, and that all the revenue from minerals is used for public investment. An SBI value greater than 1.0 means that consumption relies in part on the mineral revenues, which is an unsustainable stance in the long term. One downside of relying on the SBI as an economic planning tool, however, is that it encourages the overreliance of the economy on public sector investments. In the long term this overreliance has resulted in continued growth in public sector investment for a variety of expenditures, including for defense or for other non-productive investments, such as agricultural subsidies and assistance programs, and some pure transfer payments. Public expenditures have also risen because of the government's efforts to combat the HIV/AIDS epidemic in Botswana, including its recent commitment to provide affordable medicine to the entire population.

One of the key investment strategies on the part of the government has been to increase foreign exchange reserves and financial assets.

The main rationale has been to save windfall gains from mineral revenues for use when export earnings decline, both during short-term busts and in the long run once mineral reserves are depleted. Overall, this strategy has been successful. In recent years income from foreign financial assets has become the next largest source of government revenue after mineral taxes and royalties.

The government has also been able to foster modest diversification of the economy, particularly in labor-intensive manufactures and services. This has been achieved both directly through public investment in the manufacturing sector and indirectly through adopting stabilization policies that prevented the appreciation of the domestic currency, even during periods of commodity booms. Although the share of manufacturing value added in GDP remains only 5 percent, the sector is expanding. Employment in manufacturing and services has also grown, and accounts for 25 and 32 percent of formal employment, respectively.

Less successful have been the official programs to promote agricultural growth. Although on average 7 percent of the government's development budget has gone to agriculture, and public sector expenditure in support of agriculture averages more than 40 percent of agricultural GDP, over the past decade the sector's contribution to overall GDP has declined to less than 4 percent. The main reason for the decline has been prolonged periods of drought combined with continuing excessive pressure on rural resources, including the depletion of village water reserves, water pollution problems, overgrazing, rangeland degradation and the running down of wood supplies.

To sustain and build on its economic success, there are some additional structural imbalances that Botswana needs to tackle in the near future. First, the economy is overly reliant on public sector investment, to the extent that the relative share of private sector capital in the economy has declined significantly. Second, although growth in manufacturing and services shows signs that the economy is diversifying, these sectors produce mainly non-tradable goods.

Overall, the economy is still dominated by mining, especially for export earnings, and the declining relative share of private capital in the economy suggests that full economic diversification is likely to be unrealized for some time. Finally, the government programs for investing in agriculture have been largely a failure. Agricultural development is still critical for the economy, however. Agriculture accounts for over 70 percent of the labor force, and will remain a significant source of income for the rural poor. As indicated in box 3.1, over half the population still lives in rural areas, and 30 to 50 percent of the population is on fragile land. Moreover, around 47 percent of the population continues to live in poverty.

Sources: Barbier, Edward B. 2005. *Natural Resources and Economic Development.* Cambridge, Cambridge University Press; Gylfason, Thorvaldur. 2001. "Nature, power, and growth." *Scottish Journal of Political Economy* 48 (5): 558–88; Iimi, Atsushi. 2007. "Escaping from the resource curse: evidence from Botswana and the rest of the world." *IMF Staff Papers* 54 (4): 663–99; Kaufmann, Daniel, Aart Kraay and Massimo Mastruzzi. 2003. *Governance Matters III: Governance Indicators for 1996–2002.* Policy Research Working Paper no. 3106. Washington, DC, World Bank; Lange, Glenn-Marie, and Matthew Wright. 2004. "Sustainable development and mineral economies: the example of Botswana." *Environment and Development Economics* 9 (4): 485–505; Sarraf, Maria, and Moortaza Jiwanji. 2001. *Beating the Resource Curse: The Case of Botswana.* Environment Department Working Paper no. 83. Washington, DC, World Bank; and World Bank. 2008. *World Development Indicators 2008.* Washington, DC, World Bank.

Several lessons for improving the sustainability of primary production in other resource-dependent economies can be learned from these three country examples.

First, the types of natural resource endowment and primary production activities do not necessarily constitute an obstacle to implementing a successful strategy. Botswana's economy is largely dependent on minerals, Thailand started out as almost exclusively an agriculture-based food exporter, and Malaysia built its success first on mineral and timber reserves, then on plantation tree crops and finally on the development of a highly diversified economy.

Second, because resource endowments, primary production activities and the historical, cultural, economic and geographical circumstances of each country are different, the type of development strategy adopted by each will also vary. For example, Thailand and Malaysia initially embarked on similar strategies to encourage sustainable primary production and resource use, but the primacy of agriculture in Thailand plus differing economic and social conditions meant that its diversification strategy eventually diverged from that of Malaysia.

Third, the development strategy has to be comprehensive. Targeting the main primary production activities of an economy to improve their competitiveness, attain their export potential, limit resource overexploitation and waste and generate increased returns and revenues is necessary but not sufficient. All three countries' policies show that the financial returns and funds generated from primary production activities must be reinvested in the industrial activities, infrastructure, health services, education and skills necessary for long-term economic development.

Finally, no strategy is perfect. In all three countries, important sectors and populations have yet to gain significantly from improving the sustainability of the main primary-producing sectors. In Malaysia, there is concern about the continuing destruction of forests, especially in the more remote Sabah and Sarawak provinces, and the plans to expand oil palm plantations. In Thailand, the loss of mangroves, growing pollution problems and the failure to instigate development in upland regions are major issues. Botswana has still to grapple with a stagnant agricultural sector, large numbers of people living in fragile environments and widespread rural poverty. Finding ways to broaden the benefits of measures to improve the sustainability of resource-dependent economies must be an important additional goal.

IMPROVING THE LIVELIHOODS OF THE POOR
The high concentration of poor populations in the fragile environments and marginal lands of many developing economies is of pressing concern in the efforts to reduce extreme global poverty.

Not only do these rural households depend directly on exploiting the land and natural resources available in these environments for their economic livelihoods, but poor people are particularly vulnerable to the deteriorating ecological conditions in these environments, which are the result of the widespread loss of tropical forests, coral reefs, mangroves and other ecosystems. Box 3.5, for example, provides many examples of this complex interrelationship from across the developing world. Thus, managing these environments and ecosystems is an important aspect of efforts to improve the economic livelihoods of the poor. Equally, fostering more economic opportunities and raising the standard of living of the poor located in fragile environments can contribute to lessening pressure on surrounding ecosystems.

Box 3.5 Ecosystems and the economic livelihoods of the poor

The importance of the coastal ecosystems, coral reefs, forested watershed and floodplains to the economic livelihood of the poor is well documented.

For example, estimates from Thailand suggest that the net present value (NPV) (in 1996 US dollars) between 1996 and 2004 arising from the net income to local communities from collected forest products from coastal mangroves ranged from $484 to $584 per hectare. The NPV of mangroves as a breeding and nursery habitat in support of offshore artisanal fisheries ranged from $708 to $987 per ha, and the storm protection service was $8,966 to $10,821 per ha. Such benefits are considerable when compared to the average incomes of coastal households; a survey conducted in July 2000 of four mangrove-dependent communities in two different coastal provinces of Thailand indicates that the average household income per village ranged from $2,606 to $6,623 per annum. The overall incidence of poverty (corresponding to an annual income of $180 or lower) in all but three villages exceeded the average incidence rate of 8 percent found across all rural areas of Thailand. Excluding the income from collecting mangrove forest products would have raised the incidence of poverty to 55.3 percent and 48.1 percent in two of the villages, and to 20.7 percent and 13.6 percent in the other two communities. The Thailand example is not unusual; poor households across the developing world typically obtain many benefits from mangroves, and also value their continued existence beyond what the ecosystems yield in economic goods and services.

Coral reefs are another critical habitat throughout the developing world that both support near-shore fisheries harvested by poor coastal communities and provide valuable shoreline protection. For example, estimates were made of the losses, in NPV per square kilometer (km^2), in terms of support for near-shore artisanal fisheries and coastal protection from the destruction of coral reefs in Indonesia. The main threats to coral reefs are from poison fishing, blast fishing, coral mining, sedimentation from logging onshore, and overfishing. Together, these threats account for present value losses in coastal fisheries of around US$0.41 million per km^2 of coral reef destroyed, and present value losses in coastal protection of US$0.011 to US$0.453 million per km^2 of coral reef destroyed. Evidence from Kenya indicates that coral reefs may also be critical to the dispersal of larvae to fishing areas, which could affect the effectiveness of marine reserves and closed fishing grounds in inducing stock recovery and thus their eventual reopening to fishing. Coral reefs also have important cultural and non-use value to neighboring coastal communities; many cultural and religious traditions have evolved in tropical coastal zones that honor the dependence of local communities on adjacent reefs and reflect the value of preserving this way of life into the future.

Forested watersheds in developing regions also provide a number of hydrological services that can impact on the livelihoods of the poor, such as water filtration/purification, seasonal flow regulation, erosion and sediment control, and habitat preservation. These services will become increasingly important as more and more river basins in developing areas experience rising water use relative to freshwater supplies. Moreover, the forests of upper watersheds provide a number of direct uses to poor communities living there, including timber, collected non-timber products and community forestry. Overwhelmingly, though, the benefits of maintaining and improving land uses in upper watersheds appear to be additional hydrological services downstream. In the central highlands of Bolivia, for example, a project to improve watershed protection and reduce soil erosion on farmers' fields in the uplands yielded an NPV of nearly US$34.9 million, with the majority of the benefits attributable to flood prevention and the increased water availability due to aquifer recharge in the lower watershed. Similarly, improvements to the upper watersheds in Karnataka, India, through afforestation and the construction of tanks, artificial ponds, check dams and other reclamation structures led to significant benefits to downstream farmers as a result of improving groundwater recharge and availability, thus reducing the cost of irrigation and the need for developing new wells or extending existing wells. Increased water flow associated with the afforestation of watersheds in eastern Indonesia generates economic values for downstream farmers equivalent to 1 to 10 percent (US$3.5 to US$35) of annual agricultural profits. Land uses other than forests in some tropical watersheds may also yield beneficial hydrological flows, however; for example, forest conversion to livestock pasture in the upper watersheds of Río Chiquito, Costa Rica, actually increased water flow downstream, generating NPVs in the range of US$250 to US$1,000 per hectare of pasture.

In many developing regions, important downstream ecosystems in river basins are the seasonally inundated savanna or forested floodplains. During seasonal flood events, water often leaves the main river channel and inundates these floodplains. As the floods abate and recede, crops are planted in the naturally irrigated soils, fish are caught more easily in the retreating waters, and the increased alluvial deposits increase the biological productivity of forests, wildlife and other harvested resources. Around a half of Africa's total wetland area consists of floodplains, and includes huge large-scale ecosystems of several thousand square kilometers, such as the Inner Niger Delta in Mali, the Okavango Delta in Botswana, the Sudd of the Upper Nile in Sudan and the Kafue Flats in Zambia. Millions of people across the continent depend directly on the floodplains for their economic livelihoods through production activities such as flood recession agriculture, fishing, grazing and wood and non-wood harvesting of riparian forest resources, and millions more in surrounding arid land depend on the groundwater recharge service of floodplains for drinking water and irrigation. Similar benefits are found in other extremely poor countries, such as Bangladesh, where 80 percent of the country consists of floodplains created by the confluence of the Ganges, Brahmaputra, Meghna and other rivers.

For example, upstream dam developments threaten the economic livelihoods of millions of poor agricultural households dependent on the Hadejia-Jama'are floodplain in northeast Nigeria. Full implementation of all the upstream dams and large-scale irrigation schemes is forecast to produce overall net losses in terms of agricultural, fuelwood and fish production to these households of around US$20.2 to US$20.9 million in NPV terms. In addition, the reduction in mean peak flood extent is predicted to cause a 1 meter fall in groundwater levels in the shallow aquifers that are recharged by the standing water in the floodplain wetlands, leading to additional annual losses of around $1.2 million in tubewell-irrigated dry season agriculture and US$4.76 million in domestic water consumption for rural households. In Bangladesh, fishing and flood recession agriculture are important joint products to poor rural households utilizing natural floodplains. Floodplain fish production benefits mainly the landless households. As a consequence, a natural floodplain means more land devoted to fishing rather than agriculture, but actually yields higher overall net economic returns, especially compared to traditional management scenarios of upstream dam developments to limit flooding, increase agricultural area and expand crop production downstream.

Source: Barbier, Edward B. 2008. "Poverty, development, and ecological services." *International Review of Environmental and Resource Economics* 2 (1): 1–27. For additional case studies, see Sukhdev, Pavan. 2008. *The Economics of Ecosystems and Biodiversity: An Interim Report.* Brussels, European Communities.

Both approaches have a role in a GGND that aims to improve the livelihoods of the poor. Current efforts to reconcile development pressures with the maintenance of key ecosystem benefits focus on payment for environmental services and other incentives to protect critical ecosystems and habitat in developing countries. To the extent that such payments and incentives benefit the poor directly, the result will be to improve their livelihoods and conserve more critical habitats. Geographical targeting and other means of tackling poverty more directly should also be considered, however. Designing investment programs and policies targeted to the poor is likely to reduce the development pressures on fragile environments and ecosystems as well.

If the livelihoods of the poor depend on ecosystem services, then developing markets that provide incentives for protecting critical ecosystems and habitat may also help reduce poverty. Such markets to establish "payment" for providing ecosystem services in developing regions have focused largely on forest systems, and in particular four services from such systems: carbon sequestration, watershed protection, biodiversity benefits and landscape beauty.[13] Beginning in the 1990s, payment for ecosystem services started,

---

[13] See, for example, Alix-Garcia, Jennifer, Alain de Janvry, Elisabeth Sadoulet and Juan Manuel Torres. 2005. *An Assessment of Mexico's Payment for Environmental Services Program.* Rome, Food and Agriculture Organization of the United Nations [FAO]; Barbier, Edward B. 2008. "Poverty, development, and ecological services." *International Review of Environmental and Resource Economics* 2 (1): 1–27; Grieg-Gran, Mary-Anne, Ina T. Porras and Sven Wunder. 2005. "How can market mechanisms for forest environmental services help the poor? Preliminary lessons from Latin America." *World Development* 33 (9): 1511–27; Landell-Mills, Natasha, and Ina T. Porras. 2002. "Silver bullet or fool's gold? A global review of markets for forest environmental services and their impact on the poor." In Verweij, P. A. (ed.). *Understanding and Capturing*

principally in Latin America, but in recent years it has been adopted in sub-Saharan Africa and Asia. Hydrological services from watershed protection tend to predominate, although carbon sequestration schemes through the Clean Development Mechanism of the Kyoto Protocol have increased in number in recent years. One reason that countries and companies are increasingly eager to finance forestry sector CDM projects in developing countries to meet Kyoto obligations is that carbon sequestration costs in tropical regions are significantly lower compared to other locations; for example, forest CDM projects in Europe cost around US$777 per tonne of carbon sequestered, whereas in the tropics the most expensive projects cost US$128 per tonne of carbon sequestered.[14]

There are three principal ways in which market mechanisms for ecosystem services might also alleviate poverty. First, if payments for ecosystem services are made directly to poor rural households to maintain or enhance these services, then they provide needed cash income. Second, whether or not the rural poor receive direct payments, they may benefit indirectly from any resulting improvement in the provision of ecosystem services. Third, the rural poor may also gain from any additional economic opportunities created by payment schemes, such as the employment created by reforestation or other conservation investments. In all these instances, however, there appear to be limits on the success of payment schemes in alleviating poverty.

To date, the main purpose of introducing payment for ecosystem services is to influence land use decisions by enabling landholders to

the Multiple Values of Tropical Forest. Wageningen, the Netherlands, Tropenbos International: 89–92; Pagiola, Stefano, Agustin Arcenas and Gunars Platais. 2005. "Can payments for environmental services help reduce poverty? An exploration of the issues and the evidence to date from Latin America." World Development 33 (2): 237–53; Ravnborg, Helle Munk, Mette Gervin Damsgaard and Kim Raben. 2007. Payments for Ecosystem Services: Issues and Pro-poor Opportunities for Development Assistance. Report no. 2007–6. Copenhagen, Danish Institute for International Studies; and Sukhdev 2008 (see ch. 1, fn 15).

[14] Van Kooten, G. Cornelis, and Brent Sohngen. 2007. "Economics of forest ecosystem carbon sinks: a review." International Review of Environmental and Resource Economics 1 (3): 237–69.

capture more of the value of these environmental services than they would have done in the absence of the mechanism. While in some cases participants in such schemes do not have to demonstrate formal land titles to be eligible for payments, many of the rural poor in developing regions lack not only formal but also actual access to land. Others are near-landless or have holdings so small that they would have difficulty in participating in forest protection or planting schemes on their land. In Latin America, the land users who receive payments for preserving the hydrological services of watersheds tend to be wealthier households, and in at least one case, namely Costa Rica's program, many participants were urban dwellers with substantial non-agricultural income.[15] Similarly, the payment for forest ecosystem services in Mexico is specifically targeted to community-owned forests, and, although 86.3 percent of the hectares enrolled belong to poor communities, only 31 percent of the participating households are classified as being below the poverty line.[16]

Programs paying for ecological services may have unintended side effects on the poor, both positive and negative. In Indian watersheds, community cooperation in managing forest commons was enhanced for villages participating in payment schemes. The livelihoods of the landless who could not participate, such as women and herders, were harmed, however, if their access to forest commons for gathering non-timber products was restricted by the schemes.[17] In Latin America, some programs are thought to have improved tenure security by granting legal status to idle forest land and providing protection against squatting or land invasions. By increasing the value of marginal land, though, some payment schemes for ecosystem services have created incentives for more wealthy groups to appropriate the land, especially if tenure and ownership are in dispute.[18] Finally,

---

[15] Pagiola, Arcenas and Platais 2005 (see fn 13).

[16] Alix-Garcia *et al.* 2005 (see fn 13).

[17] Kerr, John. 2002. "Watershed development, environmental services, and poverty alleviation in India." *World Development* 30 (8): 1387–400.

[18] Pagiola, Arcenas and Platais 2005, Landell-Mills and Porras 2002 (see fn 13 for both).

payment programs can also have mixed effects on employment opportunities for the landless poor. Ecosystem service schemes that result in considerable replanting or afforestation in rural areas can generate significant demand for unskilled labor; alternatively, if the introduced schemes set aside large areas of local forests that would otherwise have been logged or converted to agriculture, then there may be less work for the landless poor.[19]

In sum, because their primary aim is to provide incentives to landowners for protecting critical ecosystems and habitat, payment programs for ecosystem services cannot always be targeted to areas of high poverty. Nor can such schemes always guarantee high participation rates by the rural poor or that their livelihoods will be significantly improved. By definition, the landless and near-landless are often excluded. Nonetheless, wherever possible, the payment schemes should be designed to enhance the participation of the poor, to reduce any negative impacts on non-participants while creating additional job opportunities for rural workers and to provide technical assistance, access to inputs, credit and other support to encourage poor smallholders to adopt the desired land use practices. More effort has to be devoted to designing projects and programs that include the direct participation of the landless and near-landless.

The alternative to investing in the enhancement of ecosystem services, and hoping that rural poverty is also reduced as a consequence, is instead to target investments directly to improving the livelihoods of the rural poor, thus reducing their dependence on exploiting environmental resources. Such "geographical targeting" of the rural poor has proved to be successful if designed correctly.[20]

---

[19] Grieg-Gran, Porras and Wunder 2005 (see fn 13).

[20] Barbier 2005 (see fn 6); Barbier 2008 (see fn 13); Binswanger, Hans P., and Klaus Deininger. 1997. "Explaining agricultural and agrarian policies in developing countries." *Journal of Economic Literature* 35 (4): 1958–2005; Coady, David, Margaret Grosh and John Hoddinott. 2004. "Targeting outcomes redux." *World Bank Research Observer* 19 (1): 61–85; Dasgupta *et al.* 2005 (see ch. 1, fn 18); Elbers, Chris, Tomoki Fujii, Peter Lanjouw, Berk Özler and Wesley Yin. 2007. "Poverty alleviation through geographic targeting: how much does disaggregation help?" *Journal of Development Economics* 83 (1): 198–213.

For example, in Ecuador, Madagascar and Cambodia, "poverty maps" have been developed to target public investments to geographically defined subgroups of the population according to their relative poverty status, which substantially improved poverty alleviation.[21] The maps in particular benefited the design and implementing of the investments by targeting smaller administrative units, such as districts or villages. Some gains were partially offset by the higher costs of administrating schemes at the village as opposed to the district or province level, however. In addition, it is unclear whether wealthy and powerful local groups were able to influence the allocation of targeted investments.

A World Bank study examined 122 targeted programs in forty-eight developing countries to analyze their effectiveness in reducing poverty.[22] The study concluded that the median program transferred 25 percent more benefits to households in the bottom income groups than would be the case in programs without targeting. Some targeted programs, however, such as those including food subsidies, were regressive, yielding fewer benefits to the poor compared to universal allocation. In comparison, geographic targeting programs that included a mandatory work requirement were associated with an increased share of benefits going to the poorest 40 percent of the population. The institutional context in which targeted schemes operated, such as the effectiveness and accountability of government, the security of tenure and property rights and bureaucratic competence, influenced greatly the ability of the schemes to alleviate rural poverty. Clearly, the careful design and implementation of geographic targeting programs will have considerable impact on the outcome and the chances of success in assuaging poverty.

In some cases, targeting "institutional failures," such as the inability of governments to deliver or manage services effectively in the remote areas where the poor are located, is important for overcoming key obstacles to improving the livelihoods of the poor

[21] Elbers *et al.* 2007 (see fn 20).
[22] Coady, Grosh and Hoddinott 2004 (see fn 20).

in fragile environments. A variety of case studies of managing irrigation water, potable water, fisheries and forest land in developing countries show that, in the absence of effective governance, encouraging private sector participation in natural resource management can enhance a variety of environmental benefits while achieving development and poverty goals.[23] Developing complementary regulatory capacity and monitoring by government is the key to securing long-term public environmental benefits and their widespread distribution to the poorest members of the population, however, and, in addition, the effective functioning of markets will vary from place to place, depending on legal, economic and cultural factors.

For persistent problems of poor institutional arrangements for managing natural resources for the benefit of local communities, entirely new institutional frameworks may need to be developed. For instance, one study found that the lack of effective property rights and conflicts between local communities and outside investors were persistent problems underlying the problem of excessive mangrove conversion by shrimp aquaculture expansion and other commercial developments in coastal areas of Thailand.[24] Developing a new institutional framework for coastal mangrove management in Thailand could enhance the incentives to restore and protect local mangroves while improving the economic livelihoods of local communities. Such a framework might contain the following features. First, remaining mangrove areas should be designated into conservation – i.e. preservation – and economic zones. Shrimp farming and other extractive commercial uses – e.g. wood concessions – should be restricted to the economic zones only. Local communities that depend on the collection of forest and fishery products from mangrove forests should be allowed access to both zones, however, as long as such harvesting activities are conducted on a sustainable basis. Second, the

[23] Johnstone, Nick, and Joshua Bishop. 2007. "Private sector participation in natural resource management: what relevance in developing countries?" *International Review of Environmental and Resource Economics* 1 (1): 67–109.

[24] Barbier, Edward B., and S. Sathirathai (eds.). 2004. *Shrimp Farming and Mangrove Loss in Thailand*. Cheltenham, Edward Elgar.

establishment of community mangrove forests should also occur in the economic and conservation zones alike. The decision to allow such local management efforts should be based on the capability of communities to enforce effectively their local rules and manage the forest to prevent overutilization, degradation and conversion to other land uses. Moreover, such community rights should not involve full ownership of the forest but be in the form of user rights. Third, the community mangrove forests should be co-managed by the government and local communities. Such effective co-management will require the active participation of existing coastal community organizations, and will allow the representatives of such organizations to have the right to express opinions and make decisions regarding the management plan and regulations related to the utilization of mangrove resources. Finally, the government should provide technical, educational and financial support for the local community organizations participating in managing the mangrove forests. For example, if only user rights (but not full ownership rights) are granted to local communities, then the latter's access to formal credit markets for initiatives such as investment in mangrove conservation and replanting may be restricted. The government may need to provide special lines of credit to support such community-based activities.

Targeting the poor is even more urgent during major economic crises. Underinvestment in human capital and lack of access to financial credit are chronic features of the extreme poor, especially those poor households concentrated on fragile land. These households generate insufficient savings, suffer continual indebtedness and rely on informal credit markets with high short-term interest rates.

As a result, private investment in human capital improvement is a luxury for most poor rural households, and, similarly, the lack of education and marketable skills limits not only the earning potential of the rural poor but also their political bargaining power relative to wealthier rural and urban households.[25] The lack of financial

[25] See, for example, Barbier 2005 (fn 6); Binswanger and Deininger 1997 (fn 20); Development Research Group. 2008. *Lessons from World Bank Research on*

and human capital available to the poor makes them particularly vulnerable to the economy-wide shocks during crises. In addition, during prolonged crises the poor often take drastic action to salvage their livelihoods in the short term: they incur greater household debt, they sell important assets, such as land and livestock, and they forgo educational expenses. An economy-wide shock can therefore have a lasting impact on the poor. For example, a study of the longer-term impacts of the 1997/8 east Asian crisis found that about a half of Indonesia's poverty count in 2002 was attributed to the effects of the crisis, even though the recovery of the Indonesian economy occurred well before then.[26]

Two types of policies and investment programs targeted at the poor are essential in these circumstances.

The first is the design and targeting of specific social safety net programs, which effectively act as insurance for those who lack any, or face high costs of, self-insurance. Although under normal economic conditions even the poor have access to informal sources of insurance, usually through community or family-based risk-sharing, large economy-wide crises often affect entire communities and even regions, thus negating informal insurance mechanisms. Unfortunately, many developing countries have weak safety net programs, which provide limited protection to the poor during an economic crisis. Even worse, governments often implement programs in haste, such as economy-wide food and fuel subsidies, with the result that they are inefficient, entailing huge financial costs, rarely benefiting the poor and proving difficult to reverse. As discussed in box 3.6, however, it is possible to design a comprehensive and targeted safety net for the poor that insures them adequately in time

Financial Crises. Policy Research Working Paper no. 4779. Washington, DC, World Bank; Ravallion, Martin. 2008. *Bailing out the World's Poorest*. Policy Research Working Paper no. 4763. Washington, DC, World Bank; and World Bank. 2005. *World Development Report 2006: Equity and Development*. Washington, DC, World Bank.

[26] Ravallion, Martin, and Michael Lokshin. 2007. "Lasting impacts of Indonesia's financial crisis." *Economic Development and Cultural Change* 56 (1): 27–56.

of crisis. The ideal program involves a relief work component that assists those poor who are either temporarily unemployed or underemployed as a result of the crisis, and includes cash or food transfers that are often conditional on ensuring that poor households do not forgo educational or health expenditures.

Box 3.6 Bailing out the world's poorest

The World Bank's advice is that, during an economy-wide crisis, it is essential for a developing economy to design and implement a comprehensive safety net program targeted at the poor. Targeting the program, by use of "poverty maps" to direct funds to where the poor are located or by ensuring that the main recipients are the women in poor families, can reduce the costs significantly. A safety net that provides effective insurance to protect the poor from a crisis usually builds in design features that encourage participation in the program only by those who need help, and just temporarily until economic conditions improve again. The features that work best are a combination of transfers to households, usually in the form of cash or food, and a relief work program. Cash or food transfers can be targeted to specific groups who are unable to work or who would otherwise forgo important expenditures during a crisis, such as the education of children. Relief work assists the working poor who are either temporarily unemployed or underemployed as a result of the crisis.

An ideal safety net program would have the following features.

It should have a guaranteed low wage for relief work, set at a rate that discourages the non-poor from participating and encourages the poor to leave the scheme for better-paid work once the crisis is over.

The work should be proposed by community groups in poor areas, to make certain that the relief effort is responsive to local needs and produces outputs valued by the poor.

The budget must be sufficiently large to employ anyone who wants to work at the guaranteed wage; if work has to be rationed, then its effectiveness as insurance for the poor is diminished.

A rapid expansion of demand for relief work should be taken as a signal to implement cash or food transfers, targeted either at specific groups who cannot work or at households that would otherwise forgo educational or health expenditures.

Well-designed relief work programs have been an important part of economic recovery programs since Roosevelt's New Deal. More recently, during the east Asian financial crisis of 1997/8, both Indonesia and South Korea introduced large relief work initiatives. Mexico implemented such programs in the 1995 "peso crisis," Peru during its recession of 1998–2001 and Argentina in its 2002/3 financial crisis. Conditional cash transfer (CCT) programs have been increasingly used in developing economies during crises to ensure that poor people do not go without educational or health expenditures. A typical scheme requires the children of the recipient family to demonstrate adequate school attendance or the family to provide evidence of maintaining basic health care. Such CCT programs have been used successfully in Bangladesh, Brazil, Indonesia and Mexico.

There are also economy-wide benefits of a comprehensive safety net program. If a crisis does create the opportunity for implementing an effective safety net for the poor, then it should become a permanent and automatic policy, expanding in times of crises but still functioning under normal economic conditions to alleviate persistent poverty problems in some areas. Some of the features of the program, such as incentives to encourage the children of poor families to stay in school or using relief work to build assets of value to poor communities, could be maintained to enhance longer-term poverty reduction in the economy. The safety net program should also provide an additional and immediate stimulus to aggregate demand in the economy. The extra income targeted to the poor is likely to translate rapidly into increased consumption in the local and wider economy.

Sources: Development Research Group. 2008. *Lessons from World Bank Research on Financial Crises.* Policy Research Working Paper no. 4779. Washington, DC, World Bank; and Ravallion, Martin. 2008. *Bailing out the World's Poorest.* Policy Research Working Paper no. 4763. Washington, DC, World Bank.

During a crisis, educational and health services targeted at the poor should be maintained, and, if possible, expanded. The economic impacts of a crisis on the poor are long-lasting and can continue well after the rest of the economy has recovered, as the example of Indonesia during the 1997/8 east Asia financial crisis illustrates. Primary education and health services, especially for the poor, rural inhabitants and women, are important for mitigating the long-term impacts of a crisis, not only because such investments foster growth and help reduce poverty but also because they reduce income inequality. Unfortunately, during financial and economic crises, publicly funded health and education services are often the first expenditures reduced by developing country governments.

Asking national governments of developing economies to implement policies, reforms and investments to improve the sustainability of primary production, invest in social safety net programs and maintain if not enhance educational and health services seems a tall order during a deepening global economic crisis. As argued by the World Bank in its submission to the G20 meeting in November 2008, developing countries, and especially low-income economies, "will be impacted through slower export growth (global trade is projected to decline in 2009), reduced remittances, lower commodity prices (which will reduce incomes in commodity exporters) and the potential for reduced aid from donors. The crisis may also lead to a reduction in private investment flows, making weak economies even less able to cope with internal vulnerabilities and development needs... Higher commodity prices have raised the current account deficits of many oil-importing countries to worrisome levels (they exceed 10 percent of GDP in about one-third of developing countries), and after having increased substantially, the international reserves of oil-importing developing countries are now declining as a share of their imports. Moreover, inflation is high, and fiscal positions have deteriorated both for cyclical reasons and because government spending has increased to alleviate the burden of higher commodity prices."[27]

[27] World Bank 2008 (see ch. 1, fn 5).

The World Bank also argues, however, that, during a crisis, "the countries that are likely to perform better are those that have managed to reduce macro-financial vulnerabilities, increase investment rates, diversify export markets, and restore productivity growth ... Developing countries must ensure that resources are put to their best and most efficient use, including by putting in place well-targeted social safety nets and improving the targeting of resources provided to the poor."[28]

In a major economic recession, the main policy priorities should be improving the sustainability of primary production activities, with the aim of ensuring that they generate sufficient investible funds for diversifying the economy; building up human capital; and investing in social safety nets and other investments targeted at the poor. The failure to implement such policies simply makes the problem of addressing extreme poverty in developing economies worse and raises the costs of implementing these measures once economic conditions improve.

For example, the World Bank estimates that a one percentage point reduction in growth in developing economies could consign 20 million more people to poverty. As a result of the food and fuel crises, the number of extremely poor is estimated to have increased by at least 100 million. Moreover, many of those who were already poor are slipping even more deeply into poverty; for instance, 88 percent of the recent increase in extreme urban poverty arose from poor households becoming poorer and only 12 percent from households falling into poverty. Because of these impacts, the annual cost of lifting the incomes of all the poor to the poverty line rose by US$38 billion, equivalent to 0.5 percent of aggregate developing country GDP.[29]

Furthermore, too many developing economies are wasting their scarce resources on short-term but inefficient responses to these

---

[28] World Bank 2008 (see ch. 1, fn 5). See also Development Research Group 2008 (fn 25).
[29] World Bank 2009 (see ch. 1, fn 1); World Bank 2008 (see ch. 1, fn 5).

crises, such as tax reductions to offset higher prices and increased spending on economy-wide subsidies and income support. An IMF study of 161 developing countries found that, in response to the fuel, food and economic crises, nearly 57 percent of countries reduced taxes on food while 27 percent lowered taxes on fuels. Almost one in five countries increased food subsidies while 22 percent raised fuel subsidies.[30] As noted in box 3.6, the reliance on such "across-the-board" tax reductions and subsidies is a poor and costly substitute for a comprehensive safety net and other investments targeted at the poor. General tax reductions and subsidies are often more regressive, more costly and more difficult to remove once in place. Fuel subsidies are usually much more regressive than food subsidies and often have further adverse environmental consequences. Reliance on such inefficient fiscal measures also means that developing country governments have less fiscal resources to invest in increasing the size and scope of targeted safety nets and publicly funded health and education services, which are much more essential policies during prolonged economic crises.

IMPROVING WATER MANAGEMENT

As noted in the introduction to this chapter, the emerging worldwide water crisis is one global ecological scarcity problem that the Global Green New Deal must address if it is to have a lasting impact on reducing worldwide poverty while at the same time ensuring that the ensuing global economic recovery is sustainable.

There are two aspects of this emerging water crisis: the scarcity of freshwater supplies relative to increasing demand, and the lack of clean water and sanitation available for millions of the poor in developing regions.

Experts may debate whether or not there is an impending global water scarcity problem; but the pressures on available freshwater supplies are mounting, for four principal reasons. First, there is the

---

[30] As quoted in World Bank 2008 (see ch. 1, fn 5).

increasing demand from growing populations. Second, as the world's population becomes urbanized, more water has to be allocated to meet highly concentrated and larger sources of demand. Third, as economic development increases and poverty diminishes, per capita water consumption will also rise. Fourth, climate change and modification of freshwater ecosystems and watersheds are likely to affect the availability of water supplies.[31]

There is no clear agreement on the definition of "water scarcity" and its measurement, and limited evidence of how its impacts will be manifested (see box 3.7). Developing countries already account for 71 percent of global water withdrawal, and their demand is expected to grow by 27 percent by 2025. Although current evidence suggests that water availability is not constraining economic growth in most countries, the exceptions are countries in the west Asia/north Africa region that exhibit moderate or extreme water scarcity, which is expected to worsen in the near future. By 2025 Asia is also expected to show signs of medium to high stress. The two most populous countries, China and India, account for around 35 percent of global water withdrawal. Both countries are already displaying medium to high water stress, which is expected to worsen by 2025. The problem is worse still for specific river basin regions within each country, however. Some of these river basins have, or will have in coming years, critical ratios exceeding 100 percent, suggesting chronic problems of extreme water scarcity. Other countries facing worsening water stress and scarcity include Pakistan, the Philippines, South Korea and Mexico.

Box 3.7 Water scarcity and its impacts
The most common measure of aggregate freshwater availability is the total renewable water resources of a country or region, which

---

[31] UNDP 2006 (see ch. 1, fn 15); UNEP. 2007. "Water." In UNEP. *Global Environmental Outlook GEO-4: Environment for Development*. Geneva, UNEP: 115–56; FAO. 2007. *Coping with Water Scarcity: Challenge of the Twenty-first Century*. Rome, FAO; UN. 2006. *Water: A Shared Responsibility*. World Water Development Report no. 2. New York, UN.

consists of adding up average annual surface run-off and groundwater recharge from precipitation, plus surface inflows from other countries or regions. Hydrologists usually measure the degree of water stress or scarcity by comparing total renewable water supply to the total water withdrawals per year in a country or region. "Withdrawal" refers to water removed or extracted from a freshwater source and used for human purposes – i.e. industrial, agricultural or domestic water use. The ratio of water withdrawals to total freshwater resources per year is often referred to as *relative water demand* or the *water criticality ratio*. Hydrologists typically consider criticality ratios for a country or a region between 0.2 and 0.4 (or 20 percent and 40 percent) to indicate medium to high water stress, whereas values greater than 0.4 reflect conditions of severe water limitation.

Developing countries already account for 71 percent of global water withdrawal. Water demand in these countries is expected to grow by 27 percent by 2025. Although criticality ratios are projected to remain low across all developing countries, there are important regional exceptions. By 2025 Asia is expected to show signs of medium to high stress. West Asia/north Africa is currently facing severe water limitation, and this problem is expected to reach critical levels by 2025. As shown in the table below, the problem of water stress and scarcity is likely to be worse for key developing countries and regions. The two most populous countries of the world, China and India, account for around 35 percent of global water withdrawal. Both countries are already displaying medium to high water stress, which is expected to worsen by 2025. The problem is worse still, though, for specific river basin regions within each country. Some of these river basins have or will have in coming years criticality ratios exceeding 100 percent, suggesting chronic problems of extreme water scarcity. Other countries facing worsening water stress and scarcity include Pakistan, the Philippines, South Korea, Mexico, Egypt and virtually all other countries in west Asia/north Africa.

Developing countries and regions with critical water ratios

Region/country	Total water withdrawal (km³)			Total withdrawal as a share of renewable water supply (%)		
	1995	2010	2025	1995	2010	2025
Huaihe	77.9	93.7	108.3	83	100	115
Haihe	59.2	62.1	62.9	140	147	149
Huanghe	64.0	71.1	79.5	89	99	111
Changjian	212.6	238.5	259.1	23	26	29
Songliao	51.5	59.2	67.6	26	30	34
Inland	89.5	98.9	111.2	299	330	371
Southwest	8.3	9.7	12.3	1	1	2
ZhuJiang	77.1	84.9	96.9	19	21	24
Southeast	38.8	41.4	47.7	27	29	33
China total	678.8	759.5	845.5	26	29	33
Sahyadri Gats	14.9	18.7	20.8	14	17	19
Eastern Gats	10.5	13.7	11.6	67	87	74
Cauvery	11.8	12.8	13.1	82	89	91
Godavari	30.2	33.3	38.8	27	30	35
Krishna	46.2	51.4	57.5	51	57	63
Indian-coastal-drain	34.8	46.9	43.6	108	145	135
Chotanagpur	7.2	10.9	14.3	17	26	34
Brahmari	25.5	27.2	31.0	24	22	26
Luni river basin	41.9	43.1	50.8	148	140	166
Mahi-Tapti-Narmada	31.4	34.3	36.3	36	39	42
Brahmaputra	5.5	7.2	9.2	1	1	1
Indus	159.1	178.7	198.6	72	81	90
Ganges	255.3	271.9	289.3	50	54	57
India total	674.4	750.0	814.8	30	33	35
Pakistan	267.3	291.2	309.3	90	98	105

Table (cont.)

Region/country	Total water withdrawal (km³)			Total withdrawal as a share of renewable water supply (%)		
	1995	2010	2025	1995	2010	2025
Philippines	47.0	58.2	70.0	24	29	35
South Korea	25.8	34.9	35.9	56	75	78
Mexico	78.6	86.2	94.2	24	26	29
Egypt	54.3	60.4	65.6	89	99	108
Other west Asia/ north Africa[a]	143.2	156.0	171.5	116	125	139

Notes: [a] Excluding Turkey.
Source: Adapted from Rosegrant, Mark W., and Ximing Cai. 2002. "Water for food production." In Ruth S. Meinzen-Dick and Mark W. Rosegrant (eds.). Overcoming Water Scarcity and Quality Constraints. Washington, DC, International Food Policy Research Institute: tab. B.3.

The fact that water scarcity and stress are occurring in specific river basins and regions and not necessarily across entire economies may be one reason that it is difficult to determine whether current patterns of water use relative to supply are hampering economic development. A study of water use and economic growth across 163 countries found little evidence of a widespread problem of global water scarcity at present in terms of physical water limits constraining economic development worldwide. The exceptions are the handful of countries in the west Asia/north Africa region that exhibit moderate or extreme water scarcity. Nevertheless, as the table above indicates, increased water utilization in critical river basins may become sufficiently severe to hamper economy-wide growth in more countries in the near future.

Sources: Barbier, Edward B. 2004. "Water and economic growth." Economic Record 80 (1): 1–16; Cosgrove, William J., and Frank R. Rijsberman. 2000.

World Water Vision: Making Water Everybody's Business. London, Earthscan; Rosegrant, Mark W., and Ximing Cai. 2001. "Water for food production." In Ruth S. Meinzen-Dick and Mark W. Rosegrant (eds.). *Overcoming Water Scarcity and Quality Constraints.* Washington, DC, International Food Policy Research Institute: 4–5; Vörösmarty, Charles J., Pamela Green, Joseph Salisbury and Richard B. Lammers. 2000. "Global water resources: vulnerability from climate change and population growth." *Science* 289 (July 14): 284–8.

There is a consensus that growing scarcity and competition for water are major threats to poverty alleviation, especially in the rural areas of developing economies, or, as UN-Water (the United Nations' mechanism coordinating the work of the many UN agencies in all aspects related to freshwater) states, "First and foremost, water scarcity is an issue of poverty."[32]

Several indicators of water availability, sanitation and health point to the scale of the problem in the developing world. About 700 million people in forty-three countries currently live under conditions of water stress (less than 1,700 cubic meters per person), including 538 million people in northern China. By 2025, as water stress and scarcity intensifies in developing regions (see box 3.7), 1.8 billion people will be living in countries or regions with moderate or extreme water scarcity, and 3 billion could face water stress. Today, one in five people in the developing world lacks access to sufficient clean water, and the urban poor typically pay five to ten times more per unit of water than do people with access to piped water. The poorest 20 percent of households in El Salvador, Jamaica and Nicaragua spend on average 10 percent of their household income on water, whereas, in comparison, paying 3 percent of household income for water is considered a hardship in the United Kingdom. Millions of women in developing regions spend several hours a day collecting water, which is an extra non-monetized cost of water supply. About half the developing world's population, 2.6 billion people, do not have access to basic sanitation. More than 660 million of the people without sanitation live on

[32] FAO 2007 (see fn 31).

less than US$2 a day, and more than 385 million on less than US$1 a day. Close to one-half of the population in the developing world have endured health problems linked to unclean water and poor sanitation, which is the second leading cause of deaths in children after acute respiratory infection. Sickness in children from water-related illness has also led to the loss of 443 million school days each year.[33]

In many economies, including high-income countries, freshwater is routinely wasted and inefficiently used because of considerable distortions in the way in which water is allocated. The problem is particularly serious in irrigated agriculture, which uses about 70 to 90 percent of the world's freshwater supplies. In addition, many of the world's surface water irrigation systems lose between one-half and two-thirds of the water in transit between source and crops. In many countries, irrigation water is subsidized, so that the price does not reflect the costs of delivery to farmers, let alone its value in use. Managing the demand for all water consumption, and reducing inefficiency in irrigated water use in particular, is therefore an important objective in a world in which freshwater is increasingly scarce relative to competing uses. Water pricing, tradable water rights and other market-based instruments are increasingly being employed as means to ensuring the efficiency of future water management activities.[34] Some institutional reforms have also encouraged a greater role for the private sector in providing certain water services to improve

---

[33] UNDP 2006 (see ch. 1, fn 20); FAO 2007 (see fn 31).

[34] See, for example, Cantin, Bernard, Dan Shrubsole and Meriem Ait-Ouyahia. 2005. "Using instruments for water demand management: introduction." *Canadian Water Resources Journal* 30 (1): 1–10; Easter, K. William, and Sandra Archibald. 2002. "Water markets: the global perspective." *Water Resources Impact* 4 (1): 23–5; Howitt, Richard, and Kristiana Hansen. 2005. "The evolving Western water markets." *Choices* 20 (1): 59–63; Rosegrant, Mark W., and Sarah Cline. 2002. "The politics and economics of water pricing in developing countries." *Water Resources Impact* 4 (1): 5–8; Schoengold, Karina, and David Zilberman. 2007. "The economics of water, irrigation, and development." In Robert Evenson and Prabhu Pingali (eds.). *Handbook of Agricultural Economics*, vol. III. Amsterdam, Elsevier: 2933–77; Stavins, Robert N. 2003. "Experience with market-based environmental policy instruments." In Karl-Göran Mäler and Jeffrey Vincent (eds.). *The Handbook of Environmental Economics*, vol. I. Amsterdam, North-Holland/Elsevier: 355–435; Tsur, Yacov, Terry Roe, Rachid

the efficiency of delivery and utilization. For example, around 7 percent of the world's population is currently supplied with water and wastewater services by privately financed water companies or projects.[35]

A further complication in water management is that many of the world's important river basins and other major sources of fresh-water do not respect international boundaries (see box 3.8). Two out of five people in the world live in rivers shared by more than one country, and thirty-nine countries currently receive most of their water from external sources. While most countries have institutional mechanisms and policies for allocating internal water resources and resolving water disputes, negotiating and implementing workable agreements to manage and share international water resources has proved more difficult.

Box 3.8 Transboundary water availability

Many countries share their sources of water, as river basins, large lakes, aquifers and other freshwater bodies often cross national boundaries. Such transboundary water sources are important for global supply; for example, two out of five people in the world live in international water basins shared by more than one country. The river Amazon has nine countries sharing it, and the Nile eleven countries. Sometimes transboundary water resources are equally distributed between countries, making it reasonably easy for the countries to

---

Doukkali and Ariel Dinar. 2004. *Pricing Irrigation Water: Principles and Cases from Developing Countries.* Washington, DC, Resources for the Future; and Young, Mike, and Jim McColl. 2005. "Defining tradable water entitlements and allocations: a robust system." *Canadian Water Resources Journal* 30 (1): 65–72.

[35] Allison, Peter. 2002. "Global private finance in the water industry." *Water Resources Impact* 4 (1): 19–21; Brook, Penelope J. 2002. "Mobilizing the private sector to serve the urban poor." *Water Resources Impact* 4 (1): 9–12; Dosi, Cesare, and K. William Easter. 2003. "Water scarcity: market failure and the implications for markets and privatization." *International Journal of Public Administration* 26 (3): 265–90; Johnstone, Nick, and Libby Wood (eds.). 2001. *Private Firms and Public Water: Realizing Social and Environmental Objectives in Developing Countries.* Cheltenham, Edward Elgar.

agree on sharing arrangements. Alternatively, the external sources of water may not be the most important source of supply for countries. As the table below indicates, however, thirty-nine countries currently receive most of their water from outside their borders. All but two of the countries are developing economies.

Countries receiving water from external sources

Region	Countries receiving 50–75% of their water from external sources	Countries receiving > 75% of their water from external sources
Middle East	Iraq, Israel, Syria	Bahrain, Egypt, Kuwait
East Asia and the Pacific	Cambodia, Vietnam	
Latin America and the Caribbean	Argentina, Bolivia, Paraguay, Uruguay	
South Asia		Bangladesh, Pakistan
Sub-Saharan Africa	Benin, Chad, Congo, Eritrea, Gambia, Mozambique, Namibia, Somalia, Sudan	Botswana, Mauritania, Niger
Eastern Europe and central Asia	Azerbaijan, Croatia, Latvia, Slovakia, Ukraine, Uzbekistan	Hungary, Moldova, Montenegro, Romania, Serbia, Turkmenistan
High-income OECD	Luxembourg	Netherlands

Source: UNDP. 2006. *Human Development Report 2006: Beyond Scarcity: Power, Poverty and the Global Water Crisis.* New York, UNDP.

A Global Green New Deal should aim to improve water management worldwide, and at the same time contribute to the goal of providing water services to the poor. Achieving these objectives is possible through progress in three main areas in all economies.

- Targeting investments and other policy measures to improve the supply of clean water and sanitation services to the poor.
- Removing subsidies and other incentive distortions and implementing, where appropriate, market-based instruments and other measures to improve the efficiency of water delivery and utilization and to manage water demand.
- Facilitate transboundary water governance and cooperation over shared management and use.

The next section provides examples of the type of national actions that can be adopted by all governments in these three areas.

MANAGING WATER SCARCITY, RISK AND VULNERABILITY

The most pervasive manifestation of the global water scarcity problem is that the poorest people in the world have the least access to clean water and sanitation but pay some of the highest prices, and bear the highest risks, for the water they do obtain and use. Thus providing safe drinking water and improved sanitation are critically important development and poverty alleviation goals that should be a key focus of the Global Green New Deal.

The United Nations has set as a Millennium Development Goal the objective of halving, by 2015, the proportion of people in the world without sustainable access to safe drinking water and basic sanitation. Even if this target is met there will still be more than 800 million people without clean water and 1.8 billion without sanitation in 2015.[36] Even before the current economic crisis, however, there was concern about whether international efforts were on track to meet the clean water and sanitation MDG by that year. The safe drinking water target has already been achieved in south Asia,

---

[36] UNDP 2006 (see ch. 1, fn 20).

Latin America and the Caribbean, and could be attained by east Asia and the Pacific by 2018, but sub-Saharan Africa and the Arab states were regarded as unlikely to reach the target before 2040. All of Asia, the Arab states, Latin America and the Caribbean were projected to meet the sanitation target by 2015 or soon thereafter, but sub-Saharan Africa was thought unlikely to halve the proportion of its population without sanitation before 2076. As discussed earlier in the chapter, a major concern is that developing country governments are already reducing expenditures on health and related expenditures. Private investment has also declined significantly, and official development assistance has not increased adequately. The current global recession is therefore seriously endangering the efforts of developing regions to achieve these MDG targets.

A top priority of the GGND must be to revive the necessary investments to attain the MDG for clean water and sanitation by 2015.

The United Nations Development Programme estimates that the minimum additional cost of achieving the MDG for clean water and sanitation is an additional US$10 billion a year globally.[37] To achieve this target, the UNDP recommends that governments in developing economies – which before the recession typically spent less than 0.5 percent of GDP on the provision of clean water and sanitation – should aim at a minimum of 1 percent of GDP.

As part of the GGND, all developing economies should follow the UNDP recommendation and allocate an amount equivalent to at least 1 percent of their GDP to clean water and sanitation investments.

The UNDP estimates that the total economic benefits of the global investment in achieving the MDG would come to about US$38 billion annually. The benefits for sub-Saharan Africa alone would amount to US$15 billion annually, which is equivalent to approximately 60 percent of the continent's current aid flows. Other

---

[37] UNDP 2006 (see ch. 1, fn 20).

benefits include around 1 million children's lives saved over the next decade as the investments are made, averaging 203,000 fewer child deaths per year by 2015. In addition, there would be 272 million days gained in school attendance as a result of reduced illness from diarrhoea alone. As summarized in box 3.9, poor households would also benefit from the income gains from the reduced number of days spent ill, the money savings from less health service use and expenditures on medicines, and the increased time spent on income-generating and productive activities. Across all developing countries, when such wider benefits are included, the return on each US dollar invested in clean water and sanitation interventions ranged from US$5 to US$11, and from US$5 to US$28 for some low-cost interventions.

Box 3.9 The economic benefits of improved drinking water and sanitation

An increasing number of studies in developing economies illustrate the economic benefits to poor households in having access to clean water and sanitation services. Most of the benefits occur not only because households gain from access to these vital services but also because of the reduction in the implied costs of the coping or averting strategies that the households have to employ when they do not have access.

For example, a study in Manaus, Brazil, estimated that households are willing to pay more than US$6.12 per month for improved water treatment services. This amount is well below what the households are currently paying for "unclean" water, however. A study in Kathmandu, Nepal, found that households cope with unsafe water by spending time on collecting water from public sources, storing water and treating it before consumption. Some households also spend money on bottled water, as well as water from public tanker trucks and private vendors. In addition, households invest in storage tanks, water filters, tube wells and chemicals, plus the costs of maintaining these facilities. These "coping costs" average as much as US$3 per household per month, equivalent to about 1 percent of current incomes. Not only are these coping costs almost twice as much as monthly water utility bills but also they are significantly lower than the average household's estimated willingness to pay for improved water services.

These results are typical across many developing economies and regions. A global assessment for the World Health Organization (WHO) of the costs and benefits to households of clean water and sanitation interventions amounted to US$5 and US$11 economic benefit per US$1 invested, respectively, for most developing country subregions and for most interventions. The return on a US$1 investment was in the range of US$5 to US$28 for interventions that met the MDG of halving by 2015 the proportion of the target population without clean water or sanitation, that increased access to improved water and sanitation for everyone or that provided disinfection at the point of use over and above increasing access to improved water supply and sanitation. The main contributions to the high benefits of these interventions were the income gains from the reduced number of days spent ill, the money savings from less health service use and expenditures on medicines, and the increased time spent on income-generating and productive activities by the household.

Sources: Casey, James F., James R. Kahn and Alexandre Rivas. 2006. "Willingness to pay for improved water service in Manaus, Amazonas, Brazil." *Ecological Economics* 58 (2): 365–72; Hutton, Guy, and Laurence Haller. 2004. *Evaluation of the Costs and Benefits of Water and Sanitation Improvements at the Global Level.* Geneva, WHO; and Pattanayak, Subhrendu K., Jui-Chen Yang, Dale Whittington and K. C. Bal Kumar. 2005. "Coping with unreliable public water supplies: averting expenditures by households in Kathmandu, Nepal." *Water Resources Research* 41 (2): 1–11.

Large-scale improvements in water supplies, sanitation and hygiene require substantial investments in major projects and management programs. The resulting increases in water quality often yield multiple benefits, including opportunities for increased employment for the poor. As box 3.10 shows in the case of the

Ganga Action Plan (GAP) in India, the latter employment benefits can be substantial. The net present value of the GAP in terms of the employment of unskilled labor amounted to nearly US$55 million, on account of increased income from employment and from the redistribution of income to the unskilled laborers. If greater weight is attached to employing unskilled laborers from poor households, the present value of these benefits rises to nearly US$190 million.

Box 3.10 Cost–benefit analysis of the Ganga Action Plan, India

The Ganga Action Plan was launched in February 1985 to raise the water quality levels of the river Ganges in India. The final investment cost of implementing the GAP from 1985/6 to 1995/6 was US$318 million (in 1995/6 prices), with an operating cost over the same period of US$10 million. In addition, water-polluting industries were required to invest in abatement, which amounted to an annual cost of effluent treatment of US$10.5 million. As a result of the plan, water quality in terms of dissolved oxygen improved and biochemical oxygen demand and concentrates of phosphates and nitrates were observed, although some places along the Ganges were affected only marginally. The result, however, was that the clean-up of the river produced multiple benefits to many different stakeholders.

The main benefits from cleaning the Ganges accrued to residents, tourists and pilgrims (at bathing ghats) who visit the river for bathing, including for religious purposes. There were other important benefits, however, arising from wanting to bequeath the biodiversity the river supports to future generations, from reassurance that the Ganges is kept clean and its aquatic life protected and from the desire to protect people living along the river from waterborne diseases. These benefits from the GAP were estimated through surveys of households. In addition, improving the water quality in the Ganges led to various health benefits to nearby residents using the water, which were estimated by the increased income due to the reduced number of working days lost from illness by river water users. As sewage sludge and wastewater from towns and cities along the Ganges are used as organic fertilizer and irrigation by small farmers, the increased number of sewage treatment plants built by the GAP allowed farmers to irrigate more hectares and to substitute treated sewage for conventional fertilizers. By estimating the fertilizer cost savings and the increased yields from irrigation, the additional agricultural benefits arising from the GAP could be calculated. Finally, there were substantial social benefits from employing unskilled labor in the GAP projects, due to the increased income from employment and from the redistribution of income to the unskilled laborers, who belonged to the lowest income group in the Indian economy.

Cost–benefit analysis of GAP and income effects, US$ million (1995/6 prices)

		Income distribution effects[b]	
	Present value[a]	$\varepsilon = 1.75$	$\varepsilon = 2.00$
Benefits from:			
recreation and amenities	0.83	0.08	0.06
non-use	195.20	12.49	8.39
health effects	23.49	72.42	81.64
agricultural productivity	16.33	48.58	56.76
employment of			
unskilled labor	54.53	162.17	189.49
Costs to:			
industry	42.74	4.10	2.91
government	129.81	129.81	129.81
Net present value	117.83	161.83	203.62
Benefit–cost ratio	1.68	2.21	2.53

Notes: [a] Estimated over 1985/6 to 1996/7 at 10 percent discount rate.
[b] The value of ε is the weight attached to the costs and benefits of each stakeholder group relative to the costs and benefits of a group with income equal to the national per capita income.

The table above summarizes the NPV estimates of the various benefits and costs of the GAP, along with a sensitivity analysis of the likely income distribution effects. As the analysis indicates, the NPV of the Ganga Action Plan is significantly positive. In addition, because many of the benefits accrue to poor income groups, such as farmers, river water users and unskilled labor, the income distribution effects of the GAP are substantial. When these are taken into account, the NPV and the benefit–cost ratio of cleaning up the river Ganges rise considerably.

Sources: Markandya, Anil, and M. N. Murty. 2000. *Cleaning up the Ganges: A Cost–Benefit Analysis of the Ganga Action Plan.* New Delhi, Oxford University Press; and Markandya, Anil, and M. N. Murty. 2004. "Cost–benefit analysis of cleaning the Ganges: some emerging environment and development issues." *Environment and Development Economics* 9 (1): 61–81.

Removing water subsidies and other incentive distortions, adopting market-based instruments and implementing other measures to increase the efficiency of water allocation should be actions taken by all economies.

The reform of pricing policies and other allocation methods is critical to improving the performance of water services and the productivity of water in all sectors of the economy. Enhancing public–private partnerships in the delivery of water services, including sanitation, might well also be significant. As noted above, the use of such measures is growing globally, not just in high-income economies but in developing countries too. Active water markets are emerging in Australia, Canada and the United States, but also in Brazil, Chile, China, Mexico, Morocco, South Africa and Turkey, as well as in many other countries and regions. As shown in box 3.11, the application of market-based instruments and water market reforms is proving to be varied and tailored to the needs of specific sectors.

Box 3.11 Market-based instruments and market reforms in water sectors

The growing international experience with market-based instruments, market reforms and similar measures in various water sectors suggests that familiarity with these policies is growing. The table below summarizes the measures that have been applied in different water sectors.

Market-based instruments applied to water sectors

Sector or application	Market-based instrument or market reform
Clean water supply	Private sector involvement; private–public partnership; tariffs and taxes; water trading and markets.
Stream flow modification; excessive surface water withdrawal; excessive groundwater withdrawal; protection of fresh-water ecosystems and watersheds	Licensing supply sources and with-drawals; realistic water pricing; reducing or eliminating energy and agricultural subsidies and subsidized credit facilities; water and wetland banking; payment for ecosystem services.
Sanitation and sewage treatment	Private sector involvement; pri-vate–public partnership; tariffs and taxes; bond issuance.
Water quality management (nutrient, pesticide, sus-pended sediments)	Regulations, penalties and taxes for industrial pollution and agricul-tural run-off; tradable permits; payment for ecosystem services; subsidies for soil conservation and organic farming.
Hazardous chemical management	Regulations and penalties.

Despite their growing prevalence, the use of market-based instruments and market reforms is still relatively limited. One problem, as a study of global water markets found, is that certain conditions must exist for water markets and trading to be effective:

water rights or water usage rights are well established, quantified and separate from the land;

water rights are registered, and people are well informed about water trading;

organizational or management mechanisms are in place to ensure that the traded water reaches the owner or owners;

the infrastructure for conveying water is sufficiently flexible for water to be rerouted to the new owner;

mechanisms are in place to provide "reasonable" protection against damages caused by a water sale for parties not directly involved in the sale; and

mechanisms are in place to resolve conflicts over water rights and changes in water use.

Source: Easter, K. William, and Sandra Archibald. 2002. "Water markets: the global perspective." *Water Resources Impact* 4 (1): 23–5

Although the use of market-based instruments and reforms across a wide range of water sectors and applications is growing, their potential for improving the efficiency of allocating water and providing services has not been realized. One problem with the spread of water markets and trading, as outlined in box 3.11, is that these mechanisms are effective only if certain conditions are met. For example, one reason why establishing irrigation water pricing in Egypt has proved less successful than in Morocco is that the irrigation system in Egypt is not designed for the use of volumetric charges and tradable water rights in the way that the system in Morocco is. Similar problems exist with the irrigation systems in India and Indonesia. There are also no legally defined groundwater rights in Egypt and India. In the Ukraine, there are problems with the smaller scale of privatized farms relative to the larger "block" supply of irrigation water. Finally, in all countries, farmers are resistant to switching to water markets when the predominant method of allocation has been the rationing of irrigation water, which does not involve charges to recover costs.[38]

Currently there are around 200 treaties and agreements that govern transboundary water allocation. Such agreements are necessary because of the interdependencies that such shared resources imply. For example, how an upstream country uses a river will affect the availability, timing and quality of water downstream. Countries that share an aquifer or lake are also affected by common water use. In recent years the international community has adopted conventions, declarations and legal statements concerning the management of international transboundary water bodies, while countries sharing river basins have established integrated basin management initiatives. Many international river basins and other shared water resources still lack any type of joint management structure, however, and some international agreements and joint management structures need to be updated or improved. Although the potential for armed conflict between countries over shared water resources remains low, cooperation to resolve disputes over water is often lacking.[39] In some cases, such as the shrinkage of Lake Chad in sub-Saharan Africa, the lack of cooperation is having a detrimental effect on the shared water system.[40] In south Asia, the 1996 treaty between India and Bangladesh for sharing the water of the river Ganges may be in serious jeopardy because of projected future water uses relative to basin supply, unless the treaty

---

[38] Hellegers, Petra J. G., and Chris J. Perry. 2006. "Can irrigation water use be guided by market forces? Theory and practice." *Water Resources Development* 22 (1): 79–86.

[39] Giordano, Meredith A., and Aaron T. Wolf. 2003. "Sharing waters: post-Rio international water management." *Natural Resources Forum* 27 (2): 163–71; Wolf, Aaron T. 2007. "Shared waters: conflict and cooperation." *Annual Review of Environment and Resources* 32: 241–69.

[40] UNDP 2006 (see ch. 1, fn 20).

is extended to allow the augmentation of river flows through water transfers from Nepal.[41]

Facilitating transboundary water governance and cooperation over shared management and use must therefore be an important objective of the GGND.

SUMMARY AND CONCLUSION

A Global Green New Deal needs to aim to reduce ecological scarcity worldwide, and at the same time to contribute to the goal of reducing significantly extreme world poverty. Targeting the poor is even more urgent during major economic crises. Underinvestment in human capital and a lack of access to financial credit are chronic features of the extreme poor, especially those poor households concentrated on fragile land. In a major economic recession, the main policy priorities should be improving the sustainability of primary production activities, with the aim of ensuring that they generate sufficient investible funds for diversifying the economy, building up human capital and investing in social safety nets and other investments targeted at the poor. The failure to implement such policies simply makes the problem of addressing extreme poverty in developing economies worse and raises the costs of implementing these measures once economic conditions improve.

The global scarcity of freshwater supplies relative to increasing demand and the lack of clean water and sanitation available for millions of the poor in developing regions must also be priorities addressed by a GGND. Because providing clean water and sanitation is fundamental to the poverty alleviation and economic development goals of developing economies, and can also yield wider employment, health and other economic benefits, developing country governments should spend an amount equivalent to at least 1 percent of their GDP on this sector, as recommended by the UNDP. All economies should

---

[41] Bhaduri, Anik, and Edward B. Barbier. 2008. "International water transfer and sharing: the case of the Ganges River." *Environment and Development Economics* 13 (1): 29–51.

consider removing water subsidies and other incentive distortions, adopting market-based instruments and implementing other measures to increase the efficiency of water allocation in all sectors, and especially in agricultural irrigation. National efforts to facilitate transboundary water governance and cooperation over shared management and use should also be important objectivesof the GGND.

4 Challenges facing developing economies

The various proposed actions for reducing carbon dependency and ecological scarcity discussed in the previous two chapters pose a number of difficulties for low- and middle-income economies. This chapter reviews the main constraints.

Developing economies in particular face a number of important challenges in their efforts to move quickly to a low-carbon economic growth path, such as a lack of finance, a technology and skills gap, and uncertainty over a future global carbon market.

Access to financing is a major constraint if developing countries are expected to invest in clean and low-carbon energy alternatives. The large-scale adoption of low-carbon and clean energy technologies by rapidly developing low- and middle-income economies will be necessary over the coming decades in order to reduce their greenhouse gas emissions and improve energy security. This will require, in turn, a massive injection of capital investment. For example, for all Asian economies to reach a target of having 20 percent of their total energy supply from clean energy sources by 2020 would require capital financing of almost US$1 trillion, of which nearly US$50 billion a year would be needed until 2020.[1] Similarly, if all developing countries honor their commitment to the International Action Programme (IAP) agreed at the 2004 International Conference for Renewable Energies in Bonn, this would mean an additional 80 gigawatts of renewable energy capacity by 2015, requiring about US$10 billion per year in investments. Official development assistance currently contributes on average US$5.4 billion per year to all forms of energy projects in developing countries worldwide, and is unlikely

---

[1] As quoted in Carmody and Ritchie 2007 (see ch. 2, fn 13).

to contribute to less than a fifth of current commitments under the IAP.[2] Sufficient capital is available from the private sector, both in terms of private investments within developing countries and financing from global and regional capital markets, but only if there is a stable regulatory framework for investment in the developing economy, favorable market conditions and incentives, and reduced uncertainty regarding the long-term price signal for carbon.

In addition to the "capital gap" there is also a substantial "skills and technological gap" for low- and middle-income economies in adopting clean and low-carbon technologies. Many developing economies spend little on research and development on these technologies and have a chronic shortage of workers with the complementary skills needed to develop and apply low-carbon technologies. Instead, most low- and middle-income countries, with the possible exceptions of China, India and perhaps a few other large emerging market economies with domestic capacity in clean technologies, are highly dependent on the importation and transfer of technologies and skills developed elsewhere. It is recognized that the transfer of new technologies and skills facilitates the development of an indigenous technological capacity and workforce, which in turn enable future innovations and the long-term adoption of low-carbon technologies. Most developing economies lack even the minimum R&D capacity and skilled workforce capable of attracting the transfer of many clean energy and low-carbon innovations, however.[3]

The Clean Development Mechanism is increasingly viewed as an important mechanism for solving some of the constraints to reducing the carbon dependency of developing economies (see box 4.1). Certainly, the CDM has achieved success in securing the financing

---

[2] "Content analysis of the International Action Programme of the International Conference for Renewable Energies, renewables2004," Bonn, June 1–4, 2004. Available at www.renewables2004.de/pdf/IAP_content_analysis.pdf; and UN ESCAP 2008 (see ch. 2, fn 7).

[3] Ockwell, David G., Jim Watson, Gordon MacKerron, Prosanto Pal and Farhana Yamin. 2008. "Key policy considerations for facilitating low carbon technology transfer to developing countries." *Energy Policy* 36 (11): 4104–15.

and transfer of clean and low-carbon technologies in developing countries, and, above all, in effectively creating a global trading market. Some problems remain with the current system, however. One concern is the geographical concentration of CDM projects in a handful of large emerging market economies, such as China, India, Brazil and Mexico, and the virtual absence of projects in low-income economies and, in particular, Africa. Most of the expected certified emission reduction (CER) credits earned by 2012 are from mainly large-scale projects, such as the incineration of greenhouse gases, grid-connected renewable electricity generation, fuel switching, reducing transmission losses and capturing fugitive methane emissions. A further problem is the growing investment uncertainty over the future of the CDM and the global carbon market after 2012. This uncertainty arises from the continuing lack of an international consensus on a post-Kyoto climate change agreement. The result could be a large decline in the future expected number of projects approved and CERs earned as 2012 approaches. Similar uncertainty faces the Joint Implementation scheme of the Kyoto Protocol, which allows recipient countries to earn emission reduction units (ERUs), each equivalent to 1 tonne of CO_2. In contrast to the CDM, the JI mechanism targets projects in industrialized countries, although it is aimed particularly at transition economies. Investment uncertainty over the post-2012 global carbon market and price is also likely to affect future JI projects in these economies and the ability to attract ERU credits.

Box 4.1 The Clean Development Mechanism

The Clean Development Mechanism is a provision of the Kyoto Protocol, which was designed originally as a bilateral mechanism through which entities in high-income economies could gain certified emission reductions by investing in clean energy technologies in developing economies. A CER is equal to 1 tonne of CO_2 equivalent. In practice, the CDM has become an international institution through which low- and middle-income countries can earn income from reducing greenhouse gas emissions by earning CER credits. In addition, by effectively setting an international price on carbon, the CDM has facilitated the commercial viability of low-carbon technology transfer, in terms of both equipment and know-how; has reduced some barriers to the information and capital flows necessary for investing in clean energy technologies in recipient countries; and, finally, has improved the quality of technology transfers to developing economies by providing assistance in project design and collaboration in management.

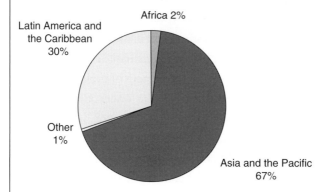

Registered CDM projects by region (total: 1,306)

As of January 2009 there were 1,306 registered projects. Two-thirds of them were located in the Asia and Pacific region, 30 percent were in Latin America and the Caribbean and only 2 percent were in Africa. The expected annual average CERs of these projects currently total nearly 244 million, which suggest an equivalent amount of reduction in tonnes of GHG emissions. More than 4,200 projects are currently in the CDM pipeline, and, if they are approved, they are expected to yield 2.9 billion CERs until the end of 2012. Thus, in a very short time, the CDM has mobilized billions of public and private investments to reduce GHG emissions in developing economies.

No fewer than 85 percent of the CERs from current registered projects are paid to just five large emerging market economies, however: China (132 million CERs), India (32.7 million), Brazil (19.8 million), South Korea (14.6 million) and Mexico (8 million). There is a similarly high degree of concentration with the CDM projects, 85 percent of which are concentrated in nine countries: India (380 projects), China (356), Brazil (148), Mexico (110), Malaysia (thirty-five), Chile (twenty-seven), Indonesia (twenty-one), the Philippines (twenty) and South Korea (also twenty). A further eight developing countries have between ten and fifteen projects. The remaining thirty-six economies have seven or fewer CDM projects, with the vast majority having only one or two projects currently.

Although the investments in CDM projects and the accumulation of CER credits in large emerging market economies are welcome, particularly as these economies are increasingly important sources of current and future global GHG emissions (see box 2.1), the virtual absence of CDM projects in many low-income economies and in Africa is of concern. One problem is that poorer countries lack the investment climate or the basic technological capacity to attract the foreign capital flows and technology transfers required for most projects. In addition, the type of small-scale clean energy projects required by many low-income economies, such as micro-hydropower, biomass and solar systems aimed at providing decentralized energy services to poor communities, are not the type of large-volume/low-cost sources of GHG emission reductions that will earn substantial CER credits under the CDM. For example, an analysis of the CDM projects currently in the pipeline by Benoit Leguet and Ghada Elabed finds that most of the expected CERs issued to 2012 will come from a handful of large-scale initiatives: the incineration of hydrofluorocarbons, nitrous oxide and perfluorocarbons (40 percent of all CERs); grid-connected renewable electricity generation, fuel switching and reductions in transmission losses (45 percent); and capturing fugitive methane emissions, such as pipelines, coal methane and landfill gas (10 percent). There are a growing number of small-scale wind, solar, hydro and biomass CDM projects, but these are overwhelmingly concentrated in large emerging market economies, such as China, India, Brazil and Malaysia.

Perhaps a greater problem is the investment uncertainty surrounding the CDM beyond 2012. While the general expectation is that a global carbon market will exist in some form after 2012, the lack of international consensus to date on a post-Kyoto climate change agreement means that there is considerable uncertainty over any future carbon market or the CDM. An Asian Development Bank report concludes that such uncertainty forces investors either to discount CERs deliverable after 2012 or not to price them at all. As 2012 approaches, CDM income is increasingly viewed as contingent income. Financial analyses of project cash flows are therefore made without reference to revenues from CERs, and thus the requirement for project entities to prove that the project is "additional" and would not have proceeded without CDM revenues becomes difficult to fulfill. If this uncertainty over the post-2012 carbon market and the CDM persists it could lead to a large decline in the future expected number of projects approved and the CERs earned.

Sources: Carmody, Josh, and Duncan Ritchie. 2007. *Investing in Clean Energy and Low Carbon Alternatives in Asia.* Manila, ADB; CDM statistics. Available at http://cdm.unfccc.int/Statistics/index.html; Collier, Paul, Gordon Conway and Tony Venables. 2008. "Climate change and Africa." *Oxford Review of Economic Policy* 24 (2): 337–53; Hepburn, Cameron, and Nicholas Stern. 2008. "A new global deal on climate change." *Oxford Review of Economic Policy* 24 (2): 259–79; Leguet, Benoit, and Ghada Elabed. 2008. "A reformed CDM to increase supply: room for action." In Karen Holme Olsen and Jørgen Fenhann (eds.). *A Reformed CDM – Including New Mechanisms for Sustainable Development.* Roskilde, Denmark, UNEP Risoe Centre: 59–72; Lloyd, Bob, and Srikanth Subbarao. 2009. "Development challenges under the Clean Development Mechanism: can renewable energy initiatives be put in place before peak oil?" *Energy Policy* 37 (1): 237–45; Schneider, Malte, Andreas Holzer and Volker H. Hoffmann. 2008. "Understanding the CDM's contribution to technology transfer." *Energy Policy* 36 (8): 2930–8; and Wheeler, David. 2008. "Global warming: an opportunity for greatness." In Nancy S. Birdsall (ed.). *The White House and the World: A Global Development Agenda for the Next US President.* Washington, DC, Center for Global Development: 63–90.

Developing economies face comparable challenges in implementing the sustainable transport strategy outlined in chapter 2. The constraints on progress in implementation are similar to those that developing countries face in adopting a low-carbon development path generally: shortfalls in public and private financial capital mobilization; a lack of skills, know-how and R&D capacity to absorb, adapt and develop novel transportation and vehicular technologies; and the failure of international mechanisms and institutions to help developing economies overcome such challenges.

For example, the United Nations Framework Convention on Climate Change (UNFCCC) estimates that a global transport strategy similar to the one outlined in chapter 2 would require additional investments worldwide of approximately US$88 billion by 2030, or an increase of about US$3 billion annually from now until that year, of which 40 percent would need to be targeted at developing economies.[4] Globally, US$79 billion is necessary for the development of hybrid and other alternative fuel vehicles and for improved fuel efficiency in all motorized transport, and the remaining US$9 billion is for biofuels. Around two-thirds of the investment should be financed domestically, one-sixth from foreign direct investment and the remaining sixth from international debt and official development assistance.

In contrast, at present in the five largest developing economies that are rapidly expanding their transport networks (Brazil, China, India, Mexico and South Africa), domestic finance accounts for 90 percent of transport investment, foreign direct investment for approximately 8 percent and international debt and development

---

[4] UNFCCC. 2007. *Investment and Financial Flows to Address Climate Change.* Bonn, UNFCCC.

assistance less than 1 percent. Across all developing countries, total development assistance in transport amounts to US$8.2 billion, which represents just 4 percent of the US$211 billion total investment in the transport sector of developing economies today. Of this development assistance, 66 percent went to Asia, 24 percent to Latin America and 10 percent to Africa (excluding South Africa). Thus, all forms of public and private investment flows to developing economies, but especially foreign direct investment, international debt financing and development assistance, need to be increased rapidly if the goal of developing sustainable transport systems globally is to be attained.

A further difficulty for developing economies is that existing international funding sources, such as the CDM, currently do not provide much financing for transportation projects. Although transportation was designated as a priority for the CDM, at present the sector accounts for just 0.12 percent of all registered CDM projects.[5] These projects include a bus rapid transit system in Bogotá, Colombia, and an urban railway system in Delhi, India. There appears to be a growing consensus that, as currently structured, the CDM is not well suited as a financing mechanism for fostering sustainable transportation in developing economies.[6]

Most developing economies, with perhaps the exception of large emerging market economies such as Brazil, China, India, Malyasia, Mexico, South Africa, South Korea and Thailand, lack the R&D capacity and skilled workforce capable of adapting and developing the technology and know-how necessary for the widespread adoption of clean and fuel-efficient vehicles, rapid transit systems, second-generation biofuels and other advances necessary for rapid progress in sustainable transportation. The necessary training in

---

[5] CDM statistics. Available at http://cdm.unfccc.int/Statistics/index.html.
[6] Sanchez, Sergio. 2008. "Reforming CDM and scaling up: finance for sustainable urban transport." In Karen Holme Olsen and Jørgen Fenhann (eds.). *A Reformed CDM – Including New Mechanisms for Sustainable Development*. Roskilde, Denmark, UNEP Risoe Centre: 111–26.

sustainable land use and urban planning ideas to complement such a strategy is also lacking in many low-income countries. Similarly, many of these economies also have limited financial and administrative capability to implement some of the more sophisticated transport economic and regulatory instruments, such as road pricing, vehicle taxation, fuel economy or greenhouse gas emission standards and even fuel taxes.

The current global economic crisis also imposes serious constraints on the capacity of developing economies to implement the policy priorities emphasized in chapter 3. Of particular concern is the decline in global trade, coupled with the continuing lack of agreement by the international community on key aspects of primary production trade in the Doha Round of international trade negotiations sponsored by the World Trade Organization. Fluctuating commodity prices are also disruptive to the finances of developing economies and their ability to plan and implement appropriate policy responses. Shortfalls in development assistance impose a severe handicap, especially since such assistance will be essential for developing countries to design and implement comprehensive and targeted social safety nets, maintain or boost health and education expenditures and develop and expand schemes for paying for ecosystem services.

For many low-income countries, especially in sub-Saharan Africa, simply meeting the MDG of halving the proportion of the population without access to clean water and sanitation will mean that development assistance is critical. Even before the current economic crisis, not only had overall development assistance to poor countries fallen in real terms over the previous decade but the share of assistance to the water and sanitation sector of developing economies had declined even more. For example, in its 2006 report on water, the UNDP estimated that the sector accounted for less than 5 percent of development assistance, and that aid flows would need to double to bring the MDG within reach, rising by US\$3.6 to US\$4 billion annually.[7] With the

[7] UNDP 2006 (see ch. 1, fn 20).

advent of the economic crisis and the revenue falls of national govern-ments, addressing the gap in overseas aid for clean water and sanita-tion in developing economies needs to be a priority of the international community under a GGND.

Developing economies will need technical and institutional assistance as well. The transfer of technologies may be important for developing large-scale water supply and sanitation projects, but the lack of skills and R&D capacity to absorb, adapt and develop new technolo-gies is a problem. For example, the availability of supplies is not the chief barrier to more efficient and productive groundwater utilization in developing economies; instead, the major obstacles are poor data on the extent of the resource, underdeveloped regulatory frameworks for governing groundwater use, and the limited knowledge of water authorities on managing the resource. Basic technologies available in richer countries for managing water resources, such as geographical information systems and remote sensing, are scarce in many develop-ing economies or underutilized. Advanced technologies, such as desa-linization plants, have become more cost-effective and affordable to large emerging market economies, such as China, Mexico, and Turkey, and to the Gulf states, but the technology has yet to be disseminated to many low-income economies, even though it would be ideal for small island states and countries with large coastal populations.[8]

As discussed in chapter 3, the effective implementation of mar-ket-based instruments and reforms in the water sector is dependent on overcoming a number of specific conditions. Many low-income countries need assistance in assessing which measures are appropri-ate for application in their economies. Unfamiliarity with public–private partnerships in providing clean water, sanitation and other water services may also be a factor deterring the more widespread use of this activity in developing economies.

[8] Lopez-Gunn, Elena, and Manuel Ramón Llamas. 2008. "Re-thinking water scarcity: can science and technology solve the global water crisis?" *Natural Resources Forum* 32 (3): 228–38.

5 National priorities for a Global Green New Deal

The major components proposed in the previous three chapters for the Global Green New Deal have been shaped by the four main crises that have afflicted the world in recent years: the current global recession, the fuel and food crises of the past several years, and the emerging water crisis. The GGND must also consider actions today that can address urgently the impending problems of global climate change, ecological degradation and extreme poverty.

Part II has been concerned with actions by national governments under a Global Green New Deal. These actions have focused on measures in two principal areas (reducing carbon dependency and ecological scarcity) and policies, investments and reforms that current evidence suggests that governments can enact fairly swiftly – i.e. in the next several years.

This chapter concludes part II by summarizing the main national actions that are essential for the success of the proposed GGND. Already one major economy has proposed public investments that accord with these proposals. In January 2009 South Korea announced a Green New Deal plan that adopts many of the national actions proposed for reducing carbon dependency and ecological scarcity. The plan involves spending US$36 billion over three years to create nearly a million jobs. The final section of this chapter describes the South Korean Green New Deal in more detail.

PROPOSED NATIONAL ACTIONS

As emphasized in part I, to be truly global, a GGND strategy must encompass the widespread adoption by national governments of fiscal measures and other policies in the short term that will expedite economic recovery and create jobs while being consistent with the medium-term objectives of reducing carbon dependence, environmental deterioration and extreme world poverty. The national actions suggested in part II generally fit these criteria.

Some actions have clearly identifiable and immediate impacts in terms of stimulating an economic recovery and creating jobs, however. Although these measures are also likely to reduce world poverty, it is more difficult to assess their impact on this goal. Other actions tackle the pressing problems faced by the world poor more directly, and in doing so should stimulate growth and employment, but the latter effects are often hard to evaluate.

It has also been difficult to put a precise "price tag" on the costs to the national governments of the proposed actions. It is possible, however, to give an approximate indication of what governments should spend in two broad priority areas of the GGND.

For instance, chapter 2 describes a low-carbon strategy for high-income OECD countries consisting of stimulus policies aimed at immediate economic recovery and job creation that also promote the transition to a less carbon-dependent economy through market-based incentives, the removal of fuel subsidies, and investments that would lead to the expansion of clean energy, energy efficiency, mass transit and freight rail networks, fuel-efficient vehicles and other low-carbon investments. As outlined in chapter 2, the cost of such a program for reducing carbon dependency implemented over the next several years in the United States and other high-income economies would amount to at least 1 percent of GDP.

Thus, as part of a GGND, the United States, the European Union and other high-income OECD economies should spend over the next two years amounts equivalent to at least 1 percent of their GDP on the national actions proposed in chapter 2 for reducing carbon dependency, including removing subsidies and other perverse incentives and adopting complementary carbon pricing policies.

As indicated in chapter 2, China is not only a major world economy but now the leading source of global greenhouse gas emissions. The elements of a comprehensive program for reducing the carbon dependency of China's economy were suggested in box 2.3. As noted in the chapter, China also needs urgently to invest and implement other measures to improve the sustainability of its transport. Already, China is committed to spending nearly 3 percent of its GDP over the next few years on low-carbon and other green stimulus measures (see box 1.1). China is not alone among large emerging market and transition economies in needing to implement such a strategy, however. In addition, if more of these economies, such as Brazil, India, Indonesia, Mexico and Russia, as well as the remaining developing economies comprising the G20 group, joined China in such a strategy, then the effects of the GGND would be magnified. The global economy and employment would recover more quickly, and world energy use and GHG emissions would decline more rapidly.

To date, however, only a handful of G20 governments have launched carbon-reducing strategies amounting to at least 1 percent of GDP (see figure 2.1). They include China (3.0 percent), South Korea (3.0 percent), Sweden (1.3 percent) and Australia (1.2 percent).[1] To improve the effectiveness of any GGND, then, all G20 governments should follow the lead of these countries and invest at least 1 percent of their GDP over the next two to three years in reducing carbon dependency. The total amount spent would amount to about one-quarter of the nearly US$3 trillion in G20 stimulus investments to date (see box 1.1). If the G20 economies coordinated the timing and implementation of these investments globally, the overall impact on moving the world economy to a low-carbon recovery path would be boosted.

If the world's twenty biggest rich and emerging economies, which together account for almost 80 percent of the world's population, 90 percent of global gross domestic product and at least

---

[1] Although figure 2.1 indicates that Saudi Arabia is spending the equivalent of 1.7 percent of its GDP on green stimulus, this expenditure is almost exclusively for water, sewage and desalinization projects. See Robins, Clover and Singh 2009, 24 (ch. 1, fn 10), for further details.

three-quarters of global GHG emissions, adopted this national action strategy for reducing carbon dependency, it would be a powerful signal to the rest of the world that these measures are critical both for reviving the world economy and for ensuring sustainable development in the future. As discussed in chapter 2, considerable economic, employment and poverty alleviation benefits would also accrue to developing economies if they adopted these proposed actions. It is therefore in their interests to pursue the recommended strategy, even though it is difficult to establish how much each economy should spend on these activities under the current economic conditions.

Chapter 3 nonetheless identifies two urgent priority areas for developing economies as part of the GGND. Because the poor are most vulnerable during economic crises, it is imperative that these countries design and implement as soon as possible a comprehensive safety net program targeted at the poor, and that they maintain, if not expand, educational and health services. To address the problem of the lack of safe drinking water and sanitation for millions of the poor in developing regions, low- and middle-income economies should follow the UNDP recommendation and spend at least 1 percent of their GDP for improved water and sanitation. These two measures will also generate important economy-wide benefits, which are difficult to quantify but should translate into immediate economic stimulus and job creation effects.

As part of the GGND, developing economies should therefore spend an amount equivalent to at least 1 percent of their GDP on improving clean water and sanitation for the poor. They should also develop urgently comprehensive, well-targeted safety net programs and at least maintain, if not expand, educational and health services for the poor.

Chapter 3 also highlights a number of other important national actions that developing economies should adopt to improve the sustainability of their primary production activities. As discussed in the chapter, adopting such measures is even more important during a major economic recession, especially if improving the sustainability of primary production generates sufficient investible funds for diversifying the economy, building up human capital and investing in social safety nets and other investments targeted at the poor. Although, as part of the GGND, developing economies should adopt the national actions outlined in chapter 3 for improving the sustainability of their primary production activities, under the current economic conditions it is difficult to determine what the costs of these activities will be for each economy.

Chapter 3 also suggests other national actions that all economies need to adopt to improve water management globally. As a top priority, all economies should consider removing water subsidies and other distortions, adopting market-based instruments or similar measures to increase water efficiency, and facilitating transboundary water governance.

Finally, chapter 4 outlines the key challenges facing developing economies in implementing the above national actions. These challenges can be overcome only through concerted action and cooperation at the international level. In addition, as a result of greater cooperation and coordination of policy efforts, the international community can also ensure the effectiveness and success of the GGND. Part III addresses the necessary international actions required for the Global Green New Deal.

THE SOUTH KOREAN GREEN NEW DEAL[2]

As noted in chapters 1 and 2, the major Asia-Pacific economies, Australia, China, Japan and South Korea, have already signaled a commitment to promoting low-carbon investments and other environmental improvements as part of their strategies for economic

[2] I am grateful to Heewah Choi, Peter Poschen and Kristof Welslau of the International Labour Organization for providing me with this information on the South Korean Green New Deal. The source for this information is "Briefing note for foreign correspondents," Ministry of Strategy and Finance, Government of South Korea. January 19, 2009.

recovery. Overall, the Asia-Pacific region accounts for 63 percent of all global green stimulus spending during the current recession, with most of the investments targeted to reducing carbon dependency. China accounts for 47 percent of global green fiscal spending to date, Japan and South Korea around 8 percent each, and Australia 2 percent (see figure 1.2).

As discussed in chapter 2, China has included a number of green stimulus investments, amounting to around 3 percent of its GDP, in its government spending in response to the economic recession. Many of the initiatives discussed in chapter 2 and box 2.3 have been adopted, including the promotion of wind energy, fuel-efficient vehicles, rail transport, electricity grid improvements and waste, water and pollution control. Some market-based incentives have been adopted, such as raising taxes on gasoline and diesel and reducing the sales tax on more fuel-efficient vehicles. Japan's green stimulus measures, which amount to 0.8 percent of its GDP, include grants for solar energy installation, incentives for the purchase of fuel-efficient cars and electronic goods, energy efficiency investments, the promotion of biofuels and recycling. The Australian government is spending around 1.2 percent of its GDP on green stimulus measures aimed at reducing carbon dependency (see box 1.1). The investments include initiatives for promoting renewable energy, carbon capture and storage, energy efficiency, the development of a "smart" electricity grid and the development of rail transport. The government is also developing a cap-and-trade permit system, which is likely to be implemented in 2012.[3]

Perhaps the strongest commitment to including green stimulus measures in an economic recovery program has occurred in South Korea. Concerned by the fall in the growth rate and employment in late 2008, in January 2009 the Ministry of Strategy and Finance announced a Green New Deal plan. At a cost of around US$36 billion from 2009 to 2012, the initiative aims to create 960,000 jobs.

---

[3] See Robins, Clover and Singh 2009, 14–20 (ch. 1, fn 10), for further details of the green recovery plans for China, Japan and Australia.

As table 5.1 indicates, the bulk of the Green New Deal is based on nine major projects involving a range of actions similar to those advocated in this book for reducing carbon dependency and ecological scarcity. The low-carbon projects include developing railroads and mass transit, fuel-efficient vehicles and clean fuels, energy conservation and environmentally friendly buildings. These measures alone will account for over 1.2 percent of the country's GDP, which indicates that South Korea is already conforming to the above recommendation that G20 economies should spend at least 1 percent of their GDP on a low-carbon strategy. There are three major additional projects in the South Korean plan that aim to improve water management and ecological protection, including the restoration of four major rivers, building small and medium-sized dams and forest restoration. By launching this initiative, the South Korean government is committing expenditures equivalent to around 3 percent of its GDP on the Green New Deal.[4] By undertaking these investments, the South Korean government is also signaling that economic recovery and employment creation are completely consistent with environmental and low-carbon goals; the Green New Deal accounts for nearly all (95.2 percent) of South Korea's fiscal response to the global recession (see figure 1.3).

In addition to the Green New Deal, the South Korean government has also announced that it plans to establish a US$72.2 million renewable energy fund to attract private investment in solar, wind and hydroelectric power projects, including developing technologies and plant construction.[5] It is hoped that the development of renewable energy will create 3.5 million jobs by 2018.

---

[4] Estimates of the GDP shares of the Green New Deal are based on 2007 estimated GDP in PPP terms from the CIA's "The world factbook." Available at www.cia.gov/library/publications/the-world-factbook/rankorder/2001rank.html. In 2007 South Korea's GDP was estimated at US$1,206 billion.

[5] See www.upi.com/Energy_Resources/2009/02/02/South_Korea_creates_renewable_energy_fund/UPI-41851233616799.

Table 5.1 *The South Korean Green New Deal*

Project	Employment	US$ million
Expanding mass transit and railroads	138,067	7,005
Energy conservation (villages and schools)	170,702	5,841
Fuel-efficient vehicles and clean energy	14,348	1,489
Environmentally friendly living spaces	10,789	351
River restoration	199,960	10,505
Forest restoration	133,630	1,754
Water resource management (small and medium-sized dams)	16,132	684
Resource recycling (including fuel from waste)	16,196	675
National green information (geographic information system) infrastructure	3,120	270
Total for the nine major projects	702,944	28,573
Total for the Green New Deal	960,000	36,280

Source: Ministry of Strategy and Finance, Government of South Korea.

In July 2009 South Korea announced the launching of a five-year Green Growth Investment Plan. The initiative essentially extends the Green New Deal into a five-year economic development plan for the country, spending an additional US$60 billion on the same priority areas for reducing carbon dependency and other environmental improvements (see table 5.1).[6] The additional funding on Green New Deal initiatives will be spent principally on clean energy technologies, energy-efficient lighting, producing energy from waste, providing credit guarantees for environmental projects and establishing funds for green investments through the Korean Development Bank. Under the plan, the government is committed to spending an amount equivalent to around 2 percent of GDP each year on these green measures through 2013. In addition to moving the economy to a low-carbon and greener development path, the plan is also expected to create around 1.5 to 1.8 million jobs and to boost economic output by US$162.7 billion by 2020.

[6] Robins, Nick, Robert Clover and Charanjit Singh. 2009. *A Global Green Recovery? Yes, but in 2010.* New York, HSBC Global Research, 7–8. Available at www.research.hsbc.com.

Part III The Role of the
International Community

The various national actions proposed in part II are necessary components of the Global Green New Deal; but they are not sufficient.

To overcome the challenges facing developing economies will require additional actions by the international community. International cooperation and policy coordination across countries will also assist the effectiveness of the national actions described in part II. The purpose of part III is to suggest how the international community can facilitate the adoption of a GGND strategy by national governments and enhance the benefits gained from such policies in terms of stimulating economic recovery, generating jobs, reducing poverty and sustaining economic development.

Chapter 4, in part II, identifies a number of challenges facing developing countries in implementing the GGND. For example, there is a serious "capital gap" preventing developing economies from implementing the proposed national actions over the next one to two years. Equally constraining is the "skills and technology gap"; most developing economies, with the possible exceptions of Brazil, China, India, Russia and other large emerging market economies, do not have the research and development capacity or the skilled workforce to import and adapt the new skills and technology for many of the proposed investments. Both these gaps can be overcome by increased financing, but during the current global economic crisis new financial flows are in short supply. Potential aid flows from donors are likely to be reduced rather than increased. The crisis has unquestionably reduced private investment flows, especially to more risky investments with longer-term returns. The political will to develop new and innovative financial mechanisms to spur global investments may also weaken. Such a financial climate is likely to affect the ability of all national governments to implement the proposed actions in part II over the next two years, but it will hamper developing economies especially.

Trade is also an important incentive for some actions proposed under the GGND. The volume of world trade declined in 2009, however, as global per capita income contracted.[1] As the world economic recovery is likely to be weak in the coming years, trade will also rebound slowly. In addition, the last few years have seen tremendous volatility in international commodity prices, especially for energy and food, with prices first rising and then falling sharply as the global recession deepened. Developing economies, especially those that are highly resource-dependent, face balance of payment problems and uncertainty over export and government revenues. Under such conditions it is difficult to implement investments and reforms, such as those required to improve the sustainability of primary production activities, increased health and educational expenditures, the development of comprehensive safety net programs targeted at the poor and the financing of clean energy and transport technologies. The current economic climate also hinders the progress needed in the Doha Round of world trade negotiations that are necessary to support the GGND.

The recommendations of part II highlight the need for global policy coordination to overcome these financial and trade challenges and make the GGND effective. There are also a number of failures in current global governance that have to be addressed. In the absence of a post-Kyoto climate change agreement, there is growing investment uncertainty over the future of the global carbon market and the Clean Development Mechanism after 2012. Future Joint Implementation projects may also be affected. New trade and financial mechanisms are required, and international agreements on transboundary pollution and water management need to be negotiated, but what is the appropriate global policy forum for promoting these initiatives over the next few years?

[1] World Bank 2009 (see ch. 1, fn 1).

Only if the international community agrees to actions and mechanisms in support of the GGND will it be possible to overcome these challenges. There are three areas in which these actions are needed:

- promoting global governance;
- facilitating access to financing; and
- enhancing trade incentives.

In formulating international actions in these three areas, an important criterion must be whether significant progress and agreement can be made by the international community within the next one to two years. The GGND is an urgent priority, given the current recession and the multiple crises facing the world. If the proposed global initiatives are to be effective in facilitating the GGND and enhancing its benefits, then they must be implemented at the same time as the actions by national governments advocated in part II.

The following chapters discuss the specific international actions proposed for each of the above three areas.

6   Promoting global governance

Improving global governance is crucial for meeting the financial, trade and policy coordination challenges to implementing the Global Green New Deal. The key question is whether there is an appropriate global policy forum that can provide the leadership necessary to overcome these global challenges and facilitate the GGND over the next several years.

To date, the most likely global policy forum for promoting urgent international action on the GGND is the G20 forum of the world's twenty largest rich and emerging economies, although all international fora, and especially the UN system, have a role to play in promoting, developing and enhancing the GGND.

There are several reasons why the G20 constitutes the appropriate environment for coordinating and innovating international policy in support of the GGND. First, the G20 has emerged as the global forum for coordinating policy action during the immediate economic crisis. The G20 is therefore well placed to consider the proposed GGND actions as part of its response to the current crisis. The indications from the Washington and London summits of the G20 are that it has the capacity to take on this role.

For example, some experts on global governance have already recommended that it do so: "The communiqué of the November 15, 2008 Summit locked in the next G20 summit and hence ordained a sequel that appears to have enshrined the G20 as the new format to address the current global financial and economic crisis over the coming months and perhaps years… [W]e strongly believe that it is best for the new US administration to focus its attention on making the G20 summit format work, in terms of its ability to address the immediate crisis, and in terms of subsequently dealing with other pressing problems, such as global warming and global poverty."[2] Although the following summit failed to address all these concerns, it appears that the London G20 meeting on 2 April 2009 was "a sincere attempt by the leaders of the G20 countries to come up with a multilateral and coherent set of proposals to deal with the problems that the world economy is facing."[3] At the April meeting, the G20 demonstrated this new global governance ability by promoting the International Monetary Fund to a lead role in the current world recession, by tripling its lending capacity, allocating more resources to the IMF and endorsing recent institutional changes to its facilities. The G20 has thereby demonstrated that it has the capability to turn into action the promise made in its London communiqué: "We will identify and work together on further measures to build sustainable economies."[4]

Second, coordinated action by G20 economies would have a profound effect on "greening" the world economic recovery and moving global economic development towards a low-carbon path. The G20 economies together account for almost 80 percent of the world's population, 90 percent of global GDP, and at least three-quarters of global greenhouse gas emissions. The leading economies in the G20 are also the dominant sources of international aid, including the funding of multilateral institutions. If the G20 leads the coordination and innovation in international policy required to support the GGND, it would be an important message to the rest of the world that this strategy is critical for reviving the world economy and addressing pressing global challenges.

There are two ways, in particular, that concerted policy action by the G20 could signal its commitment to greening the global economic recovery.

---

[2] Bradford, Colin, Johannes Linn and Paul Martin. 2008. *Global Governance Breakthrough: The G20 Summit and the Future Agenda*. Policy Brief no. 168. Washington, DC, Brookings Institution.

[3] Bird, G. 2009. "So far so good, but still some missing links: a report card on the G20 London summit." *World Economics* 10 (2): 149–58.

[4] The full text of the G20 London communiqué is available at www.londonsummit.gov.uk/en.

As pointed out in chapter 5, one signal would be if all G20 governments followed the lead of South Korea, China and a handful of other economies and invested at least 1 percent of their GDP over the next two to three years in reducing carbon dependency (see figure 2.1). The total amount spent would amount to about one-quarter of the nearly US$3 trillion in G20 stimulus investments to date (see box 1.1). If the G20 economies coordinated the timing and implementation of these investments globally, the overall impact on moving the world economy to a low-carbon recovery path would be boosted.

The second signal would be if the G20 also instigated pricing and regulatory reforms for reducing carbon dependency, including the removal of perverse subsidies and other distortions in energy, transport and similar markets. One quick way in which this could be achieved is through tackling fossil fuel subsidies. As noted in chapter 2, globally around US$300 billion annually, the equivalent of 0.7 percent of world GDP, is spent on fossil fuel subsidies. Over two-thirds of these subsidies occur in G20 economies, which could coordinate their phased removal. Cancelling these subsidies could reduce GHG emissions globally by 6 percent and add 0.1 percent to world GDP.[5] The financial savings could be redirected to investments in clean and renewable energy R&D and energy conservation, further boosting economies and employment opportunities.

Finally, as the dominant sources of international aid and funding for multilateral institutions, the G20 could mobilize international policy in support of the GGND.

For example, the G20 could secure a post-Kyoto global climate change framework. Uncertainty over future global climate policy and the delay caused by inaction both sharply increase the costs of an agreement to reduce global GHG emissions. The expiration of the Kyoto agreement in 2012 also increases the risks to global financing of carbon-reducing projects and clean energy investments in developing economies.

[5] UNEP 2008 (see ch. 2, fn 21).

Any new climate change agreement must also include developing countries, especially those whose emissions are expected to rise rapidly in coming years (see box 2.1). The longer participation of developing economies in a global agreement is delayed, the higher the costs of an agreement and the less efficient it is in reducing global GHG emissions.[6] Various policy frameworks have been proposed, with the general consensus being that a more flexible framework is likely to work best in accommodating large emerging economies such as China and Russia.[7] As these key developing economies are already part of the G20, it makes this international forum ideal for initiating negotiations towards a comprehensive framework on a climate change agreement.

A post-Kyoto international agreement is urgently needed. Many of the low-carbon and sustainable transport investments advocated

---

[6] Bosetti, Valentina, Carlo Carraro and Massimo Tavoni. 2008. *Delayed Participation of Developing Countries to Climate Agreements: Should Action in the EU and US be Postponed?* Working Paper no. 2008.70. Milan, FEEM; Hepburn, Cameron, and Nicholas Stern. 2008. "A new global deal on climate change." *Oxford Review of Economic Policy* 24 (2): 259–79; McKibbin, Warwick J., Peter J. Wilcoxen and Wing Thye Woo. 2008. *Preventing the Tragedy of the CO_2 Commons: Exploring China's Growth and the International Climate Framework.* Global Economy and Development Working Paper no. 22. Washington, DC, Brookings Institution; Nordhaus, William D. 2007. "To tax or not to tax: alternative approaches to slowing global warming." *Review of Environmental Economics and Policy* 1 (1): 26–44; Wheeler, David. 2008. "Global warming: an opportunity for greatness." In Nancy S. Birdsall (ed.). *The White House and the World: A Global Development Agenda for the Next US President.* Washington, DC, Center for Global Development: 63–90.

[7] Discussing and comparing these various post-Kyoto climate frameworks is beyond the scope of this book. For an indication of the different frameworks proposed, see Aldy, J. E. and R. Stavins (eds.). 2007. *Architectures for Agreement: Addressing Global Climate Change in the Post-Kyoto World.* Cambridge, Cambridge University Press; Aldy, J. E., A. J. Krupnick, R. G. Newell, I. W. H. Parry and W. A. Pizer. 2009. *Designing Climate Mitigation Policy.* Working Paper no. 15022. Cambridge, MA, National Bureau of Economic Research; Barrett, Scott. 2009. "Rethinking global climate change governance." *Economics: The Open-access, Open-assessment E-journal* 3 (2009–5). Available at www.economics-ejournal.org/economics/journalarticles/2009–5; Hepburn and Stern 2008 (see fn 5); Lewis, Joanna, and Elliot Diringer. 2007. *Policy-based Commitments in a Post-2012 Climate Framework*: Working paper. Arlington, VA, Pew Center on Global Climate Change; Nordhaus 2007 (see fn 5); and Wheeler 2008 (see fn 5).

that are an essential part of the GGND will be affected by the growing uncertainty over the future global carbon market after 2012 when the Kyoto treaty expires. Although it helps that the European Union has agreed to a 20 percent cut in GHG emissions by 2020, and to increase this reduction to 30 percent within the framework of "an ambitious and comprehensive global agreement in Copenhagen on climate change," rapid progress is needed in climate change negotiations.[8] The uncertainty over future global climate policy and the delay caused by inaction both increase steeply the costs of an agreement.[9] Delays in adopting effective climate policies will affect the cost of any future agreements required to abate an even larger amount of emissions. Such inaction in the short term increases significantly the costs of compliance in the long term, which is compounded by the effects of uncertainty on investment and policy decisions.

One of the most comprehensive frameworks for a post-Kyoto climate agreement has been suggested by Cameron Hepburn and Nicholas Stern, in which each country takes on its own responsibilities and targets within a larger global agreement, which in turn contains the following six features.

- A pathway to achieve the world target of 50 percent reductions by 2050, whereby rich countries contribute at least 75 percent of the reductions.
- Global emissions trading to reduce costs.
- Reform of the CDM to scale up emission reductions on a sectoral or benchmark level.
- The scaling up of R&D funding for low-carbon energy.
- An agreement on deforestation.
- Adaptation finance.[10]

Whether or not the final post-2012 climate change agreement follows this exact structure, such comprehensive frameworks should

[8] Council of the European Union. 2008. "Brussels European Council 11 and 12 December 2008: presidency conclusions." Brussels, Council of the European Union.

[9] Bosetti, Valentina, Carlo Carraro, Alessandra Sgobbi and Massimo Tavoni. 2008. *Delayed Action and Uncertain Targets: How Much Will Climate Policy Cost?* Working Paper no. 2008.69. Milan, FEEM.

[10] Hepburn and Stern 2008 (see fn 6).

form the basis for negotiations towards such an agreement. As the inclusion of all the G20 high-income and emerging market economies is fundamental to the successful conclusion of such an agreement, the G20 forum again provides an ideal opportunity for these large economies to begin the negotiation process.

Two of the most important features of any new international climate policy are the enhancement of global emissions trading to reduce costs and reform of the CDM. As argued in part II, guaranteeing the future of a global carbon market and the CDM mechanism beyond 2012 is essential to the success of many actions under the proposed GGND. It has been suggested that, in lieu of an inclusive international climate agreement, the continued existence of a global carbon market allowing developing economies to finance their mitigation measures would still permit the attainment of global GHG emission reduction targets.[11]

As discussed in part II, although the CDM has achieved success in securing the financing and transfer of clean and low-carbon technologies in developing economies, there are three concerns about it as currently constituted.

First, its projects tend to be concentrated in a handful of large emerging market economies, such as China, India, Brazil and Mexico. Low-income economies, and particularly sub-Saharan African countries, host very few CDM projects.

Second, most of the expected certified emission reduction credits earned by 2012 are from mainly large-scale projects, such as the incineration of greenhouse gases, grid-connected renewable electricity generation, fuel switching, reducing transmission losses and capturing fugitive methane emissions. Important sectors, such as transportation, building and construction, afforestation and reforestation, small-scale rural energy projects and energy efficiency, are poorly represented in the present CDM project portfolio. For example, more projects in low-income economies along the lines of the micro-credit

---

[11] Bosetti, Carraro and Tavoni 2008 (see fn 6).

scheme pioneered by Grameen Shakti in Bangladesh to provide a range of affordable renewable energy technologies to the rural poor (see box 2.7) or the transfer of second-generation cellulose biofuel technology to sub-Saharan Africa (see box 2.9) need to be funded through the CDM.

Third, although the pipeline of projects coming through the CDM has increased, the scale of the mechanism itself needs to be increased, so that it can deliver significantly greater finance and emission reductions globally. In addition, scaling up may require a much simpler and more transparent mechanism, such as sectoral benchmarks that enable entities to receive CER credits for achieving a targeted emissions intensity per unit output, or technological benchmarks, which would allow the inclusion of new techniques, such as carbon capture and storage, second-generation biofuels or simple home photovoltaic solar systems.[12]

A variety of proposals have been suggested for scaling up and reforming the CDM, increasing its coverage of countries to more low-income and sub-Saharan economies and including more sectors and technologies in the mechanism.[13] Such ideas should help the international community agree on the best way to extend the CDM and global carbon market beyond 2012.

Thus, it is essential to the success of any GGND that the international community should reach agreement on extending the CDM beyond 2012, preferably as part of a global climate change agreement, and to include reforms of the mechanism to increase the coverage of

---

[12] Hepburn and Stern 2008 (see fn 6).

[13] Collier, Paul, Gordon Conway and Tony Venables. 2008. "Climate change and Africa." *Oxford Review of Economic Policy* 24 (2): 337–53; Lloyd, Bob, and Srikanth Subbarao. 2009. "Development challenges under the Clean Development Mechanism (CDM): can renewable energy initiatives be put in place before peak oil?" *Energy Policy* 37 (1): 237–45; Hepburn and Stern 2008 (see fn 6); Stehr, Hans Jürgen. 2008. "Does the CDM need an institutional reform?" In Karen Holme Olsen and Jørgen Fenhann (eds.). *A Reformed CDM – Including New Mechanisms for Sustainable Development*. Roskilde, Denmark, UNEP Risoe Centre: 59–72; Schneider, Malte, Andreas Holzer and Volker H. Hoffmann. 2008. "Understanding the CDM's contribution to technology transfer." *Energy Policy* 36 (8): 2930–8; Wheeler 2008 (see fn 6).

developing economies, the sectors and technologies and the overall financing of global GHG emission reductions.

There are other areas of global governance that need to be improved if the actions proposed in the GGND are to be effective.

In chapter 3, it was noted that payment for ecosystem services is becoming an important mechanism in some developing regions for ensuring the long-term management of critical ecosystems, especially the protection of watersheds and forests for carbon capture. The success of current payment schemes in alleviating poverty has been limited, however. Greater international effort needs to be devoted to improving the design of payment of ecosystem service schemes so as to increase the coverage of ecosystems protected, to enhance the participation of poor, small landowners and the landless.

Chapter 3 also discussed the increasing importance of managing transboundary water resources, especially given the pressures of increasing water scarcity and the growing number of developing economies that depend heavily on these shared resources for freshwater supply. Although there are around 200 treaties and agreements that govern transboundary water allocation, many international river basins and other shared water resources still lack any type of joint management structure, and some international agreements and joint management structures need to be updated or improved. A key recommendation of the chapter is that countries should work to facilitate transboundary water governance and cooperation over shared management and use. Such efforts would be greatly enhanced if there was more support from the international community for greater collaboration on shared water issues globally.

For a GGND to tackle successfully the burdens that ecological and water scarcity impose on the world's poor, the international community needs to support efforts to improve payment for ecosystem services targeted to the poor and to include more ecosystems, and efforts to improve governance and the shared use of transboundary water resources.

7 Facilitating access to finance

If enacted, the international actions and reforms advocated in the previous chapter should facilitate the global financing and technology transfer necessary for the GGND. Problems will remain, though, in access to finance globally.

One difficulty is the decline in private financial investment flows compared to pre-recession levels. A major reason for this ongoing problem is the lack of confidence in the international financial system, coupled with the worldwide contraction of credit as the global economy adjusted to rid the system of overvalued and bad assets. The global financial system suffered a near-meltdown in 2008, and, although the massive bailout of the global financial system may have averted a major catastrophe in world credit and capital markets, it has proved insufficient to avoid the worst international economic crisis since the Great Depression. Not surprisingly, private financial investment flows have suffered accordingly, and this has led to demands for a new framework for the global financial system.

At the April 2009 London summit, the G20 suggested a number of proposals to shore up confidence in the international financial system and to reduce the risk of further financial turmoil of the type that precipitated the current recession. These proposals include the following.

- Strengthening financial supervision and regulation to include hedge funds and credit rating agencies, and eliciting more information on tax havens.
- Extending the mandate of the Financial Stability Board (formerly the Financial Stability Forum), which has the responsibility of overseeing global financial stability and risk.
- Tripling the lending capacity of the International Monetary Fund, and endorsing the IMF's recent lending initiatives to make substantial

amounts of finance available quickly to emerging market economies during a crisis.

- Increased lending by the IMF and multilateral development banks to low-income economies.[1]

Although the list of proposed actions is impressive, they fall short of establishing a new framework for the international financial system. In addition, as one commentator has pointed out, "[s]aying the right thing is not the same as doing the right thing, and we shall simply have to wait and see whether the words proffered in the G20 communiqué translate into actions," especially with regard to improving financial supervision and regulation.[2]

A discussion of the necessary reforms of the global financial system is beyond the scope of this book. Nevertheless, a healthy financial system is necessary for the success and effectiveness of the GGND. The recommendations in part II call for increased investment in a number of activities worldwide as part of this global strategy. Private investment flows and credit are important for achieving these objectives. Consequently, it is important to consider what general improvements in the financial system might be required to assist the implementation of the GGND over the next couple of years.[3]

Most discussion seems to assume that a new framework will mean more regulation of financial markets. This assumption may be erroneous, however, in several respects.

For one, the existing crisis may have more to do with a failure of governance and a lack of transparency than a lack of regulation. The financial system is already governed by many regulations and procedures. Most countries have a multitude of agencies supervising every aspect of financial activity – central and private banks, stock

---

[1] The full text of the G20 London communiqué is available at www.londonsummit.gov.uk/en.

[2] Bird 2009, 158 (see ch. 6, fn 2).

[3] The following discussion of general financial reforms was written with the assistance of Sanjeev Sanyal. I am grateful to him for these suggestions of reform and his input on the topic.

exchanges, securities, mortgage lenders and even other public agencies involved in the system. There are also independent assessors, such as credit rating agencies and research analysts, and all financial institutions have their own internal credit and audit procedures. In addition, it is worth noting that the financial crisis did not originate in poorly regulated emerging markets but in the most heavily regulated markets of Europe and the United States. As a result, reforms to the financial system should focus on better governance rather than more regulation. Indeed, simply adding more regulation could reduce transparency and could, in fact, worsen governance.

Thus, it seems that, instead of imposing more regulation on the financial system of individual countries, it makes more sense to support the G20 proposal of extending the mandate of an international body, the Financial Stability Board, to oversee financial stability at the global level. Such a function would be particularly important to monitor the degree of risk in the global financial system, and to ensure that national differences in supervisory arrangements and regulation do not lead to the expansion of financial services and products that increase global risk unduly. It remains to be seen, however, whether this new mandate for the Financial Stability Board is actually created and "is more successful in monitoring financial risks than it has been up to now."[4]

If the focus is on improving the governance of the financial system rather than greater regulation, reforms are needed in two key areas: (1) transparency and simplicity, and (2) aligned incentive structures. These objectives could be met by the following reforms.

• Lending norms must be harmonized by central banks to disallow imprudent lending and to set conservative benchmarks. As an example, housing loans should be allowed up to 70 percent of the market value of the property, as against the observed lending of 100 to 110 percent of collateral value that occurred in the sub-prime mortgage markets in the United States and some European countries.

---

[4] Bird 2009, 152 (see ch. 6, fn 2).

- Credit research, including ratings, should be paid for by investors and lenders, not by debt issuers, to prevent conflict of interest. Equity research is somewhat better aligned in terms of incentive structures, because investors pay indirectly for broker research. Ideally, however, all forms of research must be commissioned by investors or exchanges, and paid for by them.
- Senior executive pay in financial institutions must be reported transparently to the governing board and must be aligned to long-term performance rather than short-term earnings.
- Derivatives trading and hedge funds should be required to provision or reserve earnings more conservatively for future risks and costs, including the cost of future capital that may be needed to service risk-weighted assets arising in the future due to current transaction streams. Previous practices, such as the flexibility provided by Basle capital norms to derivatives trading banks to use their own risk management systems for risk and capital assessment, should be eliminated or restricted.

Such governance reforms are straightforward and could be implemented fairly rapidly throughout the global financial system. The adoption of these actions as soon as practicable is necessary to revive confidence in the global credit system and stimulate private investment flows. Because ensuring a healthy global financial system and credit availability should be considered an essential goal of a GGND, the international community should adopt as soon as possible such reforms to the governance of the financial system that increase transparency and simplicity, and improve the alignment of incentive structures.

A second problem for financing many of the initiatives outlined in the GGND is the shortfall in development assistance, especially in those sectors that are the key targets of the global strategy. Even before the current economic crisis, official development assistance contributed US$5.4 billion annually to energy projects worldwide, which is below the estimated US$8.3 billion in annual low-carbon energy investments needed just for the Asia-Pacific region and the US$30 billion required for all developing regions.[5] Across all

---

[5] UN ESCAP 2008 (see ch. 2, fn 7); Wheeler 2008 (see ch. 6, fn 6).

developing countries, total development assistance in transport amounts to US$8.2 billion, which represents just 4 percent of the US$211 billion total investment in the transport sector of developing economies today. As discussed in part II, however, the UNFCCC recommends that nearly US$15 billion in development assistance is required by developing countries if they are to adopt hybrid and alternative fuel vehicles, improve the efficiency of all motorized transport and develop second-generation biofuels. Shortfalls in development assistance will also severely hamper achievement of the necessary improvements in the sustainability of primary production in developing economies. It was also noted that the water and sanitation sector in 2006 accounted for less than 5 percent of development assistance, yet aid flows would need to double, rising by between US$3.6 and US$4 billion annually, to bring within reach the MDG of halving the proportion of the population without these services by 2015.

These estimates for the gap in development assistance are sobering, and the shortfall has worsened because of the current global recession. There is some positive news, however.

As noted above, in response to the current recession the G20 has endorsed a tripling of the IMF's lending capacity. The additional allocation of special drawing rights (SDRs) could permit up to US$19 billion in new lending to low-income economies. The G20 also proposes that the IMF finances an additional US$6 billion in lending to poor countries through sales of its gold reserves. Overall, the additional allocations proposed by the G20 could total as much as US$1.1 trillion in new lending to emerging market and low-income economies.

No doubt, if these resources are released, they will contribute significantly to the aid flows to developing economies during the current recession. In many ways, though, these increased allocations simply make up for the decline in international aid flows that was occurring before the crisis, as many of the richer donor countries failed to meet their promised bilateral targets and contributions to multilateral institutions.[6] Perhaps more importantly from the standpoint of the GGND, however, the additional aid flows proposed by the G20, via the IMF and the multilateral development banks, are not targeted towards the priority areas in developing economies identified above: low-carbon energy investments, sustainable transport, primary production and improvements in water and sanitation.

Because of the economic crisis, the World Bank is also planning to step up its development assistance.[7] Over the next three years it could make new commitments of up to US$100 billion. Lending in 2009 almost tripled to more than US$35 billion, compared to US$13.5 billion lent in the previous year. The World Bank is also creating a financial crisis facility to fast-track funds to developing countries. The new facility will accelerate the approval processes for money from a US$42 billion fund aimed at the world's poorest economies. An initial US$2 billion from this fund is being expedited to these countries, and the money is likely to support public spending on infrastructure, education, health and social safety net programs, such as school and maternal feeding programs. Such increased support is consistent with the GGND strategy of improving the livelihoods of the poor during the current crisis. More lending and development institutions should follow the lead of the World Bank, and not only increase their aid to the poorest economies over the next few years but also target it to the poor living within these economies.

As the current economic crisis is expected to exacerbate the worldwide problem of poverty, the president of the World Bank, Robert Zoellick, has called for every high-income economy to pledge 0.7 percent of its stimulus package to a global "vulnerability fund," which would be used in developing economies to finance a comprehensive and targeted safety net for the poor, investments in infrastructure, including low-carbon technology projects, and support

---

[6] Bird 2009, 155 (see ch. 6, fn 3).

[7] This information on World Bank Group lending plans is from the official website: www.worldbank.org/html/extdr/financialcrisis.

for small and medium-sized enterprises and micro-finance institu-tions.[8] Similarly, the UN High-Level Task Force on the Global Food Crisis has called on donor countries to double their financing for food assistance, other types of nutritional support and safety net pro-grams, and for an increase in the proportion of aid to be invested in food and agricultural development from the current 3 percent to 10 percent within five years.[9]

Overall, these are sensible areas for targeting aid during a glo-bal economic crisis, and are compatible with the aims of the GGND. Such measures need more support from international donors, how-ever. Bilateral and multilateral aid donors should increase their devel-opment assistance over the next few years, and target it at the sectors and actions that comprise the key components of the GGND.

The international community may also consider developing innovative financial mechanisms to facilitate attainment of the GGND goals. This report describes briefly three relevant proposals.

The first proposal is the expansion of the International Finance Facility (IFF), which was developed by the Treasury and the Department for International Development of the United Kingdom. The intention of the IFF is to mobilize resources from international capital markets by issuing long-term bonds that are repaid by donor countries over twenty to thirty years. This approach has already been applied to the IFF for immunization (IFFim), which was launched by the United Kingdom, other European countries and South Africa in 2006. These countries have pledged to contribute US$5.3 billion over a twenty-year period.[10] IFFim raises finance by issuing bonds in the capital markets to convert these long-term government pledges into funds for immediate investment. The government pledges are then used to repay IFFim. The initial offering in 2006 raised US$1 billion, and a second offering in 2008 added US$223 million. The

---

[8] Zoellick, Robert B. 2009. "A stimulus package for the world." *New York Times*, January 22.

[9] High-Level Task Force on the Global Food Crisis 2008 (see part II introd., fn 2).

[10] This information is from the IFFim website: www.iff-immunisation.org.

investments are disbursed through the Global Alliance on Vaccines and Immunization, a public–private partnership of major stakeholders in immunization in the developing world.

Gordon Brown, the UK prime minister, and Ngozi Okonjo-Iweala, a former finance minister of Nigeria, have proposed that a similar IFF facility to IFFim could be set up to meet the MDG for clean water and sanitation investments in developing economies.[11] Meeting this goal is also an important objective of the GGND (see chapter 4). Brown and Okonjo-Iweala suggest that the IFF mechanisms for making funds immediately available for investment while repayment is deferred until much later are ideal for water and sanitation projects, as their rates of return are extremely favorable (see chapter 5).

A study comparing the IFF approach to other potential new sources of international development financing, such as the currency transactions tax (otherwise known as the Tobin tax), taxes on airline travel or fuel, and establishing special drawing rights for development, has found that the alternatives to the IFF were less desirable, as they need international agreement involving many countries.[12] Another study, however, questions whether the IFF approach can raise sufficient funds to supplement the shortfalls in development assistance necessary to achieve the MDG.[13] If an IFF for water and sanitation emulated IFFim and raised US$1.2 billion from the bond market over three years, this amount would contribute to the estimated US$3.6 to US$4 billion required annually to achieve the MDG of halving the proportion of the population without these services by 2015, but the IFF funds would not provide the necessary financing on

[11] See Brown, Gordon, and Ngozi Okonjo-Iweala. 2006. "Frontloading financing for meeting the Millennium Development Goal for water and sanitation." In UNDP. *Human Development Report 2006: Beyond Scarcity: Power, Poverty and the Global Water Crisis.* New York, UNDP: 72–3.

[12] Addison, Tony, George Mavrotas and Mark McGillivray. 2005. "Aid, debt relief and new sources of finance for meeting the Millennium Development Goals." *Journal of International Affairs* 58 (2): 113–27.

[13] Moss, Todd. *Ten Myths of the International Finance Facility.* Working Paper no. 60. Washington, DC, Center for Global Development.

their own. All the same, an IFF for sanitation and water, and possibly also for other specific investments advocated in the GGND, might prove to be an innovative financial mechanism.

Another potential new source of finance is the Climate Investment Funds (CIFs), which currently consist of the Clean Technology Fund (CTF) and the Strategic Climate Fund (SCF), administered by the World Bank and other multilateral developments. The funds will be disbursed to developing economies as grants, concessional loans and risk mitigation instruments. The CTF will invest in projects and programs that facilitate the transfer and adoption of low-carbon technologies in power generation, transportation and energy efficiency.[14] The SCF will direct funding to programs that pilot new development approaches or scaled-up activities aimed at a specific climate change challenge or economic sector.[15] Initial programs include a pilot program for climate resilience, a forest investment program and a scaling up of a renewable energy program.

The CIFs are new, and thus it is too early to assess their performance. The United States first proposed a Clean Technology Fund in January 2008, and committed US$2 billion to the fund over its first three years. Since then other donors have pledged financing to the CIFs – including the United Kingdom (US$1.5 billion), Japan (US$1.2 billion), Germany (US$887 million) and France (US$500 million) – totaling over US$6.1 billion.[16]

One proposal is for the CIFs, and especially the Clean Technology Fund, to be expanded and incorporated into the next global climate change agreement.[17] If the next global agreement includes permit auction funds, then some of these funds could be allocated to increase the funding of the CIFs. It is estimated that at least an additional US$12 billion for the CIFs could be raised in

---

[14] World Bank. 2008. *The Clean Technology Fund*. Washington, DC, World Bank.
[15] World Bank. 2008. *Strategic Climate Fund*. Washington, DC, World Bank.
[16] Based on the World Bank website http://web.worldbank.org/WBSITE/
    EXTERNAL/TOPICS/ENVIRONMENT/EXTCC/0,,contentMDK:21713769~me
    nuPK:4860081~pagePK:210058~piPK:210062~theSitePK:407864,00.html.
[17] Wheeler 2008 (see ch. 6, fn 6).

this way. If this amount was matched by bilateral donations, then the CIFs would contain investible funds four times larger than their current funding.

The final financing proposal is a US-led Global Clean Energy Cooperation program, suggested by the United States' National Renewable Energy Laboratory (NREL).[18] The proposal recommends three implementation strategies for the United States. The first strategy involves revitalizing the portfolio of US clean energy investment facilitation programs. The government's existing international clean investment programs could be consolidated and expanded to increase significantly investment by US firms in energy efficiency and renewable energy worldwide. The second strategy calls for accelerating global cooperation in renewable energy and energy efficiency technologies. The global development and use of these technologies could be scaled up through strategic R&D, demonstration and deployment partnerships. The third strategy recommends expanding partnerships with major developing economies to accelerate clean energy market transformation in these economies. The partnerships could be targeted at large emerging market economies, such as Brazil, China and India, and through regional efforts in Africa, Asia, Latin America and the transition economies of Europe and central Asia.

Although it is difficult to estimate the total costs of these strategies, the proposal argues that they will yield considerable benefits for the United States, and globally as well. The strategies take advantage of the current US R&D capacity to innovate and develop clean energy technologies, which gives the United States an unparalleled opportunity to lead a global clean energy market transformation in cooperation with international partners. It is estimated that, by 2020, these strategies will have generated up to US$40 billion a year in new clean energy exports for the United States and between 250,000 and 750,000 new jobs. In addition, there would be around

[18] NREL. 2008. *Strengthening US Leadership of International Clean Energy Cooperation: Proceedings of Stakeholder Consultations.* Technical Report no. NREL/TP-6A0–44261. Golden, CO, NREL.

US$10 billion to US$50 billion in savings from reduced oil prices and other economic and energy efficiency gains. The anticipated global benefits include up to US$1 trillion a year in new investments in clean energy technologies, reductions in GHG emissions of 50 percent to 80 percent by 2050 relative to 2005 levels and a reduction in global oil use of 40 percent by 2050 compared to 2005 levels.[19]

Other major industrialized economies with significant capacity for clean energy innovation, such as the European Union and Japan, might consider similar global strategies, either on their own or in collaboration with the United States or all G20 economies. Although highly ambitious, such a proposal for global cooperation and partnership on innovative clean energy technological development addresses directly the issues of financing and the transfer of key technologies that are critical to the success and effectiveness of the GGND.

In sum, the international community needs to develop and expand innovative financing mechanisms, such as the International Finance Facility, Climate Investment Funds and Global Clean Energy Cooperation, as possible means to fund key components of the GGND.

[19] NREL 2008 (see fn 18).

8   Enhancing trade incentives**

The current financial and economic crisis is having a significant impact on trade volumes and revenue, because of falling global demand and a tightening of trade financing. The slowing of global trade is particularly daunting for those countries that depend on export-led growth. Low-income economies, and particularly those resource-dependent economies with a high share of primary products to total exports, will feel the consequence of the crisis more significantly through trade channels.[1]

Although trade is projected to decline as the global economic downturn worsens, and will recover slowly with the world economy, it is less clear what role trade policy can play in either addressing the immediate crisis or in supporting the implementation of the Global Green New Deal. As trade was not the underlying cause of the current economic crisis, it is doubtful that changes in trade policy, at least in the short term, will be able to reverse the current economic climate. Despite this caveat, one clear opportunity may be to focus on new trade financing and trade facilitation financing packages in order to promote the initiatives outlined in the GGND. There is also a strong argument for ensuring that trade policies "do no harm" in the short term through the adoption of protectionist measures. Finally, trade policy will have a critical role over the medium term in promoting some of the key components of the GGND.

TRADE AND TRADE FACILITATION FINANCING
It is estimated that more than 90 percent of trade is financed with some form of short-term credit, insurance or guarantee. The

** This chapter was written with the assistance of Ben Simmons, who provided much of the content. I am grateful to him for his inputs on the topic.
[1] UN 2009; World Bank 2009 (see ch. 1, fn 1, for both).

international financial crisis has affected the availability of such credit significantly, however. Exporters are increasingly demanding that overseas buyers obtain letters of credit from banks, and these are becoming more expensive and harder to get.[2] The problem is being felt most acutely by traders and banks in emerging economies. The World Trade Organization (WTO) estimates that the current liquidity gap in trade finance is about US$25 billion.[3] This lack of trade financing, coupled with waning demand, is exacerbating the downward trend in global trade.

As the world economy emerges from recession, it will become increasingly important to ensure that trade flows continue, which is why adequate trade financing is so critical. Maintaining or enhancing these flows will be essential to attaining some of the components of the GGND, especially the need for developing economies to improve the sustainability of primary production and generate sufficient investible funds for diversifying the economy, building up human capital and investing in social safety nets and other investments targeted at the poor.

Several national export credit agencies (ECAs) and international financial institutions have announced new trade finance facilities to address the problem.[4] For instance, in December 2008 the United States and China announced a new partnership to augment trade-

---

[2] *New York Times.* 2009. "Trade losses rise in China, threatening jobs." *New York Times,* January 14.

[3] WTO, 2008. "Lamy warns trade finance situation 'deteriorating.'" Geneva, WTO, November 12. Available at www.wto.org/english/news_e/news08_e/gc_dg_stat_12nov08_e.htm.

[4] Between 1988 and 1996 export credits increased fourfold, from US$26 billion to US$105 billion per year. In 2002 it was estimated that ECAs accounted for between US$50 and US$70 billion annually in support of large industrial and infrastructure projects in developing countries. Knigge, Markus, Benjamin Görlach, Ana-Mari Hamada, Caroline Nuffort and R. Andreas Kraemer. 2003. *The Use of Environmental and Social Criteria in Export Credit Agencies' Practices.* Eschborn, Germany, Gesellschaft für Technische Zusammenarbeit. The US Export-Import Bank (Ex-Im Bank) authorized US$12.6 billion in financing alone in its fiscal year 2007. Ex-Im Bank. 2008. "Export-Import Bank to provide liquidity to small business exporters." Press release. Washington, DC, Ex-Im Bank, November 25.

related financing for emerging markets. The United States plans to provide US$4 billion in new short-term trade finance facilities and US$8 billion in medium- and long-term trade financing for US goods and services to emerging markets. For its part, China has promised to provide US$8 billion in finance for exports of Chinese goods to emerging markets.[5]

International financial institutions are also responding to the crisis. The International Finance Corporation (IFC) has announced plans to double its Global Trade Finance Program from US$1.5 billion to US$3 billion. According to the IFC, this expanded facility would benefit participating banks based in sixty-six countries.[6]

These new financing facilities also provide a unique opportunity to promote the expansion of trade finance focused specifically on projects and products that could support actions advocated for the GGND. In some cases, such programs already exist. For instance, the US Export-Import Bank has supported an "Environmental Exports Program" since 1994, which has provided financing in excess of US$3 billion.[7] Some of the US$12 billion of the United States' increased trade financing that is envisioned could be focused specifically on expanding this program and on directing it to support the transfer of technology and capital goods necessary for the GGND. Similar initiatives could be taken with other national export credit agencies and international financial institutions. It may be necessary to receive exemptions for such initiatives under WTO rules, however, as they amount to discriminatory practices under existing provisions governing the use of trade financing.

Likewise, there is an opportunity to mobilize committed trade facilitation financing in support of the GGND. The OECD estimates

[5] Ex-Im Bank. 2008. "United States and China announce $20 billion in finance facilities that will create up to $38 billion in annual trade finance to assist global trade." Press release. Washington, DC, Ex-Im Bank, December 5.

[6] World Bank, 2008. "Trade is key to overcome economic crisis." Washington, DC, World Bank, December 1. Available at http://web.worldbank.org/WBSITE/EXTERNAL/NEWS/0,,contentMDK:21996518~pagePK:34370~piPK:34424~theSitePK:4607,00.html.

[7] See www.exim.gov/products/policies/environment/index.cfm.

that trade-related development assistance amounts to approximately US$25 to US$30 billion a year, which represents around 30 percent of total development assistance. The aid typically goes to one of four main areas: (i) trade policy and regulation; (ii) building productive capacity; (iii) economic infrastructure; and (iv) trade-related structural adjustment.[8]

At the WTO ministerial meeting in Hong Kong in 2005, it was agreed that the WTO's "Aid for Trade" program, which supports export industries and infrastructure, should be expanded. During the meeting the European Union and the United States pledged to increase annual spending on Aid for Trade to US$2.7 billion annually by 2010, and Japan announced that it would spend US$10 billion over three years for developing economies. The World Bank is also expanding its trade facilitation services by US$30 million over the next three years, one of the moves being the establishment of a Trade Facilitation Facility (TFF).[9]

As is the case with trade financing, there is an opportunity to promote within trade facilitation financing a focus on the projects and initiatives advocated in the GGND. The United Nations Environment Programme has already been active in advocating that sustainable development should be one of the goals for structuring Aid for Trade and similar initiatives and investments.[10]

Overall, there appears to be significant scope for the international community to develop and expand new trade financing and trade facilitation financing packages, and use them to target support to the GGND.

TRADE PROTECTIONISM

There is increasing concern that the economic crisis and accompanying job losses will lead to an increase in trade protectionism and

---

[8] WTO, 2008. "Aid for Trade fact sheet." Available at www.wto.org/english/tratop_e/devel_e/a4t_e/a4t_factsheet_e.htm.

[9] World Bank 2008 (see fn 6).

[10] United Nations Conference on Trade and Development [UNCTAD]. 2008. *Aid for Trade for Development: Global and Regional Perspectives.* Geneva, UNCTAD.

competitive devaluations. So far, the use of protectionist measures has been limited. According to the International Trade Commission (ITC) and the WTO, the number of anti-dumping cases jumped 40 percent in the first half of 2008, and only a few nations raised tariffs during the year.[11] There is widespread agreement that one of the successes of the Washington and London G20 summits in response to the economic crisis may have been that they averted the risk of increased reliance on protectionism by the world's major economies as a response to the recession.[12]

Nevertheless, the World Bank notes that a range of trade policy restrictions, such as export restrictions, biofuel subsidies, tariffs and mandates, have contributed to the rise in global food and other commodity prices since 2003, and there is concern that countries might resort to these measures if the global recovery continues to be weak.[13] Of more direct relevance to the GGND, biofuels policies that subsidize production, impose high tariffs and mandate consumption are on the increase, even though such measures have led to the rapid expansion of biofuels produced from food crops, such as maize and vegetable oils, contributing to higher food prices and environmental degradation.[14] A rise in protectionism would not only undermine the current WTO Doha negotiations, including important environmental issues such as fisheries subsidies and the liberalization of environmental goods and services, but also risk placing additional pressure on ecosystems as countries begin producing what otherwise would have been produced more efficiently abroad.

In sum, the international community should continue to resist a reversion to protectionism as a response to the economic crisis, and should periodically review existing trade agreements and shape future agreements to identify and minimize barriers, so as to enhance effective support for the proposed GGND actions.

[11] See the website www.usitc.gov/trade_remedy/731_ad_701_cvd/index.htm.
[12] Bird 2009 (see ch. 6, fn 3); Rao 2009 (see ch. 1, fn 7).
[13] World Bank 2009 (see ch. 1, fn 1).
[14] World Bank 2009 (see ch. 1, fn 1).

TRADE LIBERALIZATION

The current Doha Round negotiations offer a number of opportunities for promoting a Global Green New Deal, albeit in the medium rather than the short term.

For example, negotiations are currently focused on limiting fisheries subsidies. These subsidies are estimated to be valued at US$15 to US$35 billion annually, and include such items as direct cash grants, tax breaks and loan guarantees.[15] Although some subsidies directed at fishery management promote responsible fishing practices, most subsidies directly contribute to overfishing. This is a grave challenge, given that the FAO estimates that more than three-quarters of the world's fisheries have already been fished to their biological limits or beyond.[16] The threat facing these fisheries is not just an environmental issue; fisheries provide nutrition and employment for millions around the world. Successfully negotiating new WTO rules that limit fisheries subsidies that contribute to overfishing and overcapacity is crucial to ensuring more sustainable primary production activities in all economies.

Another opportunity exists with regard to the current negotiations aimed at reducing tariff and non-tariff barriers on environmental goods and services. As noted by WTO director-general, Pascal Lamy, in addressing trade ministers in Bali, Indonesia, during the UNFCCC conference of parties, "There is no doubt that an immediate contribution that the WTO can make to the fight against climate change is to indeed open markets to clean technology and services."[17] Although these negotiations hold the potential to increase the international flow of climate-friendly technologies, there is disagreement at present between WTO members about how they should be

---

[15] UNEP. 2008. *Fisheries Subsidies: A Critical Issue for Trade and Sustainable Development at the WTO: An Introductory Guide.* Geneva, UNEP.

[16] FAO. 2007. *The State of World Fisheries and Aquaculture 2006.* Rome, FAO.

[17] Soesastro, Hadi. 2008. "What should world leaders do to halt protectionism from spreading?" In Richard Baldwin and Simon Evenett (eds.). *What World Leaders Must Do to Halt the Spread of Protectionism.* London, Centre for Economic Policy Research: 3–6.

liberalized and whether liberalization itself will increase their use if it is not accompanied by a transfer of know-how and the building of local capacity. In considering tariff and non-tariff barrier liberalization for a number of clean energy technologies, however, a World Bank study finds that liberalization could result in a 7 percent to 13 percent increase in trade volumes in these technologies.[18] The potential benefits of overcoming obstacles to liberalizing this trade therefore suggest that it is worth exploring how to ensure a successful outcome of these negotiations at the WTO.

Perhaps the biggest gains to a GGND could come from the ongoing negotiations to liberalize agricultural trade.[19] For decades global agricultural protectionism has encouraged inefficient agricultural production in high-income economies and discouraged efficient and more sustainable production in developing economies. The World Bank estimates that the kind of agricultural trade barrier reductions under consideration in the Doha negotiations might lead to higher global commodity prices in the short run, but in the long run should generate a more transparent, rules-based and predictable agricultural trading system that would raise incomes worldwide. If the talks are concluded successfully, the removal of agricultural protectionism could reduce the incidence of global poverty by as much as 8 percent.[20]

To help enhance any GGND, the international community needs to achieve a successful conclusion to the Doha Round trade negotiations, especially on fishery subsidies, clean technology and services and reducing agricultural protectionism.

[18] World Bank 2007. *Warming Up to Trade: Harnessing International Trade to Support Climate Change Objectives*. Washington, DC, World Bank.

[19] Mattoo, Aaditya, and Arvind Subramanian. 2008. *Multilateralism beyond Doha*. Working Paper no. 153. Washington, DC, Center for Global Development; UN 2009 (see ch. 1, fn 1); World Bank 2009 (see ch. 1, fn 1).

[20] World Bank 2009 (see ch. 1, fn 1).

9 Conclusion: international priorities for a Global Green New Deal

Promoting global governance, facilitating access to financing and enhancing trade incentives are the three priority areas for actions by the international community in support of a Global Green New Deal. Without these actions, the effectiveness of the GGND may be severely constrained.

The GGND strategy outlined in this book recommends an expanded global policy role for the twenty rich and emerging economies that comprise the G20 forum. This recommendation is consistent with the strategy outlined in part II, that the G20 economies should spend at least 1 percent of their GDP over the next several years on reducing carbon dependency, including improving the sustainability of transport. The total amount spent would amount to about one-quarter of the nearly US$3 trillion in G20 stimulus investments to date (see box 1.1). If the G20 economies coordinated the timing and implementation of these investments globally, the overall impact on moving the world economy to a low-carbon recovery path would be boosted. Another way in which concerted policy action by the G20 could signal its commitment to greening the global economic recovery would be if the G20 also instigated pricing and regulatory reforms for reducing carbon dependency, including the removal of perverse subsidies and other distortions in energy, transport and similar markets. In addition, all G20 economies should agree to adopt carbon pricing policies, such as cap-and-trade or carbon taxes, to assist the transition of their economies to a low-carbon growth path. Such coordinated action by G20 economies would have a profound effect on "greening" the world economic recovery. As has been noted, the G20 economies together account for almost 80 percent of the world's population, 90 percent of global GDP and at least three-quarters of global greenhouse gas emissions.

Other components of the GGND should also be adopted by the G20 countries to demonstrate their global governance in response to the multiple crises facing the world economy. For example, the developing economies that are member countries of the G20 should take the lead in implementing the recommendation that developing economies should spend at least 1 percent of their GDP on water and sanitation.

An expanded leadership role for the G20 in implementing the GGND would be timely, given that it has emerged recently as the global forum for coordinating policy initiatives during the immediate economic crisis. The G20 is also likely to take a decisive role in promoting a global agreement on climate change – a role that the strategy outlined in this book also endorses. Such an agreement needs to address the urgent issue of ensuring that a global carbon market and a reformed CDM are extended beyond 2012. Improved global governance is also needed to facilitate the targeting of payments for ecosystem services to the poor and managing the shared use of transboundary water resources.

Although this book has advocated an important role for the leading twenty economies in the world in implementing the GGND, such a leadership role is not the exclusive preserve of the G20. All international fora have a role to play in promoting, developing and enhancing a GGND.

General reforms of the global financial system should focus on improving governance rather than introducing more regulation. These reforms should increase transparency and simplicity and better align incentive structures. Reforming the existing system is necessary to facilitate access to financing for the GGND, but it is not sufficient. The problem of declining development assistance and the lack of funding of the key sectors and investments identified in the GGND is of critical concern. At a time of global economic crisis, aid should be increasing and better targeted. This book recommends that bilateral and multilateral donors should increase aid over the next few years and target it to the sectors and actions advocated by the GGND. There appear to be two broad priority areas for increased aid in developing economies: (i) overcoming the shortfalls in aid for low-carbon energy investments, sustainable transport, primary production and improvements in water and sanitation; and (ii) financing for food assistance and nutritional support, sustainable primary production methods, and safety net programs targeted at poor households.

In addition, to support further the aims of the GGND, the international community should also consider developing and expanding innovative financing mechanisms, such as the International Finance Facility, Climate Investment Funds and the Global Clean Energy Cooperation program.

Trade policy may not appear to have a direct role in promoting the GGND, but specific trade measures may provide important incentives for the strategy. There may be a way of designing new trade finance and trade facilitation financing initiatives so as to assist the projects and actions advocated in the GGND. On the other hand, trade protectionism, which may increase as a result of the deep global recession, is an anathema to the GGND. Support for the strategy requires that trade protectionism be avoided, including the growing practice in some countries of implementing biofuels policies that subsidize production, impose high tariffs and mandate consumption. A successful conclusion to the Doha Round trade negotiations, especially with regard to fishery subsidies, clean technology and services and reducing agricultural protectionism, may not only assist the GGND in the short term but should provide an important stimulus to the medium- and long-term effectiveness of the strategy.

Part IV Towards a Greener World Economy

As stated in part I, the premise of this book is that the current global economic crisis has spurred governments to instigate a world-wide recovery. This provides a unique opportunity to address other important global economic and environmental challenges as well. The Global Green New Deal outlined in this book is aimed at achieving both objectives.

In sum, the GGND is not just about creating a greener world economy. It is about ensuring that the correct mix of economic policies, investments and incentives is adopted in order to reduce the carbon dependency of the world economy, protect vulnerable ecosystems and alleviate poverty while also fostering economic recovery and creating jobs.

Implicit in this is the recognition that the looming global problems of climate change, water scarcity and extreme global poverty mean that the world should not rely solely on massive fiscal stimulus packages for reviving the economy and creating jobs. Instead, what is called for is a balanced combination of policies and measures in a Global Green New Deal that has been carefully calibrated to meet the multiple economic and environmental challenges.

Reviving the world economy remains a necessity, however. That is why this book has included as part of the proposed GGND actions that can be implemented over the next several years and that will have an immediate and effective impact on the main objectives of the strategy. These objectives are:

- enhancing global economic recovery and creating new jobs while improving the long-run environmental and economic sustainability of the world economy;

- identifying key actions that national governments can adopt to attain a sustained and greener economic recovery; and
- identifying key actions that the international community can adopt to help overcome the critical challenges to implementing a GGND.

The policies and measures that fit these criteria had to be chosen carefully. In addition, it was necessary to take into account the fact that the specific priorities, policies, investments and incentive mechanisms adopted by each national government will differ in line with the economic, environmental and social conditions of the particular economy. There are three general types of economies, which differ markedly: high-income (mainly OECD) economies; large emerging market economies; and low-income economies. When necessary, the recommendations of the GGND strategy in this book have stressed which actions are relevant to each group of economies.

With all these factors in mind, this book suggests that a GGND should be aimed at two broad areas:

- reducing carbon dependency; and
- reducing ecological scarcity.

Part II provided details of the specific national actions required by governments in terms of achieving these aims. Part III outlined the complementary international actions – improving global governance, facilitating access to finance and enhancing trade incentives – that are necessary for the implementation of an effective GGND over the next few years.

This final part of the book has three principal objectives, with a chapter devoted to each. The first summarizes the main recommendations for national and international action under the proposed GGND that were formulated in parts II and III. The second chapter discusses some of the concerns expressed about the GGND, such as (i) whether green stimulus will add to uneasiness about government debt, inflation and global imbalances; (ii) why the private sector is not already making green investments, if they are so economically advantageous; and (iii) what the evidence is that the jobs and profits generated by green sector investments are better than in brown sectors. Finally, the third chapter explores how a GGND should be viewed as an intermediary step in the progress towards a "greener" economy, and provides recommendations for additional policies and instruments that may be necessary to take such progress further.

10 Summary of recommendations

Parts II and III outlined the national and international actions that should take place under a Global Green New Deal. In developing such a strategy, this book has focused on measures that fit within the two major aims of the GGND – reducing carbon dependency and ecological scarcity – and policies, investments and reforms that current evidence suggests that governments can enact fairly swiftly – i.e. in the next several years. Before proceeding to discuss the effectiveness of a GGND, and how it could foster progress towards a future green world economy, it is useful first to review the key proposals for national and international actions. The following is a summary of the main recommendations suggested in parts II and III.

NATIONAL ACTIONS PROPOSED FOR
THE GLOBAL GREEN NEW DEAL

(1) The United States, the European Union and other high-income OECD economies should spend, over the next few years, an amount equivalent to at least 1 percent of their GDP on the national actions proposed for reducing carbon dependency, including removing subsidies and other perverse incentives and adopting complementary carbon pricing policies.

(2) The remaining middle- and high-income economies of the Group of 20 countries should also aim, as far as possible, to spend over the next several years at least 1 percent of their GDP on the national actions proposed for reducing carbon dependency.

(3) Developing economies should also implement the national actions proposed for reducing carbon dependency. Under the current economic conditions, though, it is difficult to determine how much each economy should spend on these activities.

(4) Developing economies should spend at least 1 percent of their GDP on national actions proposed for improving clean water and sanitation for the poor. They should also develop, as a matter of urgency, comprehensive, well-targeted safety net programs and maintain, if not expand, educational and health services for the poor.

(5) Developing economies should adopt the other national actions for improving the sustainability of their primary production activities, although under the current economic conditions it is difficult to determine how much each economy should spend on these activities.

(6) All economies should consider removing water subsidies and other distortions, adopting market-based instruments or similar measures to increase water efficiency, and facilitating transboundary water governance.

INTERNATIONAL ACTIONS PROPOSED FOR THE GLOBAL GREEN NEW DEAL

(1) The most relevant global policy forum for promoting urgent international action on the GGND is the G20 grouping of the world's twenty largest rich and emerging economies, although all international fora, and the UN system especially, have a role to play in promoting, developing and enhancing the GGND.

(2) The G20 should coordinate the timing and implementation of the GGND actions recommended in parts II and III of this book, and help develop framework ideas towards securing a post-Kyoto global climate change agreement.

(3) The international community should reach agreement on extending the CDM beyond 2012, preferably as part of a global climate change agreement, and reforming the mechanism to increase the coverage of developing economies, the sectors and technologies and the overall financing of global GHG emission reductions.

(4) The international community should support efforts to improve payment for ecosystem services targeted at the poor and to include more ecosystems, and promote efforts to improve the governance and shared use of transboundary water resources.

(5) The international community should adopt as soon as possible reforms to the governance of the financial system that increase transparency and simplicity and improve the alignment of incentive structures.

(6) Bilateral and multilateral aid donors should increase their development assistance over the next few years and target it to the sectors and actions that comprise the key components of the GGND.

(7) The international community should develop and expand innovative financing mechanisms, such as the International Finance Facility, the Climate Investment Funds and the Global Clean Energy Cooperation, as possible means to fund key components of the GGND.

(8) The international community should develop and expand new trade financing and trade facilitation financing packages, and use them to target support to the GGND.

(9) The international community should review existing trade agreements and shape future agreements to identify and minimize barriers, in order to enhance effective support for the proposed GGND actions.

(10) The international community needs to reach a successful conclusion to the Doha Round trade negotiations, especially on fishery subsidies, clean technology and services and reducing agricultural protectionism.

11 Will a Global Green New Deal succeed?

As noted throughout this book, any Global Green New Deal should have three principal purposes:

- reviving the world economy, creating employment opportunities and protecting vulnerable groups;
- reducing carbon dependency, ecosystem degradation and water scarcity; and
- furthering the Millennium Development Goal of ending extreme world poverty by 2025.

To achieve these multiple objectives, a comprehensive range of national and international actions were proposed in parts II and III, which have been summarized in the previous chapter.

Fulfilling these recommendations will require a range of further initiatives, including commitments to increased public investments, new pricing policies, improving regulations, more aid disbursements and other policy changes. The need for such sweeping policy commitments inevitably raises questions about whether a Global Green New Deal will succeed.

In particular, three concerns have been expressed about the additional green fiscal stimulus measures and other public spending advocated by the GGND.

- What is the evidence that the investments in the "green" economic sectors advocated by the GGND will create more employment and profits compared to conventional fiscal stimulus spending?
- If the green sector investments are so economically advantageous, why is the private sector not making the necessary investments already?
- Would additional green stimulus add to the unease about government debt and its inflationary consequences, as well as the problem of structural imbalances in the world economy?

This chapter discusses these questions. Obviously, the GGND is not just about additional fiscal stimulus. For instance, it also advocates a role for complementary pricing policies and reform as a means to improving the efficiency and effectiveness of many of the proposed actions. In addition, the GGND is just as much about stimulating private sector investment in green sectors as it is about public spending. As we shall see in this chapter, such a comprehensive strategy is essential not only to the success of the GGND but also to addressing the above three concerns.

ECONOMIC AND EMPLOYMENT GAINS FROM GREEN SECTOR INVESTMENTS

In part II, a number of studies were cited that indicate that the job creation and economic benefits of a Global Green New Deal could be significant. For example, investments in clean energy technologies in the United States could create up to 2 million jobs across the country, and twice as many jobs per dollar invested compared with fossil-fuel-based energy.[1] A similar program to expand energy conservation and renewable energy supply in the European Union could create 1 to 2 million new, full-time jobs.[2] Investments in mass transit systems also have significant direct employment effects as well as reducing transport costs for poor households. Expanding public urban transit can create 2.5 to 4.1 secondary manufacturing jobs per direct job created. In China, the low-carbon stimulus provided by the government is motivated by the fact that its renewable energy sector already has a value of nearly US$17 billion and employs close to 1 million workers.[3] Further investments in the renewable energy sector and other "clean technologies" could have a major impact on developing new economic growth, expanding exports and creating employment. Finally, it was noted in chapter 5 that the South Korean government expects its Green New Deal initiative to create 960,000 jobs by 2012.

---

[1] Pollin *et al.* 2008 (see pt II introd., fn 6).
[2] Renner, Sweeney and Kubit 2008 (see ch. 2, fn 13).
[3] Renner, Sweeney and Kubit 2008 (see ch. 2, fn 13).

Although such evidence on the employment and other economic benefits of many of the proposed GGND actions is encouraging, the full economic and environmental implications of implementing such policies are difficult to predict. To date, we simply do not know enough about how such policies will affect national economies, and, in particular, how the green sector investments compare to conventional fiscal stimulus measures in terms of job creation and other benefits. Such comparative analysis for many major green sector investments is rare. Two studies involving the United States do provide some insights, however.

The Peterson Institute for International Economics (PIIE) and the World Resources Institute have assessed the economic and environmental impacts of a green recovery program for the United States. The program represents a set of policy options, combining specific low-carbon strategy investments, pricing policies, regulations and other measures that could be considered part of a comprehensive US recovery effort. Many of these policies were included as part of the green stimulus component in the US$787 billion American Recovery and Reinvestment Act of February 2009; others are not. Details of the PIIE–WRI study are provided in appendix 1.

Using the National Energy Modeling System (NEMS) and input-output tables, the PIIE–WRI analysis evaluates the employment impact of energy cost savings to households, firms and the federal government, as well as the corresponding reduction in revenue to the energy industry, resulting from each scenario. The policy options modeled were household weatherization; retrofitting federal buildings with energy-saving equipment; greening schools; a production tax credit (PTC); an investment tax credit (ITC); carbon capture and storage (CCS) demonstration projects; cash for old automobiles (referred to as "clunkers" in the United States); a hybrid tax cut; a mass transit investment; battery R&D; and smart metering. The economic and environmental effects of the measures were compared against those of traditional stimulus initiatives, such as tax cuts and road building.

The overall findings of the analysis are that the decreased cost and consumption of energy from the entire program have the potential to save the US economy an average of US$450 million per year for every US$1 billion invested. In addition, every US$1 billion in government spending would lead to approximately 30,000 job-years and reduce annual US GHG emissions by 592,600 tonnes between 2012 and 2020.[4] (Employment effects are measured in job-years, or the number of full-time equivalent jobs lasting one year.) The employment gains represent a 20 percent increase in job creation over more traditional infrastructure spending.

The relatively high employment effects of the green recovery package relative to conventional infrastructure investments are related to two factors. First, the green programs are expected to stimulate additional private sector investment, thus multiplying direct, indirect and induced job creation. Second, the PIIE–WRI study finds that the net employment effects of reducing energy costs to the economy as a whole are significant. Energy efficiency improvements and green tax credits have employment effects that continue well beyond the initial investment period. In contrast, the jobs created by conventional tax cuts and road infrastructure investments end once the money is spent.

The timing for implementing these different green policies is likely to vary considerably. The building efficiency programs (e.g. household weatherization, retrofitting federal building and greening schools) could be implemented swiftly, and provide immediate stimulus to the construction industry. Smart meter deployment and "shovel-ready" mass transit investments could also be initiated fairly rapidly. The "Cash for Clunkers" program has already been implemented in the United States in 2009, and consumers appear to be reacting to these incentives. Hybrid tax credit programs could

---

[4] The employment and GHG emission impacts exclude the effects of the transmission policy. See Houser, Trevor, Shashank Mohan and Robert Heilmayr. 2009. *A Green Global Recovery? Assessing US Economic Stimulus and the Prospects for International Coordination.* Policy Brief no. PB09–3. Washington, DC, PIIE and WRI for further details.

also be adopted quickly, but it may take longer for consumers to respond. The remaining programs are likely to require a longer lead time before implementation.

A report by the Pew Charitable Trusts compares the job growth and investments in the clean energy sector of the US economy to the rest of the economy for the ten years leading up to the current recession, 1998 to 2007.[5] Details of the Pew study are provided in appendix 2.

The Pew study defines the US clean economy as a sector that "generates jobs, businesses and investments while expanding clean energy production, increasing energy efficiency, reducing greenhouse gas emissions, waste and pollution, and conserving water and other natural resources." The five economic activities that comprise the clean economy are clean energy production, energy efficiency, environmentally friendly production, conservation and pollution mitigation, and training and support for the clean energy economy.

The Pew report finds that, between 1998 and 2007, jobs in these five clean energy areas grew more quickly than overall job growth in the United States. Clean energy jobs grew by 9.1 percent whereas total jobs in the United States increased by only 3.7 percent. By 2007 the five components of the clean energy sector accounted for over 770,000 jobs, or approximately 0.5 percent of all employment in the United States. In comparison, the biotechnology sector employed fewer than 200,000 workers, or approximately 0.1 percent of total US jobs in 2007. The fossil fuel energy sector, including utilities, coal mining and oil and gas extraction, employed 1.27 million workers in 2007, or about 1 percent of total US jobs.

Employment in the clean energy sector is now spread across all fifty US states and the District of Columbia. The jobs include both blue-collar and white-collar employment, from engineers, scientists and teachers to machinists, construction workers and farm laborers.

---

[5] Pew Charitable Trusts. 2009. *The Clean Energy Economy: Repowering Jobs, Businesses and Investments across America.* Washington, DC, Pew Charitable Trusts.

Although, in 2007, 65 percent of the jobs in the clean energy economy were in conservation and pollution mitigation, from 1998 to 2007 growth in the latter area had been only 3 percent, which was much less than it had been in environmentally friendly production (67 percent), clean energy production (23 percent) and energy efficiency (18 percent). The Pew study believes that the latter areas will be the future source of job growth in the clean economy, as "they represent businesses and jobs that are looking ahead to develop renewable, efficient energy sources and technologies to meet the demands of a carbon-constrained economy."[6]

The expansion of employment opportunities in the clean energy economy reflects the rapid growth in businesses and venture capital investment in the years leading up to the current recession. From 1998 to 2007 businesses in this sector grew by 10.6 percent. Venture capital investments in the clean energy economy totaled US$360.3 million in 1999, exceeded US$1 billion in 2000 and reached US$5.9 billion in 2008. Beginning in 2006, venture capital investments started increasing dramatically, growing by an average of US$1.6 billion every year from 2006 to 2008. Over the latter period, cumulative venture capital investments totaled nearly US$12.6 billion, with over two-thirds of this investment being channeled into clean energy production.

Given its findings on jobs, businesses and investments in the US clean energy economy between 1998 and 2007, the Pew study is relatively sanguine about the ability of this sector to spearhead a green recovery for the United States and the transition to a low-carbon economy. As noted by the report, "The clean energy economy has tremendous potential for growth, as investments continue to flow from both the government and private sector and federal and state policy makers increasingly push for reforms that will both spur economic renewal and sustain the environment."[7]

---

[6] Pew Charitable Trusts 2009, 17 (see fn 5).
[7] Pew Charitable Trusts 2009, 3 (see fn 5).

The study finds that, although jobs and investments have declined in the clean economy as a result of the current recession, other sectors have fared rather worse. In addition, clean economy investments are predicted to rebound more quickly than those in other sectors, because of the continuing growing demand for clean energy, the stress on water supplies and the need to reduce greenhouse gas emissions and other pollutants. The clean energy economy is also likely to benefit directly from the February 2009 American Recovery and Reinvestment Act, given that it includes US$84.8 billion of energy- and transportation-related spending that is targeted at the clean economy.

Overall, the PIIE–WRI and Pew studies confirm that green sector investments do have the potential for substantial employment and economic gains, at least in the case of the US clean energy economy. Both studies also confirm that realizing these potential gains will depend on formulating the right combination of policies. Green stimulus spending, such as the ARRA in the United States, can boost the impact of the clean energy sector on the overall economic recovery and job creation, but such spending alone is not sufficient. For example, the PIIE–WRI employment and economic scenarios assume – as advocated in the Global Green New Deal strategy proposed in this book – the adoption of complementary pricing policies and other regulations that will improve the effectiveness of clean energy and other green investments (see appendix 1). Similarly, the Pew study finds that the employment and investment expansion in the US clean energy sector from 1998 to 2007 was driven largely by state policies, such as requirements that electricity providers supply a minimum percentage from renewable sources and strong energy efficiency regulations (see appendix 2). To spur and sustain the clean energy economy nationally, the Pew report recommends the adoption of additional national policies: a federal cap-and-trade system to help reduce GHG emissions by at least 80 percent by 2050; a national renewable portfolio standard that would require that 25 percent of the nation's energy supply be derived from renewable sources by 2025; and an energy efficiency resource standard that would require a cut of 15 percent in electricity usage and 10 percent in natural gas usage by 2020.

An important issue, raised in the PIIE–WRI study, is that the effectiveness of green investments in creating jobs and boosting clean energy sectors will depend crucially on when the funds can be disbursed and the plans implemented.

For example, as indicated in box 1.1, in 2009 over US$460 billion has been allocated by governments on green stimulus investments, mostly by G20 governments. A review conducted by HSBC Global Research has found, however, that by the end of July 2009 only 3 percent of the green stimulus had been spent.[8] The bulk of the spending is not likely to occur until 2010, or even 2011. The green sectors that are most likely to see early disbursement of funds are mainly the "shovel-ready" infrastructure projects, such as improvements in rail networks, water restoration, building renovation and electricity grid enhancement. Disbursements to spur renewable energy and energy efficiency face the most delays.

If considerable time elapses between the announcement of green fiscal stimulus programs and their actual disbursement and implementation, then it can have two effects on employment and economic gains.

First, the longer the delay in implementation, the less likely it becomes that green sector investments are going to assist the economic recovery and job creation in the short term.

Second, for private investors, the asset valuations of sectors affected by such delays will be lower or encompass more risk. As indicated in appendix 1, many of the green programs supported by government stimulus spending are expected to stimulate additional private sector investment, thus multiplying direct, indirect and induced job creation. If the public investment component is delayed,

---

[8] Robins, Clover and Singh 2009 (see ch. 5, fn 6).

though, private investors are unlikely to assume all the risks of investing in many clean energy sectors. The delay in the disbursement in public sector funds could therefore lead to a postponement in private investment as well. As a consequence, overall employment creation in green sectors will be less than anticipated.

PUBLIC VERSUS PRIVATE GREEN SECTOR INVESTMENTS

The Pew Charitable Trusts report summarized in appendix 2 shows that, before the current recession, private venture capital was flowing rapidly into the US clean economy. Between 2006 and 2008 venture capital investments in the sector totaled US$12.6 billion. Global private investments in clean energy production assets, manufacturing, research and development passed the US$100 billion benchmark for the first time in 2007, and many renewable technologies and industries were growing at the rate of 20 percent to 60 percent per year.[9]

Such evidence is often cited, as in the case of the Pew study, as a reason why the clean economy sector could act as a catalyst for economic recovery and long-term growth, provided that it is supported by additional government investments targeted at that sector and complementary national policies. In parts II and III of this book, a similar conclusion is used to justify the need for a Global Green New Deal entailing a range of coordinated policy actions, especially by the G20 economies. Such actions would involve not only an increase in green stimulus spending over the next several years but also pricing and regulatory reforms for reducing carbon dependency, including the removal of perverse subsidies and other distortions in energy, transport and similar markets and the adoption of carbon pricing policies, such as cap-and-trade systems or carbon taxes, and similar environmental pricing measures.

One could also interpret the venture capital investment trends noted in the Pew and other reports differently, however. If private investments were already flowing to clean energy and other green

[9] REN21 2008 (see ch. 2, fn 24); Carmody and Ritchie 2007 (see ch. 2, fn 13).

sectors of the world economy before the current economic crisis, is there really a need for massive amounts of additional public investment aimed at these sectors? Should not the role of government be restricted to ensuring a general, economy-wide recovery, allowing private investments to flow to the economically most attractive sectors, including the green economy? To put it another way, if the green sector investments are so economically advantageous, why is the private sector not making the necessary investments already? Government intervention, including green fiscal stimulus spending, may serve only to subsidize inefficient investments in green sectors that would not otherwise be profitable.

Public funding and policies during a recession and recovery can help to support innovation and private investment in green sectors, however, which is necessary to counter both the contraction in capital financing caused by a downturn and the long-term shortfalls in environmental research and development.[10]

Since the 1990s private sector R&D expenditures and patent filings have tended to be cyclical, and thus have declined with economic downturns. Private R&D tends to be funded by the retained earnings of firms, which expand during boom periods but contract during recessions. In a credit-constrained economic crisis, such as the current one, it is even more difficult for firms to receive external funding for forward-looking investments such as R&D. Both internal and external funding is instead reoriented towards more short-term, low-risk innovations and investments. For example, a survey of around 500 businesses worldwide indicates that 34 percent expected to spend less on R&D in 2009 while 21 percent forecast an

---

[10] Fritz-Morgenthal, Sebastian, Chris Greenwood, Carola Menzel, Marija Mironjuk and Virginia Sonntag-O'Brien. 2009. *The Global Financial Crisis and Its Impact on Renewable Energy Finance.* Nairobi, UNEP; OECD. 2009. *Green Growth: Overcoming the Crisis and Beyond.* Paris, OECD; OECD. 2009. *Policy Responses to the Economic Crisis: Investing in Innovation for Long-term Growth.* Paris, OECD; REN21. 2009. *Renewables Global Status Report: 2009 Update.* Paris, REN21 Secretariat; UNEP. 2009. *Global Trends in Sustainable Energy Investment 2009.* Nairobi, UNEP.

increase. Corporate reports also show declines or slower growth in R&D expenditure.[11]

The ability of clean energy firms to invest in R&D and other activities out of retained earnings during the current economic crisis is further hampered by the overall decline in investments in this sector. In 2008 global stock market investments in clean energy firms fell 51 percent, to US$11.4 billion, from US$23.4 billion in 2007, and they were largely negligible in the first half of 2009. Asset-financing investment in renewable energy power projects also slowed down in the final three months of 2008 and continued to fall in the first half of 2009. The decline in overall investment in clean energy is attributed to multiple factors arising from the current recession, including the 70 percent decrease in fossil fuel prices, the constraints on credit availability and lending terms, and the reorientation of existing financing to more established and less risky projects.[12]

As discussed previously, the decline in venture capital investments is especially important for the green sector, given that they are an essential source of private equity for emerging technologies and business start-ups.[13] Venture capital investments have been particularly hard hit during the current recession, however. Total US venture capital investments fell 60 percent and first-sequence investments fell 65 percent in the first quarter of 2009 compared to the previous year. Venture capital investment in high-technology sectors also declined sharply in China.[14] Globally, venture capital and private equity investments reached a peak of US$4 billion in the third quarter of 2008, but they have fallen rapidly since then. In the fourth quarter of 2008 they declined to US$2.2 billion and in the first quarter of 2009 to US$1.5 billion.[15]

---

[11] OECD 2009 (*Policy Responses*), 6 (see fn 10).

[12] Fritz-Morgenthal *et al.* 2009 (see fn 10).

[13] Carmody and Ritchie 2007 (see ch. 2, fn 13); Fritz-Morgenthal *et al.* 2009 (see fn 10); Pew Charitable Trusts 2009 (see fn 5); REN21 2008 (see ch. 2, fn 24); REN21 2009 (see fn 10).

[14] OECD 2009 (*Policy Responses*), 7 (see fn 10).

[15] Fritz-Morgenthal *et al.* 2009, 9–10 (see fn 10).

In addition, the crisis has further exacerbated market failures in innovation financing as well as the long-term shortfalls in private R&D expenditures in green sectors. Given the spillover character-istics of most long-term R&D investments, especially in the new technologies required by many clean energy innovations, the private sector has always chronically underfunded such investments. As the OECD has pointed out, in such a situation, governments should share the risk of developing new technologies with the private sector, especially during a credit-constrained recession that limits private sector investments. Since the early 1980s, though, in most econo-mies, public R&D spending in support of clean energy developments has declined.[16]

Private investments in renewable energy face special barri-ers that are specific to these energy sources. For example, invest-ments in wind or solar energy for electricity are prone to variability and intermittency in terms of supply and the inadequacy of current transmission and grid capacity to carry the available supply to where it is demanded.[17] The result is that the levelized cost of the elec-tricity generation of renewable energy is extremely high, especially compared to coal and other fossil fuels, which have capacity factors of close to 90 percent.[18] Investing in new transmission lines and "smart" electricity grids to overcome the additional private costs imposed by intermittency, inadequate transmission, grid capacity

[16] OECD 2009 (*Policy Responses*), 15; OECD 2009 (*Green Growth*), 9 (see fn 10 for both).

[17] Heal, Geoffrey. 2009. *The Economics of Renewable Energy*. Working Paper no. 15081, Cambridge, MA, NBER; Komor, Paul. 2009. *Wind and Solar Electricity: Challenges and Opportunities*. Arlington, VA, Pew Center on Global Climate Change; Toman, Michael, James Griffin and Robert J. Lempert. 2008. *Impacts on US Energy Expenditures and Greenhouse-Gas Emission of Increasing Renewable-Energy Use*. Santa Monica, CA, RAND Corporation.

[18] The levelized cost of electricity is the constant price at which electricity would have been sold for the production facility to break even over its lifetime, assuming that it operates at full capacity. The capacity factor of an electricity-generating plant is the actual power output as a fraction of the amount that would be produced if the plant were to operate at its rated maximum capacity all the time. See Heal 2009 (fn 17) for further discussion of the implications for the incentives for private investment in renewable energy for electricity generation.

and electricity storage is necessary, but it is expensive and risky for private investors. As one study has noted, public investment has a complementary role to play in facilitating this necessary renewable energy supply infrastructure: "Attracting private sector investment in new transmission projects will likely require significant public/government support, and will certainly require better clarification of who pays and how much."[19] During a recession the risks and costs faced by private investors may further prohibit them from investing in large-scale capital projects with long paybacks, such as improved electricity transmission lines, grid capacity and storage.

Carefully targeted public investments, especially in support of R&D and other complementary infrastructure, not only boost shortfalls in private investment during a credit-constrained recession but also have the capability of inducing the technological innovation necessary for lowering carbon dependency in the economy (see box 11.1). "Technology-push policies," however, such as R&D subsidies, public investments and other initiatives, deal mainly with one type of market failure affecting induced innovation in low-carbon technologies: the inability of private investors to appropriate all the knowledge gains generated by R&D. A second market failure stems from the climate change externalities associated with the combustion of fossil fuels and other economic activities that generate GHG emissions. Public investments and expenditures in support of private R&D cannot address this second market failure. Instead, technology-push policies and investments must be supplemented by "direct emissions" policies, such as carbon pricing, to ensure that GHG-generating activities take into account climate change externalities.[20] As discussed in box 11.1, both types of policies – direct emissions and technology-push measures – are necessary to promote induced technological

---

[19] Komor 2009 (see fn 17).

[20] For example, based on a comprehensive review of existing studies, Heal 2009, 8 (see fn 17), calculates that the climate-change-related external costs of generating electricity from renewable sources, such as solar and wind, are as much as US$0.05 per kilowatt-hour less than for fossil fuels.

change by the private sector that reduce carbon dependency. Studies for reducing GHG emissions in the United States show that combining the two policies substantially lowers the costs of meeting targets compared to relying purely on a technology-push approach, such as an R&D subsidy for low-carbon energy options.

Box 11.1 Induced technological change and public policy for reducing carbon dependency

A report by Larry Goulder for the Pew Center on Global Climate Change highlights the role of public investment and policies for promoting induced technological change so as to reduce carbon dependency. The report emphasizes how induced technological innovation can be efficiently promoted through combining "direct emission policies," such as a cap-and-trade system, with "technology-push policies," such as research and development subsidies for encouraging private sector investment. As the table below indicates, other direct emissions and technology-push policies could be combined in order to generate the maximum amount of induced technological innovation in the private sector.

Public policies for reducing carbon dependency

Direct emissions policies	Technology-push policies
Carbon taxes	Subsidies to R&D in low-carbon technologies
Carbon quotas	Public sector R&D in low-carbon technologies
Cap-and-trade systems for GHG emissions	Government-financed technology competitions (with awards)
Subsidies to GHG emission abatement	Strengthened patent rules

Source: Adapted from Goulder, Lawrence. 2004. *Induced Technological Change and Climate Policy.* Arlington, VA, Pew Center on Global Climate Change, box 1.

From his review of a number of economic studies and empirical evidence of how policies and induced technological innovation can affect the costs of reducing carbon dependency, Goulder finds that cost reductions stem both from the boost to private sector R&D and from the learning-by-doing from firms gaining familiarity with new low-carbon technologies, products and processes. Both direct emissions and technology-push policies induce additional technological change by supporting private R&D and learning-by-doing.

For example, direct emissions policies, such as carbon taxes and cap-and-trade systems, would raise the prices of fossil fuels and of energy sources derived from them, such as electricity. Firms that utilize these fuels might find it worthwhile to invest more in R&D aimed at developing alternative production processes that reduce fossil fuel consumption, since the discovery of such processes could now yield significant cost savings. Technology-push policies, such as subsidy programs, can also induce technological change, by stimulating additional R&D. Goulder finds evidence that such R&D has led to large cost reductions in many important energy-related areas. For example, he cites a National Research Council study of thirty-nine R&D programs in energy efficiency and clean energy that found that these programs, taken together, yielded an annual rate of return of over 100 percent. The increased utilization of new products, processes and technologies in turn stimulates learning-by-doing. The result is further cost reductions in adopting low-carbon innovations. A typical estimate is that, for relatively new technologies, costs fall by 20 percent for every doubling of cumulative experience.

Based on these findings, Goulder argues that there is a strong rationale for employing both direct emissions and technology-push policies simultaneously, even when the associated cost reductions from induced technological change are uncertain. The rationale stems from two market failures in the private adoption of low-carbon technologies. First, private investment in R&D tends to be sub-optimal, as a result of the inability of private investors to appropriate all the returns to R&D. Some of the knowledge stemming from R&D spills over and benefits firms other than the investing firm. As a result, in the absence of public intervention, investments in R&D tend to fall short of the amount that would maximize social net benefits. This provides a rationale for technology-push policies, including subsidies to R&D. Second, the current economic reliance on fossil fuels generally exceeds socially efficient levels, because the market prices of these fuels fail to capture climate-related externalities. Hence the market prices are well below the full social cost – the sum of the private cost and the external cost. This promotes a dependence on fossil fuels that is excessive in terms of economic efficiency and provides a compelling rationale for direct emissions policies – such as carbon taxes or cap-and-trade systems – that can bring the prices of fossil fuels more in line with their social cost. Goulder concludes that both types of policies – direct emissions and technology-push policies – are necessary to promote induced technological change to reduce carbon dependency. Studies for reducing greenhouse gas emissions in the United States show that combining the two policies substantially lowers the costs of meeting targets compared to relying just on a technology-push approach, such as an R&D subsidy for low-carbon energy options.

Source: Goulder, Lawrence. 2004. *Induced Technological Change and Climate Policy.* Arlington, VA, Pew Center on Global Climate Change.

There is often concern that imposing more stringent environmental policies during a recession, especially those that curb economy-wide GHG emissions and other pollutants, may deter rather than boost private investments in green technologies. For instance, during the current recession, firms might want to invest in new technologies to lower carbon emissions and other pollutants but might not be able to raise the funds due to the reduced credit availability. In the presence of such credit constraints, it might seem desirable to relax environmental policies so that firms have larger retained earnings to meet additional green investments. As discussed in box 11.2, however, this argument applies only if the recession is mild. With a severe recession and credit-constrained firms, a stricter environmental policy is justified. If the recession is severe because of a large fall in economy-wide demand, there is little cash to be gained for firms from relaxing environmental policy, while society still suffers the damage from pollution. Moreover, imposing stronger environmental policy during a recession, together with the lower opportunity costs of investments, should boost green technology adoption. The resulting induced technological change should continue to lower abatement costs after the recession is ended. Hence, environmental policy can be even more stringent after the recession.

Box 11.2 Environmental policy and green technology investments during a recession

It is a common assumption that an economic recession should reduce the cost of environmental policy, since pollution-intensive production is demanded less in a recession. Hence, a tightening of environmental policy is desirable when the economy is in a recession caused by a fall in economy-wide (or aggregate) demand. Firms will in turn invest more in green technologies, as they reduce the costs to firms of the more stringent policy.

For example, the first figure (below) compares marginal abatement cost (MAC), which increases with the stringency of environmental policy, with the marginal environmental damage (MD), which increases with the level of pollution and thus declines with the stringency of environmental policy. The costs and benefits are measured at the aggregate (economy-wide) level. Environmental policy is optimal at the level of pollution (or stringency) at which marginal costs and benefits are equal (MAC = MD), which can be denoted by an equilibrium pollution "price" τ.

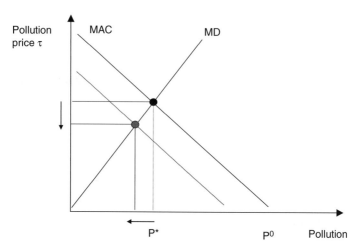

Implications of a recession – optimal policy (flow pollution)

With a fall in aggregated demand in the economy, firms choose to produce and pollute less at a given price τ. In addition, any marginal increase in the flow of pollution from a given level will result in a smaller increase in profits than without a recession, since economy-wide demand is lower. This implies that the MAC curve shifts to the left in the first figure. Lower demand reduces the productivity of inputs, so that polluting inputs are less productive, and the cost of reducing pollution is lower. The optimal response to a recession is therefore a reduction in pollution and lower prices for polluting inputs. In such a recession scenario, environmental policy should be stricter, to take advantage of the lower opportunity costs to firms of reducing pollution.

The timing of the policy might matter, however, particularly if the pollutant accumulates in the environment and then causes damage. Greenhouse gases, for example, would typify such stock pollutants. If the costs of environmental policy are incurred mainly at the time of implementation, while the benefits are reaped mainly at later dates, because of lags and the cumulative nature of stock pollutants, a recession affects marginal costs and benefits asymmetrically. Policy is optimal if the marginal abatement costs equal the net present

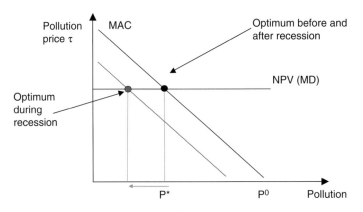

Temporary recession (stock pollution)

value of the damages caused by today's pollution. If the recession is temporary, marginal abatement costs fall, as explained in the figure above, but the NPV of a reduction in stock pollution hardly changes. The gains from abatement are reaped when the economy is "back to normal." As shown in the second figure (above), the marginal damages to which marginal abatement costs should be equated become less dependent on the current flow of pollution and the MD curve becomes flatter, as compared to the case of flow pollutants. Hence, for stock pollutants, the case for implementing stricter environmental policy becomes even more compelling.

The 2008/9 recession was not caused by falling aggregate demand, however, but by a financial crisis and a contraction of credit. Transaction costs in financial markets are now larger and the real rate of return to investments much lower than before the recession. The lower real return in private investment markets has two effects. First, total investment falls, since the average portfolio return declines. Second, investment should shift from projects that are heavily dependent on intermediation in financial markets, such as private equity and stock markets, to other investments that are less so. The first effect lowers aggregate demand, which impacts the economy as described previously. The second effect works in favor of green technology investments, however. Whereas the lowering of demand due to the recession is only temporary, the investment switching effect may not be.

As shown in the final figure (below), the shift in investment influences the MD curve. The lower return to alternative financial investments implies a lower discount rate, so the NPV of marginal damages is higher. The MD curve shifts up and optimal environment policy is more stringent (see the figure below). Note that this is a structural change, which persists after the recession. During the recession real returns to non-environmental investments, and thus the opportunity cost of environmental policy, fall. After the recession, aggregate demand should return to normal, thereby shifting the MAC curve back to its original position. Unless irresponsible behavior in financial markets comes back equally quickly, however, real returns remain lower and the MD remains at its higher position. This justifies a permanently more stringent environmental policy.

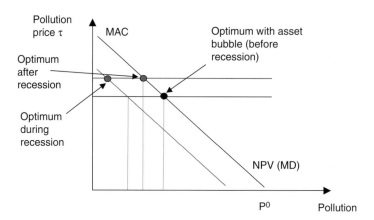

Recession with structural elements

So far, we have discussed environmental policy in terms of pollution taxes and standards. The Global Green New Deal actions discussed in this book are usually framed in terms of investments in green technologies, however – energy-saving technologies and other investments that make pollution reductions easier. Changes in environmental policy will induce innovation and investment in green technologies (see box 11.1). The analysis can be extended to take into account this induced green investment response. More stringent environmental policy, together with lower opportunity costs for investments, implies a boost to green investment. Again this introduces a structural, or permanent, effect. By the time the recession is over, the MAC curve shifts back as described above, but there is now a shift in the opposite direction as well. Marginal abatement costs are lower because of increased investments in green technologies. Hence, even after the recession, environmental policy can be more stringent.

Finally, in a credit-constrained recession, there is likely to be an interaction between problems in the financial markets and the demand for funds for green technology investments. Firms might want to invest in green technologies, for the reasons just stated, but might not be able to raise the funds in the capital market, because the financial crisis has reduced credit availability. In the presence of credit constraints, it might be desirable to loosen environmental policy in order to stimulate green investments. Investment requires cash when credit markets fail. The argument for Global Green New Deal policies is then turned on its head. Firms need extra breathing space, in the form of lower environmental standards, to get around the financial consequences of the recession.

Nonetheless, this counter-argument works only if the credit constraint is binding and the recession is relatively mild. In contrast, if the recession is severe because of a large fall in demand, there is little cash to be gained for firms from relaxing environmental policy, while society still suffers the damage from pollution. The reason is similar to the opportunity cost argument given above: With low aggregate demand, the value of an additional unit of pollution is low. Hence, with a severe recession and credit-constrained firms, more stringent environmental policy is, again, the appropriate reaction.

To summarize, during a demand-induced recession it is optimal to make environmental policy more stringent and invest more in green technology. If firms are credit-constrained, however, environmental policy might need to be less stringent, but only if the recession is mild. With a severe recession, more stringent environmental policy is still optimal.

Note: This box is based on material written by Sjak Smulders of Tilburg University: Smulders, Sjak. 2009. "The Green New Deal; a theory-based answer to a practical question." Centre for Economic Research, Tilburg University, Netherlands. I am grateful to Sjak Smulders for writing this material and allowing me to use it in this book.

Finally, like all fiscal stimulus measures, public investments and expenditures during a recession are likely to have a multiplier effect throughout the economy.[21] As discussed in box 11.3, the IMF maintains that, during the current credit-constrained global economic crisis, an export-led recovery strategy is not appropriate, since the fall in aggregate demand is global and not limited to a specific country or region. The efficacy of expansionary monetary policy through lowering central bank lending rates is limited, as these rates are already at zero or close to it in most major economies. In such circumstances, the IMF has called for a sizable, lasting and coordinated fiscal response at the global level to boost aggregate demand.[22] The IMF estimates that, for such a fiscal stimulus, every dollar spent on government investment can increase GDP by about US$3, while every dollar of targeted transfers can increase GDP by about US$1. A simultaneous and coordinated fiscal stimulus across economies globally would raise these multipliers by a factor of about 1.5.[23]

---

[21] As defined by the IMF, the term "fiscal multiplier," or the "multiplier effect" of a fiscal stimulus measure, "describes the effects of changes in fiscal instruments on real GDP. Typically, it is defined as the ratio of the change in GDP to the change in the size of the fiscal instrument or the change in the fiscal balance." See Freedman, Charles, Michael Kumhof, Douglas Laxton and Jaewoo Lee. 2009. *The Case for Global Fiscal Stimulus.* Staff Position Note no. SPN/09/03. Washington, DC, IMF, 5.

[22] Spilimbergo, Antonio, Steve Symansky, Olivier Blanchard and Carlo Cottarelli. 2008. *Fiscal Policy for the Crisis.* Staff Position Note no. SPN/08/01. Washington, DC, IMF.

[23] Freedman *et al.* 2009 (see fn 21).

Box 11.3 Multiplier effects of green stimulus investments in the current recession

The Global Green New Deal advocates that the Group of Twenty major economies should spend, over the next several years, at least 1 percent of their GDP on reducing carbon dependency, including removing subsidies and other perverse incentives and adopting complementary carbon pricing policies. In addition, the G20 economies should coordinate the timing and implementation of these investments globally. The total amount spent would amount to about one-quarter of the nearly US$3 trillion in G20 stimulus investments to date.

Evidence from the International Monetary Fund suggests that such a coordinated, global green fiscal stimulus by G20 economies would have an important multiplier effect on these G20 economies, which together account for almost 80 percent of the world's population and 90 percent of global gross domestic product.

Because the fall in global aggregate demand in the current recession was precipitated by a large decrease in real and financial wealth and a prolonged contraction in credit availability worldwide, conventional macroeconomic policies are less effective in reviving demand. First, an export-led recovery strategy is not appropriate, since the fall in aggregate demand is global and not limited to a specific country or region. Second, the scope for expansionary monetary policy in the shape of lowering central bank lending rates is limited, as these rates are already at zero or close to it in most major economies. In such circumstances, the IMF has called for a sizable, lasting and coordinated fiscal response at the global level to boost aggregate demand.

Estimations by the IMF suggest that, in an ideal scenario in which fiscal stimulus is global and accompanied by monetary expansion and government support for ailing financial sectors, every dollar spent on government investment can increase GDP by about US$3, while every dollar of targeted transfers can increase GDP by about US$1.

Multiplier effects of green stimulus by the G20[a]

| | Total stimulus (US$ billion) | Unilateral multiplier effect | | | | Coordinated multiplier effect | | | |
| | | 1.00 | | 3.00 | | 1.50 | | 4.50 | |
		US$ billion	% of GDP	US$ billion	% of GDP	US$ billion	% of GDP	US$ billion	% of GDP
Current GS[b]	454.7	454.7	0.7	1,364.1	2.2	682.1	1.1	2,046.2	3.2
GGND GS[c]	631.5	631.5	1.0	1,894.4	3.0	947.2	1.5	2,841.6	4.5

Notes: [a] Estimates of multiplier effects are from Freedman, Charles, Michael Kumhof, Douglas Laxton and Jaewoo Lee. 2009. *The Case for Global Fiscal Stimulus.* Staff Position Note no. SPN/09/03. Washington, DC, IMF. The G20 is as defined in box 1.1.

[b] Current green stimulus (GS) for the G20, as estimated in box 1.1.

[c] Global Green New Deal GS, estimated as 1 percent of total G20 GDP in box 1.1.

In addition, the IMF estimates that, due to international spillovers of demand, simultaneous and coordinated fiscal stimulus across economies globally can raise these multipliers by a factor of about 1.5.

As outlined in part II of this book, the various green fiscal measures put forward as part of the Global Green New Deal, especially to reduce carbon dependency in the G20 economies, involve a combination of public investment and targeted transfers. The table below utilizes the IMF's estimates of fiscal stimulus multipliers to calculate the likely GDP impacts of G20 green stimulus measures. Multiplier effects are estimated for both the current green stimulus investments of the G20, which are depicted in box 1.1, and the 1 percent of GDP recommended green stimulus from the GGND. In addition, both unilateral and coordinated green fiscal stimulus multipliers on GDP are estimated.

The table indicates that the existing green stimulus packages already adopted by G20 governments (see box 1.1) could produce multiplier effects in their economies from around US$450 billion to nearly US$1.4 trillion. The boost to G20 GDP could range from 0.7 percent to 2.2 percent. Coordination of these stimulus packages could increase the multiplier effects between US$682 billion and US$2.0 trillion – equivalent to a 1.1 percent to 3.2 percent increase in GDP.

If all the G20 economies adopted the GGND recommendation of spending over the next several years at least 1 percent of their GDP on the national actions proposed for reducing carbon dependency, then the GDP multiplier effect would be anything from US$630 billion to nearly US$1.9 billion – a 1.0 percent to 3.0 percent boost to GDP. A coordinated GGND green stimulus would generate a multiplier effect of almost US$950 billion to US$2.8 trillion, which would translate into an increase of between 1.5 percent and 4.5 percent in the total GDP of the G20 economies.

Sources: Freedman, Charles, Michael Kumhof, Douglas Laxton and Jaewoo Lee. 2009. *The Case for Global Fiscal Stimulus.* Staff Position Note no. SPN/09/03. Washington, DC, IMF; Spilimbergo, Antonio, Steve Symansky, Olivier Blanchard and Carlo Cottarelli. 2008. *Fiscal Policy for the Crisis.* Staff Position Note no. SPN/08/01. Washington, DC, IMF.

As outlined in part II, the various green fiscal measures put forward as part of the Global Green New Deal, especially to reduce carbon dependency in G20 economies, involve a combination of public investment and targeted transfers. Box 11.3 applies the IMF's estimated fiscal multipliers to calculate the likely GDP impacts of G20 green stimulus measures. Multiplier effects are estimated for both the current green stimulus investments of the G20, which are depicted in box 1.1, and the 1 percent of GDP recommended green stimulus from the GGND. In addition, both unilateral and coordinated green fiscal stimulus multipliers on GDP are estimated. Current G20 green stimulus measures are largely unilateral, and could have total multiplier effects of around US$450 billion to nearly US$1.4 trillion. The boost to G20 GDP could range from 0.7 percent to 2.2 percent. In comparison, if the G20 countries adopted the GGND recommendation of spending at least 1 percent of their GDP on reducing carbon dependency, and also coordinated the timing and implementation of these investments, the green stimulus would generate a multiplier effect of almost US$950 billion to US$2.8 trillion. The economy-wide benefit would translate into an increase of 1.5 percent to 4.5 percent in the total GDP of the G20 economies.

Of course, the IMF estimates of the fiscal multiplier effects assume an ideal scenario, in which fiscal stimulus is global and accompanied by monetary expansion and government support for ailing financial sectors.[24] In addition, as discussed above, if there is considerable delay in the actual disbursement and implementation of green stimulus measures, then the effects on employment and economic gains will also take longer to materialize. Any multiplier effects of the green stimulus would therefore also be postponed as a result.

In sum, public investments in the green economic sectors advocated by the GGND appear to have the potential to create employment and other economic gains, even compared to conventional

[24] Freedman et al. 2009 (see fn 21).

fiscal spending. Delays in implementing green stimulus measures may postpone these gains during an economic recovery, however. Public funding and policies during a recession and recovery can also help to support innovation and private investment in green sectors, which is necessary to counter both the likely contraction caused by a downturn and the long-term shortfalls in environmental research and development. To ensure the full benefits of induced technological change, however, through private sector R&D and learning-by-doing with green technologies, "technology-push policies," such as R&D subsidies, public investments and other initiatives, must be supplemented by "direct emissions" policies, such as carbon pricing, to ensure that GHG-generating activities take into account climate change externalities.

During a recession the risks and costs faced by private investors may become even more prohibitive for investing in large-scale capital projects with long payback times, such as improved electricity transmission lines, grid capacity and storage, which need significant public policy support. During a severe, credit-constrained recession, imposing more stringent environmental policy, together with the lower opportunity costs of investments, should boost green technology adoption. The resulting induced technological change should continue to lower abatement costs after the recession is ended. Finally, there is evidence that the various green fiscal measures put forward as part of the Global Green New Deal, especially to reduce carbon dependency in G20 economies, involve a combination of public investment and targeted transfers, which should lead to considerable economy-wide multiplier effects and help economic recovery.

DEBT, GLOBAL IMBALANCES AND A GREEN RECOVERY

As summarized in box 11.4, an IMF study of global fiscal policies warns that the positive multiplier effects of any short-term fiscal stimulus in support of an economic recovery will be counterproductive if they lead to unstably large fiscal deficits, long-run real interest rate rises and inflation. The IMF concludes that such concerns about the long-term economic consequences of the lack of fiscal discipline arising from global stimulus policies should be addressed through appropriate and credible medium-term fiscal frameworks, such as increased efforts to contain the ratio of public debt to GDP and the introduction of fiscal rules that establish a long-run target for the ratio of any deficits to GDP. The IMF is more sanguine about the ability of the advanced economies of the G20 to maintain credible fiscal discipline, however, whereas emerging market and low-income economies may be more restricted in their ability to engage in fiscal stimulus over the short term.

Box 11.4 Fiscal discipline, debt and long-term crowding out

A study of global fiscal policies by the IMF warns that the positive multiplier effects of any short-term fiscal stimulus in support of an economic recovery will be counterproductive if they lead to unstably large fiscal deficits: "A key prerequisite for a successful fiscal stimulus is that it does not undermine the medium-term sustainability of fiscal policy. But there is a significant risk that the large fiscal deficits envisaged at the current juncture might be difficult to reduce over time and could instead result in permanently lower world saving that causes higher real interest rates and therefore lowers investment and productive capacity."[25]

The IMF study first reviews the empirical evidence linking fiscal deficits and debt to real interest rates, and finds that:

a persistent increase in debt equal to 1 percent of GDP increases long-term real interest rates by between one and six basis points (a basis point is one-hundredth of a percentage point);

a persistent increase in fiscal deficit equal to 1 percent of GDP increases long-term real interest rates by between ten and sixty basis points;

although higher debt or deficits are not correlated with higher inflation in advanced economies, such correlation does exist for emerging market economies with high inflation rates; and

---

[25] Freedman *et al.* 2009, 10 (see fn 21).

the effects of deficits on interest rates are higher in economies with low financial depth, probably reflecting high risk premia or a narrow liquidity base.

From its own fiscal stimulus policy simulations, the IMF not only concurs with the above study findings but also draws the conclusion that a credible promise of fiscal discipline is critical even for the short-run effectiveness of the stimulus, and without it the stimulus might in the most extreme case become self-defeating, and could cause long-run crowding out of private investment. For example, the simulations show that, when all countries increase the ratio of their debt to GDP by ten percentage points, long-term world real interest rates increase by thirty-nine basis points, with GDP permanently contracting by 1.3 percent worldwide.

The IMF concludes that such concerns over the long-term economic consequences of the lack of fiscal discipline arising from global stimulus policies should be addressed through appropriate and credible medium-term fiscal frameworks, such as increased efforts to contain the ratio of public debt to GDP and the introduction of fiscal rules that establish a long-run target for the ratio of any deficits to GDP. The IMF is more sanguine about the capability of advanced G20 economies to maintain credible fiscal discipline, however, whereas emerging market and low-income economies may be more restricted in their ability to engage in fiscal stimulus in the short term.

Source: Freedman, Charles, Michael Kumhof, Douglas Laxton and Jaewoo Lee. 2009. *The Case for Global Fiscal Stimulus.* Staff Position Note no. SPN/09/03. Washington, DC, IMF.

Nevertheless, the unease about the economic impacts of the lack of fiscal discipline is warranted, given IMF projections that fiscal balances in G20 economies will be severely affected by the crisis in the short run.[26] For G20 advanced economies, fiscal

---

[26] IMF. 2009. *The State of Public Finances: Outlook and Medium-term Policies after the 2008 Crisis.* Washington, DC, IMF.

balances in relation to GDP were projected to worsen, on average, by six percentage points in 2009 relative to 2007, thus reaching some 8 percent of GDP in 2009. As a result, the ratio of public debt to GDP of G20 advanced economies was expected to rise by 14.5 percentage points over 2008/9 – the most pronounced upturn in the last few decades. Although the fiscal balances of G20 emerging market economies are projected to deteriorate less, they were nevertheless forecast to see a turnaround from a modest fiscal surplus equivalent to 0.2 percent of GDP in 2007 to a deficit of 3.2 percent of GDP in 2009. The debt-to-GDP ratio in G20 emerging market economies was projected to rise by almost two percentage points over 2008/9. In the medium term, fiscal balances are expected to improve, but, unless tightening measures are introduced later, fiscal balances for advanced economies would remain weaker than in 2007. As a result, the ratio of debt to GDP for advanced economies in 2014 is projected to be almost twenty-five percentage points above the 2007 level. For emerging market economies, debt ratios in 2010 will remain around their 2007 levels, and the declining trend will not resume until 2011.

The short- and medium-term projections for rises in the ratio of public debt to GDP in G20 advanced economies are especially alarming. The IMF simulations discussed in box 11.4 show that, when all countries increase the ratio of their debt to GDP by ten percentage points, long-term world real interest rates increase by thirty-nine basis points, with GDP permanently contracting by 1.3 percent worldwide. Again, this suggests that G20 economies need to develop medium-term fiscal frameworks to rein in fiscal deficits and public debt rather than engaging in prolonged expansionary fiscal policy.

Such a warning about the need for fiscal discipline is relevant to the green fiscal stimulus actions proposed in the Global Green New Deal strategy. For example, as illustrated in box 11.3, the GGND recommendation that the G20 governments spend at least 1 percent of their GDP on additional measures to reduce carbon dependency would raise current green fiscal stimulus amounts from around US\$455 billion to US\$632 billion – an increase of nearly 40 percent.

There are several reasons why such a recommended rise in green fiscal stimulus is unlikely to lead to a significant increase in fiscal deficits and public debt in the medium term, however.

First, although an increase in green fiscal stimulus amounts by G20 governments of around US\$177 billion appears substantial, this amount is a relatively small addition (6.6 percent) to the total fiscal stimulus of around US\$2.7 trillion that the G20 has already made (see box 1.1). Thus the additional debt burden of the 1 percent of GDP recommendation of the GGND is not likely to be substantial.

In addition, some G20 economies do have scope for additional fiscal expansion. For example, the ratio of public debt to GDP is expected to fall from 2007 to 2010 for Argentina, Australia, Brazil, Canada, Indonesia, Russia, Saudi Arabia and South Africa. Over the medium term, from 2010 to 2014, the debt-to-GDP ratio will continue to fall for these economies as well as for several others, such as China, India, Mexico, South Korea and Turkey.[27] As indicated in box 1.1, many of these G20 economies have yet to commit to any sizable green fiscal stimulus measures.

Moreover, as discussed in part II, the GGND strategy is not based solely on increased green fiscal stimulus spending. It is also recommended that the G20 countries instigate complementary pricing and regulatory reforms for reducing carbon dependency, including removing perverse subsidies and other distortions in energy, transport and similar markets. One quick way in which this could be achieved is through tackling fossil fuel subsidies. As noted in chapter 2, globally around US\$300 billion annually, or 0.7 percent of world GDP, is spent on fossil fuel subsidies. Over two-thirds of these subsidies occur in G20 economies, which could coordinate their phased removal.[28] Cancelling these subsidies could reduce GHG

[27] IMF 2009, tab. 6 (see fn 26).
[28] UNEP 2008 (see ch. 2, fn 21).

emissions globally by 6 percent and add 0.1 percent to world GDP. The financial savings could be redirected to fund the additional public investments in clean and renewable energy R&D and energy conservation, further boosting economies and employment opportunities. The US$200 billion in annual savings from the removal of fossil fuel subsidies in G20 economies would, in fact, on its own cover the additional US$177 billion in green fiscal stimulus advocated for these economies by the GGND.

The GGND also calls for G20 economies to adopt complementary carbon pricing policies, either in the form of taxes or cap-and-trade systems, so as to reduce carbon dependency. The previous section highlighted how such "direct emission" policies are critical for spurring private investment and induced technological change in clean energy sectors. In addition, both cap-and-trade and carbon tax policies will generate sizable revenues, which could, again, be used for financing any increases in green fiscal stimulus in the short term. For example, it was noted in chapter 2 that, for the United States, the implementation of a comprehensive cap-and-trade system for greenhouse gas emissions could eventually pay for low-carbon investment programs by generating US$75 billion a year in revenues from permit sales. Similarly, China could not only accelerate its transition to a low-carbon economy but also pay for further public investments in green sectors through the revenues earned from innovative economic policies and instruments, including carbon and other emission taxes.

The problem of global imbalances was a significant factor underlying the recent financial crisis and recession, and the persistence of such imbalances continues to add uncertainty and risk to the future stability of the world economy.[29] A major issue, therefore,

---

[29] See, for example, Caballero, Ricardo J., and Arvind Krishnamurthy. 2009. "Global imbalances and financial fragility." *American Economic Review* 99 (2): 584–8; Feldstein, Martin S. 2008. "Resolving the global imbalance: the dollar and the US saving rate." *Journal of Economic Perspectives* 22 (3): 113–25; Gros, Daniel. 2009. *Global Imbalances and the Accumulation of Risk*. Policy Brief no. 189. Brussels, Centre for European Policy Studies; Lane, Phillip R. "Forum: global imbalances and global governance." *Intereconomics* 44

is whether or not the proposed GGND strategy will exacerbate or ameliorate the ongoing structural problem of global imbalances.[30]

Although the cause of the current economic recession is widely attributed to regulatory failure in the mortgage and financial market, a major contributing factor was the structural imbalances in the world economy. While the United States has for some time been running the world's largest current account trade deficits, China, Japan, other emerging market economies, especially in Asia, and to some extent oil exporters have been generating trade surpluses. Similar structural imbalances were occurring within major regional economies, such as the European Union, where the large current account surpluses were offset by deficits in Ireland, Greece, Portugal, Spain and the United Kingdom. The result of such global imbalances was that those economies with chronic trade deficits were receiving large and sustained capital inflows from surplus economies seeking safer assets as investments.

Even before the crisis there was widespread concern about the sustainability of these structural global imbalances in the world economy.[31] Some economists were sanguine that such imbalances were part of the "new economy," however, in which foreign saving

(2): 77–81; Park, Donghyun, and Kwanho Shin. 2009. *Saving, Investment, and Current Account Surplus in Developing Asia.* Economics Working Paper no. 158. Manila, ADB; Prasad, Eswar S. 2009. "Rebalancing growth in Asia." Unpublished manuscript. Cornell University, Ithaca, NY; and Rodrik, Dani. 2009. "Growth after the crisis." Unpublished manuscript. John F. Kennedy School of Government, Harvard University, Cambridge, MA.

[30] As defined by the IMF. 2009. *World Economic Outlook: Crisis and Recovery.* Washington, DC, IMF, 34. "The phrase 'global imbalances' refers to the pattern of current account deficits and surpluses that built up in the global economy starting in the late 1990s, with the United States and some other countries developing large deficits (United Kingdom; southern Europe, including Greece, Italy, Portugal, and Spain; central and eastern Europe), and others large surpluses (notably, China, Japan, other east Asian economies, Germany, and oil exporters)."

[31] See, for example, Cline, William R. 2005. *The United States as a Debtor Nation.* Washington, DC, PIIE; Eichengreen, Barry. 2006. *The Blind Men and the Elephant.* Brookings Issues in Economic Policy no. 1; Feldstein 2008 (see fn 29); and Geitner, Timothy F. 2006. "Policy implications of global imbalances." Remarks at the "Global Financial Imbalances" conference. Chatham House, London, January 23.

would continue indefinitely to finance current account deficits in the United States and elsewhere with large capital inflows.[32] It has emerged subsequently, though, that the problem of global imbalances helped spur the real estate "bubble" and risky speculation in securitized debt in the financial sector of the United States, which precipitated the worldwide crisis of 2008/9. As overseas economies continued to invest their dollar reserves in the United States, the resulting excess demand for short-term, safe and liquid assets led to the securitization of US mortgages and other high-risk assets that obscured the inherent risk.[33] Because of the scale of the structural imbalance, and thus the amount of capital inflows into the United States, the eventual "bubble burst" in the domestic real estate market caused a massive global financial contraction.[34]

[32] See, for example, Cooper, Richard N. 2007. "Living with global imbalances." *Brookings Papers on Economic Activity* 2: 91–107. It is clear, however, that such confidence in the ability of structural imbalances to be sustained indefinitely depended on the quality of the financial assets in the United States and other debtor nations. For example, Cooper 2007, 107, argues: "The United States has a vibrant, innovative economy... It has an especially innovative financial sector, which continually introduces new products to cater to diverse portfolio tastes. The United States has a comparative advantage in a globalized market, in producing marketable securities and exchanging low-risk debt for higher-risk equity. It is not surprising that savers around the world want to put a growing portion of their savings into the US economy. The US current account deficit and the corresponding surpluses elsewhere, although conventionally described as imbalances, do not necessarily signal economic disequilibria in a globalized world economy, and they may well remain large for years to come." Unfortunately, as the financial crisis of 2008/9 attests, Cooper's faith in the ability of the US financial sector to generate "marketable securities" and in "exchanging low-risk debt for higher-risk equity" was sadly misplaced.

[33] See, for example, Caballero and Krishnamurthy 2009; Gros 2009; and Lane 2009 (all fn 29).

[34] For example, Gros 2009, 2 (see fn 29), notes: "Over the period 2000–07, the cumulated US current account deficit amounted to almost $5 thousand billion and the household debt increased by almost $7 thousand billion, of which approximately $5 trillion was in the form of mortgages. Meanwhile the foreign exchange reserves of emerging markets increased by about $4 trillion (of which the Chinese central bank accounted for about a third). The financial system thus had to transform trillions of dollars of US household mortgages (issued by private banks) into the type of assets in excess demand from those investors (foreign and domestic) who had been crowded out of the government debt market due to the reserve accumulation by EME [emerging market economy] central banks. In doing so it took an enormous macro risk."

A major concern therefore is that, if the economic recovery from the current worldwide recession does not address the problem of the global imbalances, they will continue to pose a threat to the future stability of the world economy. Although a full discussion of possible solutions to the global imbalances is beyond the scope of this book, the issue as to whether or not the Global Green New Deal strategy will help alleviate these imbalances is pertinent.

The IMF predicts that global imbalances are expected to stabilize over the medium term, with the total of all current account imbalances remaining equivalent to 4 percent of world GDP from 2009 to 2014.[35] One alarming trend during the current economic crisis, however, is the accumulation of foreign exchange reserves by emerging market and other developing economies. For example, reserves in China have risen from US$300 billion in 2003 to US$2 trillion currently. Brazil, India, Russia and South Korea each have more than US$200 billion in reserves. From 1999 to 2007 eight economies – Chile, China, Hong Kong, Israel, Malaysia, the Philippines, Singapore and Taiwan – had annual current account surpluses that were equivalent to 2 percent or more of their GDP.[36] From 2007 to 2008, with the rise in global fossil fuel prices, oil-exporting countries were also amassing huge surpluses on their current accounts, and these are also expected to become even larger after the crisis.[37] Thus, the glut in world savings has not abated as a result of the current crisis.

As a result of the recession, the US current account deficit declined from its peak of 6 percent of GDP in 2006 to about 3.5 percent of GDP in 2009. Current account deficits are also contracting in other economies, such as the United Kingdom and other European countries.[38] For the foreseeable future, however, the United States

---

[35] IMF 2009, 38 (see fn 30).
[36] Cline, William R. 2009. "The global financial crisis and development strategy for emerging market economies." Remarks presented to the Annual Bank Conference on Development Economics. Seoul, June 23.
[37] IMF 2009, 38 (see fn 30).
[38] IMF 2009, 36 (see fn 30).

and other debtor economies are still expected to need substantial foreign capital inflows to finance chronic current account deficits, especially if fossil fuel prices increase as a result of the world economic recovery. To avoid the dangers posed by any future global imbalances, it is suggested that the United States will need to hold its current account deficits to the current range of 3 percent to 4 percent of GDP, instead of the much higher level of 6 percent, reached in 2006 before the recession.[39]

The GGND strategy of reducing carbon dependency and improving energy security may therefore help both to control the large current account deficits incurred by major oil-importing economies, such as the United States, and to reduce the trade surpluses of fossil-fuel-exporting economies. For example, the US current account deficit declined from its peak of US$788 billion in 2006 to US$673 billion in 2008, and then fell further to around US$400 billion in 2009, with a similar outcome projected for 2010.[40] Despite the recession and the fall in oil and commodity prices, however, over the same period net fossil fuel imports by the United States rose, from US$294 billion in 2006 to US$410 billion in 2008.[41] When the world economy recovers, it is generally predicted that short-term demand pressures may again raise fossil fuel prices, especially for petroleum.[42] As a result, for the United States, net fuel imports are likely to rise further, putting even greater pressure on the chronic current account deficit. Similarly, for fossil fuel exporters, current account balances peaked at US$587 billion in 2008 but they are estimated to have been in deficit by US$23 billion in 2009. By 2010, however, rising fossil fuel prices and demand will push these balances back up to US$107 billion, and then more than double to US$239 billion in 2014.[43] To the extent that the measures proposed in the GGND

---

[39] Cline 2005 (see fn 31); Cline 2009 (see fn 36).

[40] IMF 2009, tab. A10 (see fn 30).

[41] Energy Information Administration [EIA]. 2009. *Annual Energy Review 2008.* Washington, DC, EIA, tab. 3.9.

[42] Adams, F. Gerard. 2009. "Will economic recovery drive up world oil prices?" *World Economics* 10 (2): 1–25.

[43] IMF 2009, tab. A10 (see fn 30).

can help to reduce both the volume of fossil fuel imports into deficit economies, such as the United States, and help stem the rise in world prices, then it may help alleviate global imbalances by curbing current account deficits and surpluses in oil-exporting economies.

The role of the GGND in reducing the persistent trade surpluses in Asian and other emerging market economies is more complex. There is general agreement that a necessary step will be a rebalancing of the pattern of economic growth in these economies, in order to absorb more of their savings domestically.[44] Most policy prescriptions advocate moderating the excessive reliance on exports and export-promoting investments, and instead expanding imports of capital goods for key sectors with future growth potential. Such an approach may actually be helped by key elements in the GGND strategy.

Although a study by the Asian Development Bank finds stronger evidence of over-saving rather than overinvestment in Asia, it also notes that the investment climate in many economies of the region was not conducive to obtaining the full investment potential from the private sector.[45] For many of these economies, there is considerable scope for shifting their output structure away from labor-intensive goods to skill-, capital- and technology-intensive production. Moreover, the financial and policy climate and complementary public infrastructure that would otherwise encourage this realignment are often lacking.

These objectives are consistent with the need to promote clean energy investments in Asian and other emerging economies under the GGND. In chapter 4, it was noted that, for all Asian economies to reach a target of 20 percent of total supply from clean energy sources by 2020, capital financing of almost US$1 trillion would be required, with nearly US$50 billion being required every year until 2020.[46] Because of the high savings rates in these economies, sufficient capital

---

[44] Cline 2009 (see fn 36); Feldstein 2008 (see fn 29); IMF 2009 (see fn 30); Prasad 2009 (see fn 29); Park and Shin 2009 (see fn 29); Rodrik 2009 (see fn 29).

[45] Park and Shin 2009 (see fn 29).

[46] Carmody and Ritchie 2007 (see ch. 2, fn 13).

is available from the private sector, both for funding clean energy investments and attracting further financing from global and regional capital markets, but only if there is a stable regulatory framework, favorable market conditions and incentives, and reduced uncertainty regarding the long-term price signal for carbon. If these conditions are met under a GGND, then a substantial amount of the private sector savings in Asian and emerging market countries could be tapped for raising the investment and growth potential of their economies. The fostering of clean energy investments from domestic sources and overseas financing would also be consistent with shifting the output structure of emerging market economies from labor-intensive goods to skill-, capital- and technology-intensive production.

As noted in chapter 4, however, in addition to the "capital gap" there is also a substantial "skills and technological gap" for many emerging market economies in adopting clean and low-carbon technologies. These economies currently spend little on research and development on these technologies and have a chronic shortage of workers with the complementary skills needed to develop and apply low-carbon technologies. The technological and skills gap also provides an opportunity, however, for emerging market economies to import low-carbon capital and technology goods rather than continuing increasing their exports of labor-intensive consumer goods. Although in the short term these economies may continue to depend on the importation and transfer of technologies and skills developed elsewhere, in the medium and long term the transfer of new technologies and skills will facilitate the development of an indigenous technological capacity and workforce, enabling future innovations and the long-term adoption of low-carbon technologies. Expanding the opportunities to import low-carbon capital and technology goods rather than emphasizing further increases in exports is consistent with the general policy prescription as to how emerging market economies can help to reduce global imbalances.[47]

---

[47] Cline 2009 (see fn 36).

In fact, the expansion of clean energy investments and the adoption of low-carbon technologies in emerging market and other developing economies also accord with the growth strategy "after the crisis" advocated by Dani Rodrik.[48] According to Rodrik, "What matters for growth in developing nations is not the size of their trade surplus, nor even the volume of their exports... What matters for growth is their *output* of non-traditional tradables, which can expand without limit as long as domestic demand expands at the same time."[49] Citing the examples of Japan from 1950 to 1973, South Korea from 1973 to 1990 and China from 1990 to 2005, Rodrik argues that what distinguished these "high-growth" economies during these periods was that they were able to undertake rapid structural transformation from low-productivity ("traditional") to high-productivity ("modern") activities. These latter activities largely involve tradable industrial products, although tradable services are also important. In the past, high-growth emerging market economies expanded their output of tradable industrial goods by promoting their export with policies such as undervalued exchange rates. Because such policies lowered the cost of exports while effectively taxing domestic consumption, the result was large trade surpluses. To foster growth after the current economic crisis while avoiding creating huge trade surpluses, Rodrik urges emerging market economies to encourage growth in the output of tradable commodities but through industrial policies, included targeted subsidies, that allow these goods and services to be consumed domestically. The GGND is consistent with this strategy; policies to target and develop clean energy, sustainable transport and

[48] Rodrik 2009 (see fn 29).

[49] Rodrik 2009, 3 (emphasis in original) (see fn 29). Note that Rodrik is making the conventional economic distinction between "tradable" and "non-tradable" goods and services. Tradables comprise all goods and services produced in an economy that are actually or potentially imported or exported – that is, they are capable of being traded, even if they are produced and consumed domestically. Non-tradables are goods and services that do not cross country borders, either because transport costs prohibit the export or the import of a good, or due to the virtually non-tradable nature of the goods in question – e.g. public services, land, housing, construction, local specialities that are not traded on the world market, highly perishable products.

other green sectors as new growth poles in emerging market and developing economies should also foster the production of modern tradable goods and services to meet expanding domestic demand. As I discuss further in the next chapter, such "green growth" investments are important not just for economic recovery from the current crisis but also for long-run economic development.

The GGND also advocates the need for developing economies to invest urgently in comprehensive, well-targeted safety net programs and maintain, if not expand, educational and health services for the poor (see chapter 10). Such investments might also help to absorb domestic savings and reduce trade surpluses. For example, Martin Feldstein maintains that the key to shrinking the chronic trade surplus of China and other emerging market economies is to reduce the high rate of national savings, not only by encouraging household consumption but also through government spending on public programs in health and education. Such services would improve primary and secondary education access and health services and also create additional demand to absorb a growing non-agricultural labor force.[50] Similarly, Eswar Prasad suggests that increased spending on safety net programs, the better provision of health care and other government insurance mechanisms could help reduce the precautionary motives for saving by households in developing countries.[51] The result would be a multiplier effect, lowering economy-wide excess saving while promoting higher household consumption.

In sum, the GGND strategy for a green economic recovery should help alleviate, rather than worsen, unstably large fiscal deficits, long-run real interest rate rises and inflation, and global imbalances. The recommended rise in green fiscal stimulus for G20 economies is unlikely to increase fiscal deficits and public debt significantly in the medium term. This will particularly be the case if G20 economies adopt complementary pricing and regulatory reforms for reducing carbon dependency, including the removal of

[50] Feldstein 2008 (see fn 29).
[51] Prasad 2009 (see fn 29).

perverse subsidies and other distortions in energy, transport and similar markets. Various GGND actions could also limit rather than increase global imbalances. Reducing carbon dependency and improving energy security should help in correcting structural trade imbalances for oil-importing economies with large current account deficits, such as the United States, and for fossil-fuel-exporting economies with accumulating foreign reserves. Promoting clean energy investments in Asian and other emerging economies should encourage domestic private investment, increase imports of low-carbon technologies and capital, and expand the output of tradables. Such policies could promote long-term growth while avoiding huge trade surpluses in developing economies. By investing in safety net programs and educational and health services for the poor, developing economies may also utilize more domestic savings and expand household consumption.

12 Beyond a green economic recovery

Most of this book has been concerned with articulating a vision for the present world economic recovery from the worst global recession since the Great Depression of the 1930s. The premise of this vision is that the right mix of policy actions can stimulate recovery and at the same time improve the sustainability of the world economy. If these actions are adopted, over the next few years they will create millions of jobs, improve the livelihoods of the world's poor and channel investments into dynamic economic sectors. Such a timely mix of policies can be referred to collectively as a Global Green New Deal.

The previous chapters have aimed to show how a GGND is critical to the lasting success of a world economic recovery. Reviving growth, ensuring financial stability and creating jobs should be essential objectives, but unless new policy initiatives also address other global challenges, such as reducing carbon dependency, protecting ecosystems and water resources and alleviating poverty, their impact on averting future crises will be short-lived. Without such progress, restarting the world economy today will do little to address the imminent threats posed by climate change, energy insecurity, growing freshwater scarcity, deteriorating ecosystems and, above all, worsening global poverty. Rather, it is necessary to reduce carbon dependency and ecological scarcity not just because of environmental concerns but because this is the correct and only way to revitalize the economy on a genuinely sustainable basis.

This final chapter is concerned with the latter objective by addressing two further questions: how we can build on the GGND to ensure that it leads to a more sustainable world economy in the medium and long term, and the additional policies and instruments that may be necessary to further such an objective.

To explore the issues posed by these questions, let us look further at the role of complementary pricing policies, global markets, green development strategies and targeting aid and development.

COMPLEMENTARY PRICING POLICIES

Throughout this book, the need to adopt complementary pricing policies to enhance the effectiveness of and sustain GGND measures has been stressed. Such policies include additional taxes, tradable permits and other market-based instruments to provide the correct incentives for reducing carbon dependency and ecological scarcity and removing perverse subsidies and other market distortions that inhibit these objectives.

For example, in chapter 2 it was argued that the removal of fossil fuel subsidies eliminates perverse incentives in energy markets. The resulting financial savings of US$80 billion in OECD economies and US$220 annually in developing countries could also be redirected to investments in clean energy research and development, renewable energy development and energy conservation. Complementary pricing incentives might include energy and carbon taxes, carbon and other tradable permit schemes, and temporary subsidies to initiate clean energy R&D. The removal of transport market and planning distortions would help cut economic waste, reduce pollution and congestion, allow greater transport choice and facilitate sustainable transport strategies that would boost economic recovery and employment. Fiscal policies, such as fuel and vehicle taxes, new vehicle incentives, road fees, user fees, vehicle insurance and fleet vehicle incentives, can have powerful impacts on encouraging the introduction of cleaner, fuel-efficient vehicles. Combining these policies with regulatory measures, such as more stringent greenhouse gas and fuel economy standards, may produce the most important shifts in vehicle demand and use.

Several chapters in part II suggested that complementary pricing policies and market reforms in developing economies were important for enhancing the sustainable and efficient use of natural resources and production processes dependent on them, and to ensure that the financial returns generated from these activities are reinvested in the industrial activities, infrastructure, health services, education and skills necessary for long-term economic development. Removing subsidies and other incentive distortions and implementing, when appropriate, market-based instruments and other measures to improve the efficiency of water delivery and utilization were also considered essential to managing growing water demand.

As we saw in chapter 11, there are other longer-term economic benefits arising from complementary pricing policies. Combined with "technology-push" policies, such as public support for clean energy R&D, carbon taxes or tradable permit systems could provide significant incentives for induced technological innovation for reducing carbon dependency. The revenues earned, or financial subsidies saved, from complementary pricing policies could pay for any additional fiscal stimulus measures and other public expenditures in support of green sector development. This would alleviate concern about the need to restore fiscal discipline once the economic recovery takes hold. To the extent that complementary pricing policies help to revive economies while reducing carbon dependency and improving energy security, they may also assist in correcting the problem of structural imbalances for oil-importing economies with large current account deficits, such as the United States, and for fossil-fuel-exporting economies with accumulating foreign reserves. For trade surplus countries, such as emerging market economies, complementary pricing policies should be part of the development strategy that shifts these economies such that they reorient domestic savings towards clean energy investments, increase imports of low-carbon technologies and capital and expand their output of tradables to satisfy growing domestic demand.

Evidence suggests that, as economies and governments become more familiar with the use of complementary pricing policies, they tend to develop these policies, improve their effectiveness and extend them to a variety of environmental management areas. An assessment by the European Environment Agency (EEA), for example, finds that, since 1996, the increased use of a variety of market-based instruments across a growing number of sectors and economies is developing an emerging "environmental tax base."[1] Table 12.1 illustrates the spread of environmental taxes in Europe since the mid-1990s. One of the advantages of the proposed GGND could be that it helps economies worldwide develop and enhance a similar environmental tax base for sustaining a healthy and efficient green economy of the future.

CREATING GLOBAL MARKETS

Most of the impending environmental crises targeted by the GGND – climate change, ecological scarcity and the declining availability of water – are examples of market failure on a global scale. That is, those who emit greenhouse gases, destroy ecosystem services and threaten water availability inflict damage on others without paying for these losses. In the case of climate change, the uncompensated damages are truly global, in that all economies are contributing to the problem, without paying fully for the costs, and the economic consequences of the market failure will be felt worldwide. In the case of ecological scarcity, it is the scale and pace of the loss of ecosystems and their services that have created a global market failure. The unprecedented modification of ecosystems worldwide over the past fifty years means that fifteen out of twenty-four of the world's major ecosystems are currently being degraded or used unsustainably, including freshwater, capture fisheries, air and water purification, and the regulation of regional and local climate, natural hazards, and pests.[2] As discussed throughout this book, the impending freshwater scarcity reflects the chronic "underpricing" of vital water resources worldwide, and countries are increasingly becoming dependent on new sources of water from outside their borders for

---

[1] EEA. 2005. "Integrated assessment." In EEA. *The European Environment: State and Outlook 2005.* Copenhagen, EEA: 24–249.
[2] MA 2005 (see ch. 1, fn 14).

Table 12.1 *The emerging environmental tax base in selected European economies*

	Austria	Belgium	Denmark	Finland	France	Germany	Greece	Iceland
Air/energy								
CO_2			★	★		★★		
SO_2			★★		★			
NO_x					★			
Fuels	★	★	★	★	★	★	★	★
Sulfur in fuels		★★★	★		★★★			
Transport								
Car sales and use	★	★	★	★	★	★	★	★
Differentiated car tax			★★			★★		
Water								
Water effluents	★	★	★	★	★	★		
Waste								
Waste – end	★★	★★★	★	★★	★★		★★	
Dangerous waste			★	★		★		★
Noise								
Aviation noise						★		
Products								
Tires	★		★★	★★				
Beverage containers		★	★	★				
Packaging	★★		★		★★★			
Bags			★					★
Pesticides		★★	★					
CFCs	★		★					
Batteries	★★	★★	★					★★★
Light bulbs			★					
PVCs			★★					
Lubrication oil				★				

Ireland	Italy	Luxembourg	Netherlands	Norway	Portugal	Spain	Sweden	United Kingdom
★★★	★★		★	★			★	★★★
	★			★★★				
	★						★	
★	★	★	★	★	★	★	★	★
			★★★	★			★	★★★
★	★	★	★	★	★	★	★	
				★★				
★	★		★	★		★	★	
	★★		★	★★		★★★	★★	★
	★		★	★				
			★★					
				★			★	
	★★			★★★				
★★★	★							
				★★			★	
	★★						★	
	★			★★		★★★		

Table 12.1 (cont.)

	Austria	Belgium	Denmark	Finland	France	Germany	Greece	Iceland
Fertilizers			**					
Paper and board			**		*			*
Solvents			**					
Resources								
Raw materials		***	*					

Notes: * = in 1996. ** = new after 1996. *** = new after 2000. NO$_x$ is nitrogen oxide. CFCs are chlorofluorocarbons. PVCs are polyvinyl chlorides.
Source: EEA. 2005. "Integrated assessment." In EEA. *The European Environment: State and Outlook 2005.* Copenhagen, EEA: 24–249, 236, fig. 10.2.

economic development. For example, as indicated in box 3.8, two out of five people in the world live in international water basins shared by more than one country, and thirty-nine countries – all but two of them developing economies – receive most of their water from outside their borders.

The most efficient solution for combating such worldwide market failures is to create global markets. To provide the best incentives for all economies worldwide to invest in clean energy technologies and reduce their carbon dependency requires establishing a long-term and credible price signal for carbon across world markets. To ensure that ecosystems yielding valuable services are more likely to be conserved than destroyed requires the establishment of a system of international payment for ecosystem services that allows individuals in one part of the world who value these services to compensate those in other parts of the world for managing the ecosystems. Tackling transboundary water allocation, which is becoming increasingly critical to global supply, will require a renewed commitment by countries sharing these resources to cooperate on governance and pricing arrangements to manage joint supply relative to demand.

Throughout this book, the need to create such global markets has been emphasized as critical to the success of any GGND.

Ireland	Italy	Luxembourg	Netherlands	Norway	Portugal	Spain	Sweden	United Kingdom
			★ ★				★	
				★ ★				
	★ ★ ★						★	★ ★ ★

Continued progress in this objective is also vital to the lasting success of any green economic recovery.

A key example is the need to reach agreement on a post-Kyoto global climate change framework. Many of the low-carbon and sustainable transport investments proposed in the GGND will be affected by the growing uncertainty over the future global carbon market after 2012, when the Kyoto Protocol expires. Uncertainty over future global climate policy and the delay caused by inaction both also increase the costs of an agreement sharply. Any delay in adopting effective climate policies will affect the cost of future agreements that will be required to abate an even larger amount of greenhouse gas emissions. Such inaction in the short term increases significantly the costs of compliance in the long term, which is compounded by the effects of uncertainty on investment and policy decisions.

As discussed in this book, even if a post-Kyoto agreement fails, it is essential that any new international climate policy achieves two aims: the enhancement of global carbon emissions trading and reform of the Clean Development Mechanism. In lieu of an inclusive international climate agreement, the continued existence of a global carbon market that allows developing economies to finance their mitigation measures would still permit the attainment of global

GHG emission reduction targets, which usually set goals for 2020 or 2030. Guaranteeing the future of a global carbon market and CDM mechanism after 2012 is therefore essential not just to the success of many actions under the proposed GGND for the next several years but also for the attainment of ambitious GHG targets for 2020 and beyond.

The world economy has made tentative steps towards international trading in GHG emissions but it is not there yet by any means. By establishing the first regional carbon market with its Emissions Trading System, the European Union has demonstrated how international trading can function to provide regional incentives for reducing GHG emissions: an EU-wide carbon price has been created; businesses began incorporating this price into their decisions; and the market infrastructure for multilateral trading in carbon has been set up.[3] Expansion and reform of the ETS are needed, however, if it is to become the basis of a global trading scheme (see box 2.5). Similarly, the CDM has become the basis for establishing projects and investments for large emerging market economies, such as Brazil, China, India, South Korea and Mexico, effectively linking them into global GHG emissions trading and financing. Reform and expansion of the CDM are also essential, for it to cover a broader range of GHG reduction projects and developing economies, and if it is truly to be the basis for a global carbon market (see box 4.1). A number of important economies, such as Australia, Canada, Japan, New Zealand, Norway and Switzerland, have proposed or implemented cap-and-trade systems, which could link into the larger international trading network. In addition, GHG trading has been

---

[3] Convery 2009 (see ch. 2, fn 19); Demailly, Damien, and Philippe Quirion. 2008. *Changing the Allocation Rules in the EU ETS: Impact on Competitiveness and Economic Efficiency.* Working Paper no. 89. Milan, FEEM; Ellerman, A. Danny, and Paul L. Joskow. 2008. *The European Union's Emissions Trading System in Perspective.* Arlington, VA, Pew Center on Global Climate Change; Stankeviciute, Loreta, Alban Kitous and Patrick Criqui. 2008. "The fundamentals of the future international emissions trading system." *Energy Policy* 36 (11): 4272–86.

established in the northeastern US states, and there is pending cap-and-trade legislation for the entire United States. The basis for a global carbon market is clearly emerging, but it needs to become a major priority not only for enhancing efforts to "green" the present economic recovery but also to provide the incentives for long-term targets to reduce carbon dependency in the world economy.

GREEN DEVELOPMENT STRATEGIES

In chapter 11, it was noted that, for many developing economies, "growth after the crisis" will require a reorienting of their development and industrial strategies to encourage expansion in the output of modern tradable goods and services, mainly to meet growing domestic demand and to absorb high rates of saving in these economies. An advocate of this policy, Dani Rodrik, argues that this was largely the development strategy and rapid structural transformation undertaken by "high-growth" economies in past periods, such as Japan in 1950 to 1973, South Korea from 1973 to 1990 and China from 1990 to 2005.[4] In the past, high-growth emerging market economies expanded their output of tradable industrial goods by means of promoting their export with policies such as undervalued exchange rates. After the crisis, though, emerging market and other developing economies should encourage growth in the output of tradable commodities but through industrial policies, including targeted subsidies, that will allow these goods and services to be consumed domestically.

As discussed in chapter 11, the GGND would support this long-term development strategy. Policies to target and develop clean energy, sustainable transportation and other green sectors should serve as the new growth poles in emerging market and other developing economies. Moreover, these sectors would be at the forefront of fostering modern tradable goods and services to meet expanding domestic demand. To overcome critical capital, technological and

[4] Rodrik 2009 (see ch. 11, fn 29).

skills gaps, developing economies should encourage the importation of low-carbon capital and technology goods. In the medium to long term the transfer of new technologies and skills will facilitate the development of an indigenous technological capacity and workforce, enabling future innovations and the long-term adoption of low-carbon technologies. Such strategies to promote "green growth" are not just about ensuring economic recovery from the current crisis but also about devising a new and sustainable long-run development path for these economies.

Some key Asian economies appear to have endorsed this view, that greening their economies may be crucial both to economic recovery and ensuring long-run growth.

As noted in chapters 1 and 2, the major Asia-Pacific economies – Australia, China, Japan and South Korea – have already signaled a commitment to promoting low-carbon investments and other environmental improvements as part of their strategy for economic recovery. Overall, the Asia-Pacific region accounts for 63 percent of all global green stimulus spending during the current recession, with most of the investments targeted to reducing carbon dependency. China accounts for 47 percent of global green fiscal spending to date, Japan and South Korea around 8 percent each, and Australia 2 percent (see figure 1.2).

China has undertaken a number of green stimulus investments, amounting to around 3 percent of its GDP, in response to the economic recession. These initiatives include the promotion of wind energy, fuel-efficient vehicles, rail transport, electricity grid improvements and waste, water and pollution control. Some market-based incentives have been adopted, such as raising taxes on gasoline and diesel and reducing the sales tax on more fuel-efficient vehicles. Japan's green stimulus measures, which are equivalent to to 0.8 percent of its GDP in total, include grants for solar energy installation, incentives for the purchase of fuel-efficient cars and electronic goods, energy efficiency investments, the promotion of biofuels and recycling. The Australian government is spending around 1.2

percent of its GDP on green stimulus measures aimed at reducing carbon dependency (see box 1.1). The investments include initiatives for promoting renewable energy, carbon capture and storage, energy efficiency, the development of a "smart" electricity grid and the development of rail transport. The government is also developing a cap-and-trade permit system, which is likely to be implemented in 2012.[5] In addition, of course, as discussed in chapter 5, South Korea has perhaps the strongest commitment to including green stimulus measures in an economic recovery program, through its Green New Deal plan. At a cost of around US$36 billion from 2009 to 2012, or over 3 percent of its GDP, the initiative aims to create 960,000 jobs through investments in a variety of low-carbon and environmental projects. The Green New Deal is South Korea's economic recovery plan; it accounts for nearly all (95.2 percent) of South Korea's fiscal response to the global recession (see figure 1.3).

So far, the efforts by China and South Korea on green initiatives and other fiscal measures appear to be paying off; they and other Asian emerging market economies appear to be the first to be recovering from the current recession. Comparing the second quarter of 2009 with the first at an annualized rate, China's GDP grew by 15 percent and South Korea's by almost 10 percent.[6] The rapid recovery in China and South Korea is attributed to the fiscal stimuli adopted by these economies, including green initiatives, which have revived domestic demand. South Korea's private consumption increased at an annualized rate of 14 percent in the second quarter of 2009. Fixed investment in China is more than 20 percent higher than a year ago, real consumer spending in urban areas is 11 percent up and car

---

[5] See Robins, Clover and Singh 2009 (*Building a Green Recovery*), 14–20 (ch. 1, fn 10), for further details of the green recovery plans for China, Japan and Australia.

[6] *The Economist*. 2009. "Briefing: emerging Asian economies: on the rebound." *The Economist*, August 15: 69–72. The only Asian economy that performed better was Singapore, which grew at an annualized rate of 21 percent between the first and second quarters of 2009. Indonesia grew by 5 percent, and other Asian emerging market economies showed positive but lower growth. Overall, on average Asia's emerging market economies grew at an annualized rate of over 10 percent between the two quarters, whereas US GDP fell by 1 percent.

sales have risen 70 percent.[7] Green stimulus measures have clearly had a role in the quick economic rebound of China and South Korea; nearly all of South Korea's total fiscal stimulus involves green initiatives, and over a third of China's (see figure 1.3).

As noted in chapter 5, South Korea has gone one step further and is extending its Green New Deal into a five-year economic development plan, spending an additional US$60 billion on the same priority areas for reducing carbon dependency and achieving other environmental improvements (see table 5.1).[8] Under the plan, the government is committed to spending an amount equivalent to around 2 percent of GDP each year through 2013 on clean energy technologies, energy-efficient lighting, producing energy from waste, providing credit guarantees for environmental projects and establishing investment funds for these initiatives. It appears that South Korea sees its future economic development as being based on "green growth," and, as advocated in this book, is using its Green New Deal not just to ensure economic recovery from the current crisis but also to devise a new, and sustainable, long-run development strategy.

The national actions advocated under the Global Green New Deal should also serve as the basis for policies to promote the transition to low-carbon and clean energy use in advanced economies. For example, box 12.1 summarizes a study by the Union of Concerned Scientists (UCS), which analyzes such a long-run policy strategy for the United States.[9] The main aim of the strategy is to reduce US greenhouse gas (GHG) emissions to 26% below 2005 levels by 2020 and 56% below by 2030. The UCS finds that the most beneficial policies for attaining these targets is an economy-wide cap-and-trade system combined with complementary policies

---

[7] *The Economist* 2009 (see fn 6). Other Asian emerging market economies that rebounded significantly in the second quarter of 2009 also have stimulus packages equivalent to at least 4 percent of GDP, including Singapore, Malaysia, Taiwan and Thailand.

[8] Robins, Clover and Singh 2009 (*Building a Green Recovery*), 7–8 (see ch. 1, fn 10).

[9] Cleetus, Rachel, Steven Clemmer and David Friedman. 2009. *Climate 2030: A National Blueprint for a Clean Energy Economy*. Cambridge, MA, UCS.

targeted at industry, buildings, electricity and transportation. In addition, the strategy will have only minimal impacts on long-run economic growth in the United States, will increase nonfarm employment slightly and yield net cumulative savings from 2010 to 2030 of US$1.7 trillion, mainly due to energy savings and auctioning carbon allowances.

Box 12.1 The 2030 blueprint for a clean energy economy

The Union of Concerned Scientists has devised and analyzed a policy strategy for establishing a clean energy economy in the United States, with the goal of reducing greenhouse gas emissions 26 percent below 2005 levels by 2020 and 56 percent below by 2030. The study estimates total GHG emissions from the US economy to be 7,180 million tonnes of carbon dioxide (CO_2) equivalent in 2005, which in the business-as-usual, or reference, case would rise to around 8,000 million tonnes by 2030.[10]

To reach the 2020 and 2030 targets in GHG emission reductions, the UCS policy strategy advocates an economy-wide cap-and-trade system for the United States combined with complementary policies targeted at industry, buildings, electricity and transportation. The specific policies are as follows.

(1) An economy-wide cap-and-trade system, with:
   - the auctioning of all carbon allowances;
   - the recycling of auction revenues to consumers and businesses;
   - limits on carbon "offsets" to reduce the capped sectors' GHG emissions; and
   - flexibility for capped businesses to over-comply with the cap and bank excess carbon allowances for future use.

---

[10] Note that the UCS estimates of GHG emissions for the US economy in 2005 indicate that 34 percent was electricity CO_2, 30 percent was transportation CO_2, 11 percent was industrial CO_2, 5 percent was residential CO_2, 3 percent was commercial CO_2 and 17 percent was non-CO_2 emissions. See Cleetus, Clemmer and Friedman 2009 (fn 9).

(2) Industrial and building policies that include:
- an energy efficiency resource standard, requiring retail electricity and natural gas providers to meet efficiency targets;
- minimum federal energy efficiency standards for specific appliances and equipment;
- advanced energy codes and technologies for buildings;
- programs that encourage more efficient industrial processes;
- wider reliance on efficient systems that provide both heat and power; and
- research and development on energy efficiency.

(3) Electricity policies that include:
- a renewable electricity standard for retail electricity providers;
- the use of advanced coal technology, with a carbon capture and storage demonstration program; and
- R&D on renewable energy.

(4) Transportation policies that include:
- standards that limit GHG emissions from vehicles;
- standards that require the use of low-carbon fuels;
- requirements for the deployment of advanced vehicle technology;
- smart-growth policies that encourage mixed-use development, with more public transit;
- smart-growth policies that tie federal highway funding to more efficient transport systems; and
- pay-as-you-drive insurance and other per-mile user fees.

As indicated in the figure below, the UCS study estimates that these policies could achieve the 2020 and 2030 GHG emission reductions targets by constraining cumulative emissions in the various sectors of the US economy to 180 billion tonnes of CO_2 equivalent between 2000 and 2030. The price of carbon allowances starts at US$18 per tonne of CO_2 in 2011, rises to US$34 in 2020 and then increases further to US$70 in 2030.

In addition, the study estimates that the above policies will result in savings for households and businesses from reductions in electricity and fuel use that will more than offset the costs of any additional investments arising from the strategy. By 2030 the net savings will be US$255 billion. Although administering and implementing the policies will cost US$8 billion, auctioning carbon allowances will generate US$219 billion revenues that should be recycled to consumers and business. Overall, the strategy should yield US$465 billion in savings by 2030. Net cumulative savings from 2010 to 2030 amount to US$1.7 trillion.

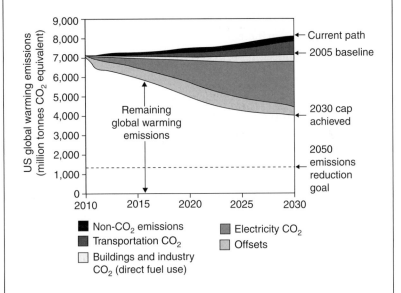

Emissions reductions under the 2030 blueprint for a clean energy economy

Finally, the strategy has only minimal impacts on long-run economic growth. Under full implementation of the policies, GDP increases by at least 81 percent between 2005 and 2030. In the reference case, the US economy grows by 84 percent. Employment trends are virtually identical in the two scenarios, although non-farm employment is slightly higher under the clean energy strategy compared to the reference case.

Source: Cleetus, Rachel, Steven Clemmer and David Friedman. 2009. *Climate 2030: A National Blueprint for a Clean Energy Economy.* Cambridge, MA, UCS.

As outlined in box 12.1, the policies advocated for the long-term clean energy strategy for the United States are similar to the GGND actions put forward in part II for reconciling the short-term objectives of enhancing economic recovery and promoting jobs in the United States while taking initial steps to reduce its carbon dependency in the long run (see box 2.4). This link between short- and long-term goals in the GGND emphasizes a key message of this book: although the principal aim of the Global Green New Deal is to spur global economic recovery from the current recession, the GGND should also be viewed as a first step in ensuring a sustainable development strategy for the world economy. As the examples of South Korea and the United States illustrate, the GGND policies should form the basis for longer-term economic development aimed at promoting "green growth" and a clean energy economy.

In moving from economic recovery from the current global recession to long-term sustainable economic development strategies, some difficult policy choices have to be made. One important issue, for example, is the role of nuclear power generation in any long-term clean energy strategy. The common perception of clean energy is that it includes renewable energy resources, such as solar, wind, biomass, tidal and other non-fossil-fuel resources, as well as the development of technologies for reducing GHG emissions from fossil fuels, such as clean coal technologies and carbon capture and storage. As discussed in this book, the support for and development of such renewable and cleaner fossil fuel technologies are critical in the short term for boosting economic recovery and employment while moving economies towards a low-carbon path. Many analysts have also noted, however, that, even with the most favorable policies in place, it will not be economically and technically feasible to develop renewable energy resources and other clean energy technologies sufficiently to reach the critical medium- and long-term goals for reducing GHG emissions.[11] Accordingly, many strategies for

[11] See, for example, Burger, Nicholas, Lisa Ecola, Thomas Light and Michael Toman. 2009. *Evaluating Options for US Greenhouse-gas Mitigation Using*

achieving energy security and climate change mitigation targets by 2020 or 2030, whether for developing or advanced economies, advocate some role for nuclear energy development.[12]

The UCS analysis of a long-term clean energy strategy for the United States shows, however, that an economy-wide carbon pricing policy, such as a cap-and-trade system, combined with complementary policies targeted at energy-intensive sectors encourages the development of advanced nuclear technologies that would improve the safety of power plants and reduce their costs.[13] Thus, the UCS study concludes that no new incentives and policy support are needed over the medium and long term to develop the next generation of nuclear power plants.[14] A study of the European Union's Emissions Trading System confirms that an economy-wide cap-and-trade scheme has the capacity to induce substitution in electricity generation to clean energy technologies, including nuclear power.[15] Carbon pricing and complementary sectoral policies that encourage the development of clean energy over the long term should also foster advanced nuclear power, without the need for additional incentives.

TARGETING AID AND DEVELOPMENT

As discussed in chapter 3, for most low- and middle-income economies, improving the sustainability of primary production must

Multiple Criteria. Occasional paper. Santa Monica, CA, RAND Corporation; Heal 2009 (see ch. 11, fn 17); Resch, Gustav, Anne Held, Thomas Faber, Christian Panzer, Felipe Toro and Reinhard Haas. 2008. "Potentials and prospects for renewable energies at global scale." *Energy Policy* 36 (11): 4048–56; and Toman, Griffin and Lempert 2008 (ch. 11, fn 17).

[12] See, for example, Burger *et al.* 2009 (fn 11); Cleetus, Clemmer and Friedman 2009 (fn 9); IEA 2007 (ch. 2, fn 7); and UN ESCAP 2008 (ch. 2, fn 7).

[13] Cleetus, Clemmer and Friedman 2009, 81–8 (fn 9).

[14] As pointed out by Cleetus, Clemmer and Friedman 2009, 86–8 (see fn 9), US policy already contains substantial incentives for nuclear energy development, including an inflation-adjusted production tax credit of US1.8 cents per kilowatt-hour for new nuclear plants that begin operation in 2020 and US$18.5 billion in incentives through the current loan guarantee program. The UCS clean energy strategy assumes that these incentives for advanced nuclear power remain in place at least until 2030.

[15] Considine, Timothy J., and Donald F. Larson. 2009. "Substitution and technological change under carbon cap and trade: lessons from Europe."

be considered both an immediate response to the current world economic crisis and a long-term sustainable development goal. Similarly, it was noted that ecological scarcity, energy poverty and a lack of access to clean water and sanitation directly impact the economic livelihoods of the poor in all developing economies. The GGND therefore focuses on three critical areas for national actions in these economies.

- Policies, investments and reforms to enhance the sustainable and efficient use of natural resources and production processes dependent on them, and to ensure that the sufficient financial returns generated from these activities are reinvested in the industrial activities, infrastructure, health services, education and skills necessary for long-term economic development.
- Targeting investments and other policy measures to improving the livelihoods of the rural poor, especially those living in fragile environments.
- Protecting and improving the provision of ecosystem services on which the extremely poor depend.

For example, two urgent priorities for immediate action under the GGND are that developing economies should spend at least 1 percent of their GDP on improving clean water and sanitation for the poor, and that they should also develop urgently comprehensive, well-targeted safety net programs and maintain, if not expand, educational and health services for the poor. It was also argued that adopting the above measures for improving the sustainability of primary production is even more important during a major economic recession, especially as it should generate funds for diversifying the economy, building up human capital and investing in social safety nets and other programs targeted at the poor.

The above recommendations under the GGND should also be the basis for devising a global strategy for alleviating poverty and enhancing sustainable development in resource-dependent

Unpublished paper. Laramie, University of Wyoming, Department of Economics and Finance.

economies over the next several decades, however. One of the key objectives of the GGND is to achieve the Millennium Development Goal of ending extreme world poverty by 2025.

Low- and middle-income economies will clearly need continuing assistance from the international community in achieving these long-term goals, though. If developing economies are to adopt the GGND actions as the basis for a long-term development strategy, then the international community must also reorient development assistance and financing to improving the sustainability of their primary production activities, the livelihoods of the poor living in fragile environments and the provision of the ecosystem services on which the extremely poor depend.

As outlined in chapter 4, developing economies will also need considerable assistance in overcoming the capital, skills and technological gaps that prevent them from adopting low-carbon and clean energy technologies, and may also limit the dissemination of simpler renewable energy technologies to poor households that lack access to basic energy services. Developing economies face similar challenges in implementing sustainable transport strategies, including improving access by the poor to basic transport facilities. For example, improving sustainable transport and access requires an increase in investments in developing economies of about US$1.2 billion annually from now to 2030, with about one-sixth of the financing coming from development assistance.[16] To achieve the goal of halving the proportion of the population without access to clean water and sanitation, aid flows would need to double to this sector, rising by between US$3.6 billion and US$4 billion annually.[17] There is also an urgent need to establish a long-term global "vulnerability fund," which would be used in developing economies to finance a comprehensive and targeted safety net for the poor, investments in infrastructure including low-carbon technology projects, support for small and medium-sized enterprises and micro-finance institutions,

[16] UNFCCC 2007 (see ch. 4, fn 4).
[17] UNDP 2006 (see ch. 1, 20).

and financing for food assistance, nutritional support for poor households and sustainable agricultural development.[18]

In sum, as argued in this book, there appear to be two broad priority areas for increased international assistance to developing economies: (i) overcoming the shortfalls in aid for low-carbon energy investments, sustainable transport, primary production and improvements in water and sanitation; and (ii) financing for food assistance and nutritional support, sustainable primary production methods, and safety net programs targeted at poor households. Current aid efforts in these areas are not sufficient to address the critical development problems facing developing economies and the poor. Reorienting current development assistance to these priority areas is more than just an essential component of a Global Green New Deal; it is also vital to achieving a more sustainable and equitable global economy over the next few decades.

Finally, it was noted in chapters 7 and 8 that successful implementation of the GGND will require both the development of innovative financing mechanisms and the enhancement of trade incentives. The recommendations for improving trade and financing globally will also have a critical impact on whether the economic recovery from the current global crisis will lead to sustained and greener growth in the long term. For example, a successful conclusion to the Doha Round trade negotiations, especially on fishery subsidies, clean technology and services and reducing agricultural protectionism, may not only assist the GGND in the short term but also provide an important stimulus to the medium- and long-term effectiveness of the strategy in fostering a greener world economy. Developing and expanding innovative financing mechanisms, such as the International Finance Facility, Climate Investment Funds and Global Clean Energy Cooperation, may also be necessary for supporting the long-term impacts of the Global Green New Deal.

---

[18] See Zoellick 2009 (ch. 7, fn 8); and High-Level Task Force on the Global Food Crisis 2008 (part II introd., fn 2).

FINAL REMARKS

The key message of this book has been that the expanded vision offered by a Global Green New Deal is critical to the lasting success of a world economic recovery. Reviving growth, ensuring financial stability and creating jobs need to be essential objectives. Unless new policy initiatives also address other global challenges, however, such as reducing carbon dependency, protecting ecosystems and water resources and alleviating poverty, their impact on averting future crises will be short-lived. Without this expanded vision, restarting the world economy today will do little to address the imminent threats posed by climate change, energy insecurity, growing freshwater scarcity, deteriorating ecosystems and, in particular, worsening global poverty. To the contrary, it is necessary to reduce carbon dependency and ecological scarcity not just because of environmental concerns but because this is the correct and only way to revitalize the economy on a truly sustainable basis.

As argued in this book, the key elements of any Global Green New Deal should focus on three main objectives:

- reviving the world economy, creating employment opportunities and protecting vulnerable groups;
- reducing carbon dependency, ecosystem degradation and water scarcity; and
- furthering the Millennium Development Goal of ending extreme world poverty by 2025.

Some G20 economies appear to be working towards some of these objectives already, by including "green" investments in their stimulus packages to reduce carbon dependency, enhance economic recovery and create jobs. The full range of GGND objectives cannot be achieved simply through injections of "green" fiscal stimulus investments by a handful of national governments, however. That is why the GGND strategy outlined in this book has called for a more comprehensive and coordinated set of national and international actions that goes beyond just green fiscal stimulus investments, involving pricing policies and reforms, better regulations, new approaches to aid, trade and financing, and improved global governance. Overall, this strategy is crucial to addressing the fundamental policy question posed by this book: what more must be done to ensure that the world economy is on a recovery path that is more economically and environmentally sustainable?

This is a question that should remain the central concern of global policymakers, not just for the next one or two years of economic recovery but also for the next critical decade or so, as we grapple with the ongoing threats posed by climate change, energy insecurity, growing freshwater scarcity, deteriorating ecosystems and, most of all, worsening global poverty.

Appendix 1 PIIE–WRI analysis of a green recovery program for the United States††

The Peterson Institute for International Economics and the World Resources Institute provide a modeling framework for assessing the economic and environmental impacts of a green recovery program for the United States.

The program represents a set of policy options, combining specific investments, pricing policies, regulations and other measures that could be considered part of a comprehensive US recovery effort. Many of these policies are currently included in the US$787 billion stimulus package proposed by the Obama administration; others are not.

The twelve specific policies considered in the PIIE–WRI analysis are as follows.

- **Household weatherization**: install insulation, new windows and better light bulbs in residential dwellings.
- **Federal building efficiency**: retrofit federal buildings to reduce overall energy demand.
- **Green schools**: provide funding to ensure that new school construction and renovations are highly energy-efficient.
- **Production tax credit (PTC)**: promote the deployment of grid-connected renewable energy through an extension of the PTC.
- **Investment tax credit (ITC)**: bolster incentives for installing distributed renewable generation options in businesses and households by an increase in the ITC.
- **Carbon capture and storage demonstration projects**: fund CCS demonstration projects around the country.
- **"Cash for Clunkers" program**: provide a tax credit towards the purchase of a new or used high-efficiency vehicle when an older and less fuel-efficient vehicle is retired.

†† This appendix is based on Houser, Trevor, Shashank Mohan and Robert Heilmayr. 2009. *A Green Global Recovery? Assessing US Economic Stimulus and the Prospects for International Coordination*. Policy Brief no. PB09–3. Washington, DC, PIIE and WRI. I would like to thank the authors, Manish Bapna, Ed Tureen, the PIIE and the WRI for allowing me to use the results of this study and copyrighted material in this appendix and book.

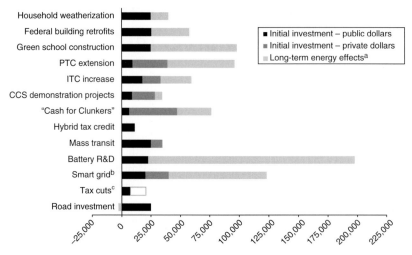

FIGURE AI.I Total employment effects

Notes: [a] These measure the net change in employment (measured in job-years) resulting from energy savings and the change in energy mix for the decade following the initial investment.
[b] "Smart grid" is a combination of "Smart metering" and "Transmission" in terms of the twelve elements of the program.
[c] The lighter field here indicates the employment effects of the share of the initial tax cut or rebate that is saved until future years. "Tax cuts" and "Road investment" together constitute conventional stimulus investments.
Sources: Houser, Trevor, Shashank Mohan and Robert Heilmayr. 2009. *A Green Global Recovery? Assessing US Economic Stimulus and the Prospects for International Coordination.* Policy Brief no. PB09-3. Washington, DC, PIIE and WRI.
©Peter G. Peterson Institute for International Economics and World Resources Institute.

- **Hybrid tax credit**: provide a tax credit towards the purchase of a new hybrid vehicle.
- **Mass transit investment**: fund "shovel-ready" mass transit projects.
- **Battery R&D**: fund strategic investment in the research, development and deployment of advanced battery systems aimed at reducing lithium battery cost and weight.
- **Smart metering**: provide matching funds to upgrade electricity metering, enabling users to better control energy costs and allowing utilities to more effectively manage demand.

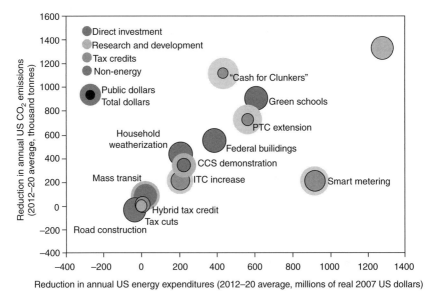

FIGURE A1.2 Economic and environmental impacts of recovery policy options

Note: The circle size indicates the amount of job creation for every US$1 billion spent.

Source: Houser, Trevor, Shashank Mohan and Robert Heilmayr. 2009. *A Green Global Recovery? Assessing US Economic Stimulus and the Prospects for International Coordination.* Policy Brief no. PB09–3. Washington, DC, PIIE and WRI.

©Peter G. Peterson Institute for International Economics and World Resources Institute.

- **Transmission**: construct high-voltage transmission lines to allow for greater renewable energy penetration.

To assess the energy and environmental impact of the green recovery program, the authors of the study employed the Energy Information Administration's National Energy Modeling System, which is used to create the Department of Energy's official *Annual Energy Outlook*. Estimates of the employment impact of each program were made using the input–output tables from the Department of Commerce's Bureau of Economic Analysis. This allowed assessment of the direct employment effects (jobs created in the sector receiving stimulus spending), indirect employment effects (jobs created in industries supplying the sector) and induced employment effects (jobs created when new direct and indirect hires spend their wages). The authors were also

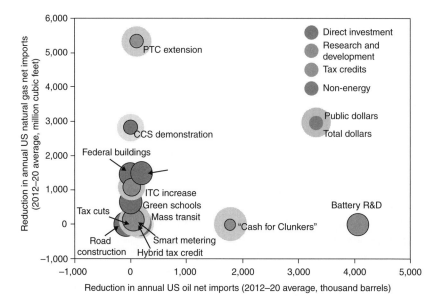

FIGURE A1.3 Economic and energy security impacts of recovery policy options

Note: The circle size indicates the amount of job creation for every US$1 billion spent.

Source: Houser, Trevor, Shashank Mohan and Robert Heilmayr. 2009. *A Green Global Recovery? Assessing US Economic Stimulus and the Prospects for International Coordination.* Policy Brief no. PB09-3. Washington, DC, PIIE and WRI.

©Peter G. Peterson Institute for International Economics and World Resources Institute.

able to evaluate the employment impact of energy cost savings to households, firms and the federal government, as well as the corresponding reduction in revenue to the energy industry, resulting from each scenario.

The PIIE–WRI study was able to estimate and compare how the twelve policies vary in terms of job creation, energy savings, emissions cuts and energy import reductions per billion dollars of government spending. For programs in which government dollars are matched by private dollars (such as tax credits, demonstration projects or some infrastructure investment), the analysis has also estimated the ratio of public to private spending.

The overall findings of the analysis are that the decreased cost and consumption of energy from the entire program have the potential to save the US economy an average of US$450 million per year for every US$1 billion invested. In addition, every US$1 billion in government spending would lead to approximately 30,000 job-years and reduce annual US greenhouse gas emissions by 592,600 tonnes between 2012 and 2020.[1] Employment effects are measured in job-years, or the number of full-time equivalent jobs lasting one year. The employment gains represent a 20 percent increase in jobs creation over more traditional infrastructure spending.

The comparatively high employment effects of the green recovery package relative to conventional infrastructure investments are related to two factors. First, the green programs are expected to stimulate additional private sector investment, thus multiplying direct, indirect and induced job creation. Second, the PIIE–WRI study finds that the net employment effects of reducing energy costs to the economy as a whole are significant. Energy efficiency improvements and green tax credits have employment effects that continue well beyond the initial investment period (see figure A1.1). In contrast, the jobs created by conventional tax cuts and road infrastructure investments end once the money is spent.

Figures A1.1 to A1.3 compare the economic and environmental impacts of the various policies analyzed in the PIIE–WRI study.

Figure A1.1 shows the total employment effects in terms of job-years created through US$1 billion in government investment, and depicts the relative sizes of public and private investment. In addition, the figure indicates the net change in employment resulting from energy savings and the change in energy mix in the economy following the initial investment. The effects of the green recovery policies are compared to conventional spending on road building and tax cuts. Almost all the green measures have a more lasting employment effect than the latter conventional policies.

In figure A1.2 the horizontal axis depicts the reduction in average annual energy expenditures between 2012 and 2020 for the US economy, measured in millions of 2007 US dollars. In figure A1.3 the horizontal axis shows the reduction in net imports of oil (in thousand barrels per year). In both figures, the vertical axis indicates the reduction in average annual GHG emissions (in thousand tonnes) over the same period. The size of the bubble shows the number of direct, indirect and induced jobs created in the year that the investments are made.

The timing for implementing these different green policies is likely to vary considerably. The building efficiency programs (e.g. household weatherization, retrofitting federal building and greening schools) could be implemented swiftly, and provide immediate stimulus to the construction industry. Smart meter

---

[1] The employment and GHG emission impacts exclude the effects of the transmission policy. See Houser, Mohan and Heilmayr 2009 for further details.

deployment and "shovel-ready" mass transit investments could also be initiated fairly rapidly. The "Cash for Clunkers" program has already been implemented in the United States, in 2009, and consumers appear to be responding to these incentives. Hybrid tax credit programs could also be adopted quickly, but it may take longer for consumers to respond. The remaining programs are likely to require a longer lead time before implementation.

Appendix 2 Pew comparative analysis of clean energy jobs and investments in the United States, 1998–2007[††]

A report by the Pew Charitable Trusts compares the job growth and investments in the clean energy sector of the US economy to the rest of the economy for the ten years leading up to the current recession, 1998 to 2007.

The Pew study defines the US clean economy as the sector that "generates jobs, businesses and investments while expanding clean energy production, increasing energy efficiency, reducing greenhouse gas emissions, waste and pollution, and conserving water and other natural resources."[1] The five economic activities comprising the clean economy are as follows.

- **Clean energy production**: jobs, businesses and investments that produce, transmit and store renewable energy from solar, wind, low-impact hydropower, hydrogen fuel cells, marine and tidal, geothermal and small-scale biopower energy sources.[2]
- **Energy efficiency**: jobs, businesses and investments that reduce the amount of energy used in the economy.
- **Environmentally friendly production**: jobs, businesses and investments that mitigate the harmful environmental impacts of existing products and

---

[††] This appendix is based on Pew Charitable Trusts. 2009. *The Clean Energy Economy: Repowering Jobs, Businesses and Investments across America.* Washington, DC, Pew Charitable Trusts.

[1] Pew Charitable Trusts 2009, 11.

[2] As explained in Pew Charitable Trusts 2009, 12: "Clean energy must have a positive net energy yield, reduce greenhouse gas emissions compared with other sources of energy, and be produced and distributed in a sustainable and safe manner. Nuclear power is not included in this category because of significant, ongoing questions about how and where to safely store its waste; a system to safely dispose of nuclear waste has not been implemented anywhere in the world. Additionally, we do not include the jobs and businesses associated with the production and distribution of liquid biofuels such as corn-based ethanol in the Clean Energy category because they do not meet its requirements."

develop and supply alternatives that require less energy and emit fewer greenhouse gases.[3]

- **Conservation and pollution mitigation**: jobs, businesses and investments that manage water and other finite natural resources more effectively, mitigating emissions of greenhouse gases and other pollutants that result from the continued use of fossil fuels.

- **Training and support**: jobs, businesses and investments that provide specialized services to the other four areas of the clean energy economy.

The Pew report finds that, between 1998 and 2007, jobs in these five clean energy areas grew more rapidly than overall job growth in the United States. Clean energy jobs grew by 9.1 percent whereas total jobs in the country increased by only 3.7 percent (see table A2.1). Moreover, the clean energy sector offers a range of blue- and white-collar employment opportunities, from engineers, scientists and teachers to machinists, construction workers and farm laborers. By 2007 the five components of the clean energy sector accounted for over 770,000 jobs, or approximately 0.5 percent of all employment in the United States. Although the total employment numbers appear modest, they contrast favorably with comparable sectors in the US economy. For example, biotechnology, which has been the focus of significant public policy support as well as substantial public and private investment, employs fewer than 200,000 workers, or approximately 0.1 percent of total US jobs in 2007. The fossil fuel energy sector, including utilities, coal mining and oil and gas extraction, employed 1.27 million workers in 2007, or about 1 percent of total US jobs.

Employment in the clean energy sector is now spread across all fifty US states and the District of Columbia. California currently has the most jobs in the clean energy economy (125,000), but Colorado, Oregon and Tennessee have clean energy economies that are both large and fast-growing, at an annual average rate of 1.9 percent. In addition to California, eleven other states have clean energy economies that generate jobs above the national average and in which employment has grown by 1 percent or more annually. These states are Florida, Georgia, Indiana, Massachusetts, Michigan, Minnesota, North Carolina, Ohio, Texas, Virginia and Washington.

In 2007 501,551 jobs in the clean energy economy, or 65 percent of the total number, were in the category of "Conservation and pollution mitigation" (see figure A2.1). The dominance of this area of the clean economy represents how

---

[3] This includes the biofuels infrastructure – i.e. facilities in which feedstocks are distilled into biofuels and centers that distribute them, but not agricultural jobs, businesses and investments that supply feedstocks to produce liquid biofuels.

Table A2.1 *Jobs, businesses and investments in the clean economy, United States*

	1998[a]	2007[b]	Total 2006–8	Growth 1998–2007[c]
Clean energy economy				
Employment	706,151,	770,385	12,570.1	9.1%
Businesses	61,689	68,203		10.6%
Venture capital investment (US$ millions)	360.3	5,900.0		1,537.5%
US economy				3.7%

Notes: [a] 1999 for venture capital investment.

[b] 2008 for venture capital investment.

[c] 1999–2008 for venture capital investment.

Source: Pew Charitable Trusts. 2009. *The Clean Energy Economy: Repowering Jobs, Businesses and Investments across America.* Washington, DC, Pew Charitable Trusts.

both public policy and business practices have responded to the growing demand to recycle waste, conserve water and reduce greenhouse gas emissions and other pollutants. As indicated in figure A2.1, however, from 1998 to 2007 growth in "Conservation and pollution mitigation" (3 percent) was much less than in three other areas: "Environmentally friendly production" (67 percent), "Clean energy production" (23 percent) and "Energy efficiency" (18 percent). Already, in 2007, these three categories comprised one in four jobs in the clean energy economy, and they will probably be the "jobs of tomorrow." According to the Pew report, "They represent businesses and jobs that are looking ahead to develop renewable, efficient energy sources and technologies to meet the demands of a carbon-constrained economy."[4]

For example, nearly six out of ten of the jobs in "Clean energy production" come from the generation of renewable energy rather than its transmission or storage. In 2007 solar energy generation accounted for 32,782 jobs, or 62.5 percent of all clean energy generation employment. Wind energy generation was the next largest source of jobs (5,068, or 9.7 percent of the total). The numbers employed in both solar and wind energy generation have expanded rapidly in

[4] Pew Charitable Trusts 2009, 17.

(a) Jobs in the clean energy economy, 2007

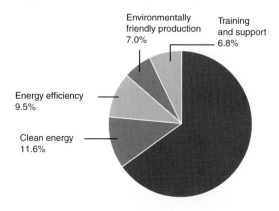

(b) Growth of jobs in the clean energy economy,
    1998 to 2007

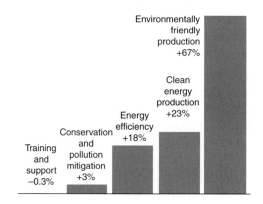

FIGURE A2.1 Jobs in the clean energy economy
Source: Pew Charitable Trusts. 2009. *The Clean Energy Economy: Repowering Jobs, Businesses and Investments across America*. Washington, DC, Pew Charitable Trusts.

recent years, and are likely to continue to grow. Between 1998 and 2007 wind energy generation employment grew by 23.5 percent and solar energy generation jobs by 19.1 percent.

The expansion of employment opportunities in the clean energy economy reflects the rapid growth in businesses and venture capital investment in the years leading up to the current recession. From 1998 to 2007 businesses in this economy grew by 10.6 percent (see table A2.1). Venture capital investments, which are an essential source of private equity for emerging technologies and business start-ups, expanded hugely. Venture capital investments in the clean energy economy totaled US$360.3 million in 1999, exceeded US$1 billion in 2000 and reached US$5.9 billion in 2008. Beginning in 2006 venture capital investments started increasing dramatically, growing by an average of US$1.6 billion from 2006 to 2008. Over the latter period, venture capital investments totaled nearly US$12.6 billion (see table A2.1). Businesses in "Clean energy production" accounted for 69 percent of this amount, or US$8.73 billion. "Environmentally friendly production" and "Conservation and pollution mitigation" attracted nearly US$3 billion of venture capital investment in this three-year period.

Given its findings on jobs, businesses and investments in the US clean energy economy from 1998 to 2007, the Pew study is relatively sanguine about the ability of this economy to spearhead a green recovery for the United States and lead the transition to a low-carbon economy. As noted by the report, "The clean energy economy has tremendous potential for growth, as investments continue to flow from both the government and private sector and federal and state policy makers increasingly push for reforms that will both spur economic renewal and sustain the environment."[5]

The study bases this optimistic conclusion on two recent trends. Although the study acknowledges that the clean economy has suffered both job losses and declining investment as a result of the current recession, the sector has not fared as badly as the overall economy. For example, investments in the clean economy declined by 48 percent in the first three months of 2009 compared with a year earlier. Total venture capital investment across all sectors of the US economy was reduced by 61 percent over the same period, however. In addition, clean economy investments are predicted to rebound more quickly than investments in other sectors, because of the continuing growing demand for clean energy, the stress on water supplies and the need to reduce GHG emissions and other pollutants.

The clean energy economy will also benefit directly from the February 2009 American Recovery and Reinvestment Act. The Pew study estimates that a total of US$84.8 billion of fiscal stimulus devoted to energy- and transportation-related spending should assist a speedy rebound for the clean economy. The expenditures include around US$21 billion extending tax incentives for wind, solar and other renewable energy businesses, US$11 billion to modernize the nation's electricity

---

[5] Pew Charitable Trusts 2009, 3.

grid, US$5 billion for the weatherization of low-income homes and US$2 billion for advanced battery technology. Other expenditures that will help spur the clean energy economy are US$500 million for job training for workers participating in the sector and US$300 million for the purchase of fuel-efficient vehicles for the federal government fleet from US automobile manufacturers.

The Pew study also notes, however, that the employment and investment expansion between 1998 and 2007 was driven more by state than federal policy. For example, the study found that, of the eighteen states that require electricity providers to supply a minimum percentage or amount of power from renewable sources as well as strong energy efficiency regulations, eleven of them had more jobs in the clean energy economy than the national average. In addition, for twelve of the eighteen states, clean energy jobs comprised a larger share of all jobs compared to the national average. Interviews with venture capitalists, business leaders and policymakers confirmed that state policies such as renewable portfolio standards are important factors in attracting more investments, businesses and jobs to a state, as such policies help to create market demand for clean energy technologies, products and services.

The Pew report recommends that, to spur the clean energy economy nationally, the United States needs to adopt a comprehensive, economy-wide "Clean Energy Plan." The study cites as the basis for such a plan the benchmark goals set by President Obama: a federal cap-and-trade system to help reduce greenhouse gas emissions by at least 80 percent by 2050; a national renewable portfolio standard that would require that 25 percent of the nation's energy supply be derived from renewable sources by 2025; and an energy efficiency resource standard that would require reductions of 15 percent in electricity usage and of 10 percent in natural gas usage by 2020.

Glossary

Biological diversity (biodiversity) The variation of life forms (genes, species or organisms) within a given habitat, ecosystem or biome, including the entire Earth.

Biomass fuel A renewable energy source derived from a variety of biological material sources, such as wood, waste, crops, grasses, algae and similar biotic matter.

Carbon dependency The degree to which production and consumption in an economy generates carbon-dioxide-equivalent greenhouse gas emissions. Carbon dependency is often measured by the greenhouse gas intensity of economies – e.g. the tonnes of CO_2-equivalent GHG emissions per million international dollars of gross domestic or national product.

Clean Development Mechanism (CDM) A provision of the Kyoto Protocol, which was designed originally as a bilateral mechanism through which entities in high-income economies could gain certified emission reductions by investing in clean energy technologies in developing economies. A CER is equal to one metric ton (tonne) of CO_2 equivalent.

Doha Round Short for the Doha Development Agenda, which is the current global trade negotiation round held under the auspices of the World Trade Organization; it commenced in November 2001.

Ecological scarcity The continued and irreversible loss of ecosystem benefits, or "services," as these systems are exploited or converted for human use and economic activity.

Economic recession A significant decline in the production and consumption of an economy, which lasts for more than a few months and is normally visible in key economy-wide indicators, such as real GDP growth, real personal income, employment (non-farm payrolls), industrial production and wholesale/retail sales.

Ecosystem service A human benefit generated by the normal functioning of an ecosystem – e.g. resources for harvesting, recreation, watershed protection, flood control, etc.

Emerging market economies Economies experiencing transition from the developing (low- and middle-income) to the developed (high-income) stage. The best-known examples are the large emerging market economies of Brazil, Russia, India and China, often referred to as the BRIC economies. Other middle-income economies are often also considered emerging market economies, however, including those in the Group of Twenty, such as Argentina, Indonesia, Mexico, South Africa and Turkey. Other important emerging market economies are Chile, Colombia, the Czech Republic, Egypt, Hungary, Malaysia, Morocco, Peru, the Philippines, Poland, Taiwan and Thailand.

Energy poverty A condition describing households in developing economies that either have no access to modern energy services or pay high prices for erratic and unreliable services.

Ethanol (ethyl alcohol) A biofuel alternative to gasoline that is produced through agricultural or biomass feedstocks.

Fiscal stimulus A short-term, net increase in government spending through rises in government spending or public investment, or, alternatively, a fall in taxation or increased public subsidies (or a combination of these policies), that has the purpose of stimulating aggregate demand – and thus growth – in an economy.

Fossil fuel subsidies Payments to producers or consumers that have the effect of artificially lowering the market prices of coal, natural gas and petroleum products, as well as the generation of electricity from burning these fossil fuels.

Fragile land Inhabited rural areas that present significant constraints for intensive agriculture and where the people's links to the land are critical for the sustainability of communities, pastures, forests and other natural resources; they include arid regions with no access to irrigation, areas with soils unsuitable for agriculture, land with steep slopes and fragile forest systems.

Fuel-efficient vehicles Vehicles with high fuel efficiency, hybrid and alternative fuel use (including electricity), low emissions and other cleaner technologies.

Global Green New Deal (GGND) A coordinated mix of global economic policies, investments and incentives with the aim of achieving three broad objectives: (i) reviving the world economy, creating employment opportunities and protecting vulnerable groups; (ii) reducing carbon dependency, ecosystem degradation and water scarcity; and (iii) furthering the Millennium Development Goal of ending extreme world poverty by 2025.

Great Depression The major and prolonged world economic recession of the 1930s, which began with the US and global stock market crash in 1929 and continued until the start of the Second World War.

Green fiscal stimulus Fiscal stimulus measures that are targeted to reducing carbon dependency and to other environmental improvements – e.g. supporting renewable energy development, carbon capture and sequestration, energy efficiency, public transport and rail; improving or modernizing electrical grid transmission and river basin management; and improving freshwater supplies and ecosystem management.

Greenhouse gas emissions Carbon dioxide and related gases from human activities that contribute to the warming of the Earth's atmosphere by trapping solar radiation reflected from the Earth's surface. In 2005 world GHG emissions consisted of CO_2 (73.6 percent of the total), methane (CH_4, 16.5 percent), nitrous oxide (N_2O, 8.5 percent), hydrofluorocarbons (HFCs, 1.0 percent), perfluorocarbons (PFCs, 0.3 percent) and sulfur hexafluoride (SF_6, 0.2 percent).

Gross domestic product (GDP) The value of all goods and services produced in an economy in a given year, less net foreign income from investments.

Group of Twenty (G20) economies The twenty richest and most populous economies of the world, which include nineteen countries (Argentina, Australia, Brazil, Canada, China, France, Germany, India, Indonesia, Italy, Japan, Mexico, Russia, Saudi Arabia, South Africa, South Korea, Turkey, the United Kingdom and the United States) plus the European Union.

High-income economies According to the World Bank's definition in the *World Development Indicators 2008*, economies in which 2006 gross national income per capita was US$11,116 or more.

Intergovernmental Panel on Climate Change (IPCC) A scientific intergovernmental body established in 1988 by the World Meteorological Organization and the United Nations Environment Programme to evaluate the risk of climate change caused by human activity.

Low- and middle-income (or developing) economies According to the World Bank's definition in the *World Development Indicators 2008*, economies in which 2006 GNI per capita was less than US$11,116.

Market-based instruments The introduction of incentives and interventions to influence the market behavior of consumers and producers to achieve a desired policy outcome. Such incentives can be applied to existing markets or used to create entirely new markets. In existing markets, the instruments usually involve correcting persistent market distortions, such as the removal of perverse subsidies incompatible with a policy objective or imposing additional taxes and subsidies to achieve an objective, such as taxes, user fees, refunds and targeted payments. Market-based instruments can help create new markets through establishing property rights, privatizing and decentralizing industries and firms, and setting up tradable permits, rights and offsets.

Millennium Development Goals (MDGs) The eight international development goals that the member states of the United Nations have agreed to achieve by 2015. The goals include reducing extreme poverty, reducing child mortality rates, improving water and sanitation, fighting disease epidemics, including AIDS, and developing a global partnership for development.

Millennium Ecosystem Assessment (MA) A program of research launched in 2001 with support from the United Nations to assess the state of global ecosystem change as well as its causes and consequences for human welfare.

New Deal The package of policies, investments and incentives that was implemented in the United States during the administration of President Franklin D. Roosevelt in response to the Great Depression of the 1930s.

Organisation for Economic Co-operation and Development (OECD) A grouping of countries that includes, from Europe, Austria, Belgium, the Czech Republic, Denmark, Finland, France, Germany, Greece, Hungary, Iceland, Ireland, Italy, Luxembourg, the Netherlands, Norway, Poland, Portugal, Slovakia, Spain, Sweden, Switzerland, Turkey and the United Kingdom and, from other regions, Australia, Canada, Japan, Mexico, New Zealand, South Korea and the United States.

Primary production The output of the natural-resource-based sectors of an economy, which usually comprise mineral and energy industries, agriculture, forestry, fishing and other extractive industries.

Renewable energy Energy generated from naturally replenished sources, such as biomass, sunlight, wind, tides and geothermal heat.

Resource dependency An indicator of the dependency of an economy on primary product exports, usually measured in terms of primary product exports in relation to total exports or total merchandise exports.

Safety net programs Initiatives that target cash or food transfers, relief work and other publicly funded programs to specific groups of the poor in developing economies, which provide either effective insurance or employment to poor households during a severe economic crisis.

Transboundary water sources River basins, large lakes, aquifers and other freshwater bodies that cross national boundaries.

Water scarcity The insufficient availability of freshwater supplies relative to the demands of human populations.

World Bank An international financial institution that provides leveraged loans to low- and middle-income economies in order to assist economic development and poverty reduction.

World Trade Organization (WTO) The international organization, which succeeded the General Agreement on Tariffs and Trade (GATT) in 1995, that provides a framework for negotiating and formalizing international trade agreements, enforcing member countries' adherence to these agreements and resolving disputes between members over trade issues.

Index